mountains of memory

AMERICAN LAND & LIFE SERIES

edited by Wayne Franklin

mountains

of memory

A Fire Lookout's Life

in the River of No Return

Wilderness

DON SCHEESE

Foreword by Wayne Franklin

Ψ

University of Iowa Press

Iowa City

University of Iowa Press,
Iowa City 52242
Copyright © 2001 by the
University of Iowa Press
All rights reserved
Printed in the United States of America
Design by Richard Hendel
http://www.uiowa.edu/~uipress

"August on Sourdough" by Gary Snyder, from
The Back Country, copyright © 1966 by Gary
Snyder, reprinted by permission of New
Directions Publishing Corp.; "Things to Do
Around a Lookout" by Gary Snyder, from
Mountains and Rivers without End, copyright
© 1996 by Gary Snyder, reprinted by
permission of Counterpoint Press, a member
of Perseus Books, L.L.C.; "Witness" by W. S.
Merwin, from *The Rain in the Trees*, copyright
© 1988 by W. S. Merwin, reprinted by
permission of Alfred A. Knopf, a division of
Random House, Inc. Chapter 15, "The Eagle
Bar Fire," appeared in a somewhat different
form as "A Season of Fire" in the Fall 1989
issue of *Idaho: The University*.

The publication of this book was
generously supported by the University of
Iowa Foundation.

All photographs by Don Scheese
Maps by Megan McCready

Printed on acid-free paper

Library of Congress
Cataloging-in-Publication Data
Scheese, Don.
Mountains of memory: a fire lookout's life
in the river of no return wilderness / by
Don Scheese; foreword by Wayne Franklin.
p.   cm.—(American land and life series)
Includes bibliographical references and index.
ISBN 0-87745-783-2 (cloth),
ISBN 0-87745-784-0 (pbk.)
1. Scheese, Don.   2. Fire lookouts—Idaho—
Frank Church–River of No Return Wilderness
—Biography.   3. Natural history—Idaho—
Frank Church–River of No Return Wilderness.
4. Frank Church–River of No Return
Wilderness (Idaho).   I. Title.   II. Series.
SD421.375.S34   2001
634.9'3—dc21   2001033292

01   02   03   04   05   C   5   4   3   2   1
01   02   03   04   05   P   5   4   3   2   1

TO ALL LOOKOUTS

past, present, and to come

*There is great good in returning to a landscape that has had
extraordinary meaning in one's life. It happens that we return
to such places in our minds irresistibly. There are certain villages
and towns, mountains and plains that, having seen them, walked
in them, lived in them, even for a day, we keep forever in the
mind's eye. They become indispensable to our well-being; they
define us, and we say: I am who I am because I have been there,
or there.*
   —N. Scott Momaday

*What is remembered
is what becomes reality.*
   —Patricia Hampl

*I am a native in this world
And think in it as a native thinks.*
   —Wallace Stevens

*You cannot overemphasize being able to get into your landscape.
There is no way to go native without it, no way to develop a sense
of place centered in the fundamental world, no way to imagine
yourself a part of the natural community of plants and animals
and the regional forces around you. For that you have to have
the full, five-sense experience of direct and repeated contact,
experiential immersion with nature.*
   —Dan Flores

& when pray tell, shall Lookouts die?
   — Gary Snyder

contents

foreword

WAYNE FRANKLIN

I first encountered Don Scheese when he was a student in my classes at the University of Iowa nearly two decades ago. I remember him on campus then — it must have been the fall of 1984 — as a solid, tanned, soft-spoken bike-rider receding from view along a bordering street after a brief conversation about John Hanson Mitchell's *Ceremonial Time*. We were working together then on books like that — books about places, especially American places, and about the idea of place in general. Don was obviously a bit older than most of my students, but only a bit, as if it had taken him somewhat longer to come up for the thin air that fills any academic town. The delay was a mark of how capacious his lungs were. He brought a sense of what I can only call outdoor reality to the classroom and the community. It wasn't that he preached about the outdoors, or about Edward Abbey, his soul brother, who already had become famous as a prophet railing against the Grossest Domestic Product and urging men — and women too, if need be, in Abbey's misogynist view — to monkey wrench the great machine of the U.S. of A. Don wasn't and isn't like that, even though a superficial reader of what ensues may see a certain resemblance to Abbey in it. With "Seldom Seen Scheese" (as he used to sign his postcards to me from God knows where, way out west, probably writing them between a bite of pizza and a swig of beer on a rare trip down from his mountain), it was more like the classroom windows all opened slightly on their own, even in that unnatural brutalist structure with brick walls *inside* where I then usually taught. What Don exuded most, like the sky's green light accompanying the death of a few long days in the Catskills or the Wind River Range, was the obvious lesson that some things simply can't be learned in school. He was there by his own sufferance, not because it was necessary. He chose to spend that time among professors much as he spent other time among wilder creatures, who also taught him much. He hadn't matriculated; he had wandered in.

Beneath a respectfully quiet surface, there was always a healthy skepticism in his manner. What things couldn't be learned in school? He shied away from such direct questions. But if you attended to his eyes as much as his words, you began to understand. You can't learn in school what it means to sit high on a mountain and wait for the slightest sign of fire as the sun comes up bright and crosses the hot sky and goes down red, day after nameless day, all through a lonely western summer. Even before I knew of Don's experience as a fire lookout, I swear I sensed it in his uncommonly clear gaze, as if he looked *through* you to regard the horizon you only temporarily interrupted. You began to feel like a corner frame on a fire tower window, structurally necessary maybe but otherwise beside the point. Don was always somehow distant — out there, so to speak, above Hells Canyon or in the Frank Church–River of No Return Wilderness.

My explanation of that gaze is a story. In the summer of 1989, having read Don's lookout journals and talked with him at length about his experience, I had a chance for a closer look. School was out, the weather was warm, and I had a few weeks on my hands. I got into my car and headed north, then turned straight west across the state. I had gone that way — through Eldora, Iowa Falls, Fort Dodge, and Sioux City — several times before, often enough to have the map inside my head. Later, I realized that *how* I reached Horse Mountain, where Don was stationed then, was very much part of what I saw there. The route and the lines it drew between nature and history, intention and circumstance, mattered to the story. What we see concludes an itinerary.

I prefer to travel light, with a small tent and sleeping bag and only enough equipment to fit in the trunk. The second night out, I remember a campground in the Missouri Valley, spread on the river bluffs above a cluster of islands. You could see the hills rolling off to the left, rising over the flat of a big oxbow just upstream. There were no other campers, so as the light failed the view merged with those painted a hundred and fifty years earlier by Karl Bodmer when he accompanied Prince Maximillian up the Missouri. Much of the landscape had changed radically since then, but most of the change you could see only if you turned your back on the river and scanned the gridded fields beginning to die behind the bluffs. Right here the hills had cushioned the imprint of human design, turning away the highways and twisting the farm roads and refusing to learn how to say "corn" and "beans" the way most of the Midwest dutifully does. Rivers in the Midwest gave all sorts of trouble to the original government surveyors, then to the farmers who came after them. If you look at the plat books of any county with a major river running through it, you see immediately the way nature erodes the grid. It is also in the river corridors that wildlife thrives. In the cottonwoods bordering the Iowa River bald eagles spend the winter each year, clawing fish in the open water of the oxbow that had made the farm and sitting up in the trees to eat and digest them. Only five miles away, living on the outskirts of the small gridded city, I never saw them.

On my trip to Horse Mountain, I followed the Missouri along the length that formed the border between Nebraska and South Dakota, passing the first of the big dams that convert the upper river into lakes, blocking or indeed reversing the old drainage patterns in the valley. The local tributaries remain, but in the lower channels where they used to run down to their clear entry points, water sponges upward, smudging the distinction. The dam also smudges the old political distinctions of the region. The boundary line between the two states here snakes beneath the placid surface of Lewis and Clark Lake, regardless of the human artifact above it. It traces on paper the way the old channel still slithers through the mud under there. Or rather it traces out *one* of the old channels. Since the Missouri long proved resistant to human management, political boundaries in the region are notoriously untidy. The Iowa-Nebraska border has been tangled in many places by the always shifting channels, and each state — because its memory derives from human rather than natural sources — has tried to hold on to its land even when, by every reasonable measure, the land ought to belong to the state on the opposite shore. The town of Carter Lake, Iowa, is on the Nebraska side of the river, bordered by the municipality of East Omaha and, on the west, by that part of Omaha proper in which Malcolm X was born. It is an island of Iowa in a sea of Nebraska. The same flatness of surface that made it so easy to imprint most of the Midwest with the human grid also made these rivers so unreliable as boundaries. If the gradient were higher, the rivers would be less likely to slip left and right, laterally eating away at the landmarks. Instead, rivers like the Missouri, except where they are temporarily confined by dams, keep chewing away at the banks. If you sit by any of them a fair period of time, chances are that a chunk of soil the size of a car will crack away and plunge in, like a glacier calving on the Alaska coast.

The border between Nebraska and South Dakota abandons the north-tending Missouri just downstream from the second big lake, turning abruptly west in the middle of a little piece of land snagged in the river. The old line up the water continues from there as a county boundary, all the way north and west through both Dakotas and across most of Montana in fact, so this nameless island is the benchmark of several human jurisdictions. Back on the Nebraska side of things, the gravel and dirt roads keep their westward heading to Anoka, where a sizable highway crosses them, leading to Butte and from there west through Brocksburg to Burton. Just beyond Valentine, an old rail town on the Niobrara, it crosses the hundredth meridian, the legendary starting point for the high plains. Nothing special happens right when you pass that, of course, but by then the landscape differs in many ways from the predominantly green, Iowa-like features of eastern Nebraska. There is less cropland — or less without irrigation — and more scrub cover, and by the time you pass the hundred and second meridian in this part of Nebraska the farthest faint tributaries of the Niobrara dry up and all the streambeds seem intermittent. Here begins a stretch of sparsely settled, nearly treeless sand hills stretching all the way to Gordon, nearly a hundred miles away.

On my 1989 trip, I noticed the altitude increasing steadily. It was not unusual to find features in the nearby landscape topping out at well over two thousand or twenty-five hundred feet. The road kept going on and on over a surface less obviously affected by the human economy, although the economy's effects are generally so pervasive and at the same time subtle that it is hard to escape them even when you cannot detect them. The road that might take you beyond such a pall of influence would itself, of course, bear it as well as you onward. So would the path. So do your eye and mind.

Soon the way led north over earth-colored hills into Pine Ridge, past Wounded Knee, where in 1890 the prayer of the Sioux Ghost Dance was answered by the *amens* spit from the government's Benjamin Berkeley Hotchkiss machine gun. Then Porcupine Butte rose near the road to almost thirty-seven hundred feet, the first really big hill, after which the road went north into the Badlands and South Dakota. Although it rained through here that day, for the most part water seemed only a memory now, something you have to look for when you need to fill a canteen or wash your face or just want to hear it make its wet sounds as it moves from one place to another. The rain wasn't real, it was an echo of things that happened elsewhere. The impression seemed especially true that night in Badlands National Park, which overlaps with Pine Ridge in the southwest and runs from there in thin strips northeast and then east. There is a wilderness area of the park centered on Sage Creek, a tributary of the Cheyenne river, as far from either visitor center as you can get and still be in the park. Here, on an open flat below mostly bare hills to the south and the depressed bed of Sage Creek to the north, seemed like a perfect place to camp. There was no marked campground per se. No water or sites to speak of, only open grass between those two features. The wind was blowing fiercely and the rain continued, less than ideal conditions to put up my small dome tent. Barely was it up before it blew flat several times, but the stakes held in the hard Dakota earth, the seams in the nylon remained tight, and the fiberglass poles bent over without contusion or fracture. Waiting out the end of the storm in the car was like watching an experiment in modern materials and ancient conditions. But eventually the rain stopped and the wind died, leaving the tent beneath a silent, clear, dark prairie sky. More stars filled it than you could imagine counting even if the night lasted forever.

And of course it didn't. Lying in the blue light that filtered through the nylon the next morning, I heard a series of shuffling noises, irregular and mysterious. Still in the sleeping bag, I rolled over and looked out the bottom of the door. My eyes searched first the bright blue sky to the north, vacant of storm as it rose over the place I remembered glimpsing the hidden stream bed the night before. As I heard the sound again, I sat up and my eyes came down, down, down, until they saw many brown spots across the way. A herd of fifty bison was grazing on the thin grass beyond the stream. Every few minutes, one of them would skid from the bank into the bed of the stream, tearing the grass at the edge and sending a plume of earth down to where the last of the water from the storm might still be running. I couldn't see them once they were in the cut, but from time to time one of them would reappear farther along, first its head and horns and then the mane. A few scrambled back up completely where the bank opened a little draw into the grass. Others never reemerged. I had seen bison before, in zoos and at animal farms, even in parks, but these wild ones, seemingly free in their immemorial landscape, made all those others fade from mind. The latter were toys, trophies, quotes from nature, pages in a human book. Here were the genuine hoofed beasts, doing what their ancestors had done long before any humans had seen or hunted them. Of course they were here only because the remnant herds — only about six hundred bison survived the slaughter — had been preserved and nurtured and individuals and agencies had reinserted them in the landscape. Later, in Oklahoma, I was to learn that the Nature Conservancy monitored its four hundred bison at the former Chapman-Barnard ranch in Osage county electronically, herding them in at regular intervals to read the transponders implanted in each one. Perhaps these, too, were electro beasts, animals on work release from extinction, only facsimiles of their old selves. Virtual creatures. But I didn't care. If this was an illusion, it worked perfectly on my imagination, restoring me to the prairie along with the bison. Oddly, it was part of the Ghost Dance become real:

> The whole world is coming
> A nation is coming, a nation is coming
> The Eagle has brought the message to the tribe
> The father says so, the father says so
> Over the whole earth they are coming
> The buffalo are coming, the buffalo are coming

Time passed. I was happy when the road led out of the Black Hills and into Wyoming. There it went across open country until, precipitating from the clouds you first take them to be, the Big Horns solidify once again into the first real mountains you encounter driving west from Iowa. You can see them long before you get to Sheridan, so you know the West hasn't forgotten to exist simply because you weren't regarding it for a while. Beyond there, the land flattens out again but the Big Horns stay in the rearview mirror until you can glimpse the Yellowstone country out front, so you know the great distances will not evaporate. After Cody, the road passes the Buffalo Bill dam and then beyond the lake recovers the north fork of the Shoshone, reversing history as it goes higher and higher and the water, ignorant of where gravity is taking it, seems wild. The route leads up a long climb past Wapiti and Pahaska and on to the eastern entrance of Yellowstone.

I had been to Yellowstone before, in 1985 I think. From that trip I recalled the bizarre plumbing that runs beneath the landscape, the timely or erratic geysers and the mud pools with those earthy stinks. This time, though, it was the black woods themselves that attracted my eye. The fires the year before, a consequence of bad luck or bad policy or both, had torn the greenery off the now lumbering trunks of trees that seemed even taller for their bareness. Big dark splotches sucked the western sunlight into them like starless holes in the night sky. Along one stream, a colony of Douglas-fir still stood straight, but the reddish bark had gone very dark, like a copper pot used so long on the stove it might be iron. Yet the regrowth that everyone was beginning to notice this next year had already started, stunning against the black. Grass speared up through the devastation. Nature had its own policy, made its own luck.

The images of that fire and rebirth kept recurring as I traveled the road to West Yellowstone for an overnight, then back through the scorched park and down into the Grand Tetons to Colter Bay on Jackson Lake. There was

a full moon during the stay there, shining off the granite and the bits of glacier until well past midnight. On my left I could see Teewinot and Mount
Owen and I thought even the Grand Teton itself. Straight ahead Mount
Moran, speckled down its front with several ice fields, seemed to give off
light, not just reflect it. I know of no place on earth where the mountains
have such an obvious beginning point, where the nearly vertical and nearly
horizontal so perfectly meet. That the mountains go up out of the water of
Moran Bay and Leigh Lake and especially Jenny Lake makes the contrast
even more perfect: it is a Zen exercise in water and rock, the flat and the up-
right, the hardest matter and the shimmering, patient liquid that over time
is harder still. You can actually walk around the lakes to the points where the
change happens. *Here* is the mountain. The fires had spared this area the
year before, perhaps because the mountains are too high to have much forest cover and there seems to have been comparatively less reason to suppress fire here over the previous decades.

After two nights in this landscape of elemental difference, I took the road
north once more into Yellowstone, around by Old Faithful to Madison
Junction and out the other side at West Yellowstone again. So the black
memory of '88 was very much with me when the road led through that dog-
leg of Montana and up over Targhee Pass into Idaho. I was wandering, with
no set route and no destination other than an eventual homecoming, but
that memory set me thinking about Don and his mountain and thus helped
set the rest of the route. The road led over some of the best Idaho country,
from Idaho Falls north between the Lost River Range and the Pioneer
Mountains. It stopped at Challis, then turned south and west toward the
Stanley Basin. After camping in a primitive area where I heard the coyotes
howling at the moon around three o'clock, I woke to a suddenly dark morning sky that led into Stanley. It had the color of night, the black clouds
snagged with lightning bolts and the rain so heavy it threatened to wash
away whatever light was left. Stanley was almost flattened beneath that
weight of sky, crouching like a soaked dog left out in the storm. Behind it
rose the West's most characteristic mountain range, the Sawtooths, their
humble workaday name suggesting something about the dead level of the
American vernacular imagination. Beyond Stanley, the wet road ran north
along Marsh Creek at the base of the range, then twisted around up the bed
of Cape Horn Creek through the rock, up and up until that creekbed cut off
west and it followed another leading farther south. The road kept a nearly
southerly heading through these vagaries of landform, cresting another divide that finally took it into one of the drainage ways of the Payette River. It

was one of those roads that followed the dictates of the land, seeking out passageways rather than engineering them the way the Interstates do. Driving it, you are constantly aware that something other than human wit and strength are in charge here. Small hot springs, venting some of the extraordinary energy seething under the terrain, pooled along the road, steaming vaguely in the summer. They invited travelers to stop and strip and immerse themselves, and along little-used roads like this people often do.

By the time the road passed between Kirkham and Banner ridges, crossed a web of new creeks, and came to Lowman, the rain had let up. The sky started clearing, a fortunate thing, since the road from there south to Idaho City led through terrain that would be difficult even in perfect weather. Although it parted company with the Payette River at Lowman, the road remained in the same large watershed, whose waters all ran north and east, as it switched back and forth up through the hills toward Beaver Creek Summit. There it crossed over into a second watershed feeding the opposite way. Amid such dramatic shifts, it was hard to sense what the map showed — that the water in both cases ultimately met in the Snake River, the stream that originated in Yellowstone, ran south out of there through Jackson Lake, past that camp at Colter Bay, then beneath the Tetons and on through Jackson Hole before it made its big loop across southern Idaho. All the settlements in that part of the state, from Idaho Falls through Pocatello and Twin Falls and back up again to Boise, are where they are because the river flows that way. They are mostly lowland towns, with borders of hills but few close-in mountains, often gridded out and regular and surrounded by extensive plains. The Snake provides the land with order, setting boundaries and shaping the ground, but it also orders the water flowing through the landscape. As they come through the mountainous heart of the state, all the streams on that side of the Continental Divide eventually collect in that big snaking arc of the Snake.

The trajectory down which the road from Lowman to Idaho City plunges is an especially rich example of the pattern. So many switchbacks distort the road that even at small scale the line denoting it on a map seems like a squiggle. It passes over another summit, then enters the last sluiceway that it manages to fit itself into, that of More's Creek. For the first few miles down, the road swaps sides with the creek at intervals, but then it crosses back over to the west flank and stays there as it enters the stretch where gulch after gulch, all quaintly named by the miners who operated in the Idaho City region, open brief lateral vistas upward. Here the flume-like streams that bore the ore out of the surrounding hills come down on More's

Creek, down through American Girl Gulch and Chinee Gulch, through Rocker and Gambrinus, Illinois and Walla Walla, Slaughterhouse, and Big Gulch and all the others. Idaho City proper sits in a cluster of gulches. From there the road passes west, into and through the Boise Basin and past more gulches until it comes out near Horseshoe Bend, a town on an oxbow of the Payette River. I had left that drainage back in Lowman and made a great circuit south and west, up and over countless mountains, but now inexorably came back into it again. Water makes the routes here.

The road passes north to the town of McCall, where the river flattens out into mountain-ringed Payette Lake. From there, leaving that watershed at last, I followed the road west before turning south to Council, where the district office of the Payette National Forest would allow a last check on local conditions and a call to alert Don that his solitude was about to be compromised. Jim Fry, the ranger, called Don on the Forest Service radio and let me talk with him directly. Don was surprised to hear my voice, but even more surprised to hear of the plan to actually come up Horse Mountain. After a visit to the local grocery store for the obligatory lookout offering, I angled the car up the dirt road along Hornet Creek. After it headed that stream and crossed over to another one, it led to the ghost town of Landore in the Placer Basin. There the road, ever thinner, hooked back around and went almost in the opposite direction. Soon the Sheep Rock turnoff appeared, and from there it wasn't long until the car lurched up the last stretch of edge-clinging trail to the summit. Don had no vehicle up there, as I recall, so my red car sat on the mountain by itself, almost seven thousand feet above sea level, looking more forlorn than a golf club on Mars. It was the opposite of Don, who was more truly at home there than anyone else anywhere. The distance was gone from his eyes, since now he literally occupied the place he belonged. Seeing what he saw there day after day, I now knew what he was looking at when he looked past me or through me in the city. He brought his mountain eyes back with him each year.

It is hard to translate into language what struck me once I'd taken in the tall green-legged lookout and the dark, tin-roofed bunkhouse nearby. Those were the only human structures. And there were no trees on the summit, no bushes even, only some grass clumps and flowers and dirt and rock. But you don't go to places like this to inspect the architecture or kick around what's under your feet. Don led up the two flights of stairs to the lookout proper. The view from such a structure is spectacular — that is the whole point of putting it where it is. But nothing can prepare the casual visitor for the effect of looking down from this height into a canyon as deep as the

Grand but much narrower and more solitary. Its nearness to the inspecting eye reminded me of the Black Canyon of the Gunnison, in Colorado, where I remembered standing right on the unfenced cliff edge and peering thirteen hundred feet straight down at a thin line of water. There are places along the Snake where you can almost simulate that vertiginous view, but Hells Canyon is four times deeper than the Black, and wider as well. And there the Snake always is, broad, strong, the force responsible for ripping away all the rock you know was once here but you see no trace of now. Horse Mountain is not high for the West, but it stands at the edge of a rare abyss, where the Snake River has had its way for what seems like forever as a viewer looks down on it.

Don led a hike to a favorite viewpoint about a mile away. There we sat and looked and talked for another couple of hours before heading back to the lookout, where the canned chicken and the red wine I'd hauled up from Council made a passable coq au vin. We ate it, along with a fresh salad Don especially appreciated, out on the catwalk as the last of the canyon light evaporated into the night sky. Then I remember stumbling down the stairs to spend the night in the bunkhouse, which was more shack than house and had no bunks at all in it. The propane-powered refrigerator made an odd white noise, humming and spewing its noxious fumes, reminding me that although I was resting so far from the precincts of civilization machines were still all too close. The next night, on special request and probably in violation of some officious rule, Don cleared more sleeping room up top in the lookout.

Before that, though, came a whole day exploring his precincts. The alarm clock was a shower of firewood sent down onto the tin roof by Don at seven o'clock, an old lookout custom. Before breakfast, I drove up to Kinney Point, below the old settlement of Helena. Here the view down into Hell's Canyon was more incisive still, as if it had been constructed just for that purpose. The river spread out wider just upstream from the point, twisting about the base of the steep slope that formed the opposite shore. Off to my left were brown spikes and blackened rock, evidence of the 1988 Eagle Bar fire that Don writes about. Other burned areas spotted the whole landscape, even up on the mountain. From Sheep Rock, a high point at the end of this particular road, other burns registered, along with the still blue Snake that coiled down there and went on, carrying everything it had gathered from most of Idaho and parts of Wyoming and Oregon slowly downhill to the Columbia River and the sea.

Around four o'clock that afternoon, back at the lookout, Don spotted a smoke across the canyon. Hence I had a chance to observe firsthand some of the procedures he outlines in the narrative that follows, especially in the chapter about the Eagle Bar fire. He called it in on the radio, giving a precise location and determining with those at headquarters that it was an old fire that had flamed up again, a not uncommon event. A plane was sent out, from McCall probably, and once it verified the location and the nature of the blaze a ground crew was dispatched to attack and extinguish it. There was more to the visit, another dinner and breakfast and more walks before departing. But this was the heart of it, a chance to see the inside of the lookout as a workplace in the wild.

That insight became more important as the rest of that odd summer unfolded. The next morning I took the car down the steep Kleinschmidt grade, a road built a hundred years earlier to transport ore from the mines scattered over this rough terrain. It dropped a mile over its ten-mile length and came out in the heart of the canyon, right along the Snake, then led farther upstream to a bridge where a traveler can cross into Oregon. Over the next weeks, I drove on to the sea, then down along it to Eureka and back up into Washington. Hard as it was to fathom after spending so much time on that wettest of our coasts, once I turned around and headed back, much of the land I had traversed on the way to Horse Mountain was on fire. Incredibly, even that road from Stanley to Lowman, along which the rain had been so heavy only the previous month, was closed due to a big burn. And from the routes that remained open farther north, like the one up through the Bitterroots to Lolo Pass that I took back, the smoke in the air a hundred miles away was visible. The Yellowstone had burned the year before, but now the country all around my ears seemed on fire.

Visiting Don Scheese at his aerie above the Snake River had not prepared me for the disaster, but it helped me understand the place of fire in the landscape of the West and its many effects on those who reside there. As I think readers of *Mountains of Memory* will discover, Don makes an excellent guide for such a trip.

preface

Tell me your landscape, wrote the Spanish philosopher José Ortega y Gasset, and I'll tell you who you are.

Exactly.

For as long as I can remember, I have been a lover of mountains.

I was born in the mountains — the Pocono Mountains of central-eastern Pennsylvania, a sub-range of the Appalachians. One of my earliest memories is of craning my neck in our backyard in order to take in the mountain—Summit Hill, we called it — that rose behind our house. Many men in my hometown and surrounding area worked literally *in* the mountains — they were coal miners. My father was a blaster, responsible for blowing out the tunnels that were burrowed into the mountainsides in order to reach the rich seams of anthracite coal for which the region was famous. People from where I grew up were called "coalcrackers" by outsiders, not exactly an honorific term. As kids, we didn't care. We played in the deep green leafy woods at the edge of town, and when the woods disappeared as strip-mining replaced underground mining and turned the earth upside down, we continued to play in and around the strip mines and patches of woods that remained, mostly copses of white birch. We thought nothing of the devastation wrought upon the land and people, though most of our fathers lost their jobs (because strip-mining employs far fewer workers) and the town slowly died. Only after I left home to attend college in the city did I notice, when I occasionally returned for visits, the — how else to put it? — ugliness of the surroundings.

My love of the mountains continued, though I simply explored farther away, discovering the Appalachian Trail, which runs along the ridgetops twenty miles from home, and the world-famous bird sanctuary Hawk Mountain, where in the spring and fall thousands of migrating raptors are concentrated above its open, windy summits. In Pennsylvania there were always more mountains to discover.

I discovered, and immediately came to love, the mountains of the American West when I drove cross-country in the summer of 1976 headed to law school in Oregon, intending to become an environmental attorney to save the planet in the heady wake of the first Earth Day. Looking back more than twenty years later, I now recognize this journey as a significant initiation. Cruising along Highway 14 somewhere in central Wyoming, I descried, from what I later calculated was a hundred miles away, the snow-capped Wind River Range, apparently levitating above a searing desert plain, an impossible juxtaposition of summer and winter. Those snowy summits struck an elemental chord in my heart and imagination that has sounded ever since.

I encountered more mountains during that same Western odyssey: the Tetons, the Blues of eastern Oregon, the Cascades. I became so enamored of high country during my first year of law school that I spent more time in the mountains than I did in the classroom. With predictable consequences. Burned out on books, tormented by torts and property law, I decided to take a leave of absence from law school (which proved to be permanent) and harangued the United States Forest Service into offering me a seasonal job. I'd heard through some people I met on the trail that the agency hired vigorous, outdoorsy young adults to work in the national forests where I'd spent the past year hiking. Doing what? Who cared? So long as I was in the mountains.

I began my job as surveyor on the Gifford Pinchot National Forest in southwestern Washington in June 1977. It mattered little that I had virtually no formal training or work experience in surveying; the technical expertise required for the survey crew (whose purpose, by the way, was to recon routes for logging roads) could be acquired quickly in the field. More important was one's physical condition and the desire to walk many miles a day in steep, heavily forested terrain where few paths existed. Essentially, we were paid to create and hike our own trails. It was a dream job.

That summer and fall I walked all over the Amboy and Mount Adams districts of the Gifford Pinchot. And on the weekends I backpacked with a couple of buddies in farther parts of the Cascades of Washington and Oregon, as well as in other mountain ranges: Goat Rocks, Indian Heaven, Glacier Peak, the Olympics, the North Cascades, the Strawberry Mountains, the Wallowas. I liked the work and the recreation so much I came back the following season. We climbed Mount Hood, Mount Adams, Middle and South Sister, and Mount Saint Helens (before the eruption of 1980) plus many lesser peaks. It was an idyllic, carefree existence: working four ten-hour days during the week, often spiked out in some camp far from any paved roads, then on weekends gassing, gearing, and beering up for a three-day backpack in some official wilderness area.

One day in the summer of 1978, my boss asked me if I'd like to transfer with him to a national forest in northern Idaho. Why not? I'd heard there were more mountains to explore in those parts. Not to mention that in the rain shadow of the Cascades it would be drier, less cloudy, and stormy — hence more chances to actually *see* the mountains in which one worked and played. My boss also mentioned the possibility of doing some firefighting in Idaho when things got really hot and dry. Lots of money and interesting tours of duty in spectacular country all over the American West, he said. Why not indeed?

Late that fall, after a series of hunter-caused fires broke out north of the Silver Valley in the Idaho Panhandle, I found myself, along with several hundred other grunts recruited for emergency firefighting duty, digging line, breathing smoke and dust, and keeping a wary eye out in the middle of the night for widowmakers (falling limbs and branches from trees on fire nearby). Surely, I thought, there must be a safer, less strenuous, more contemplative way to enjoy — yet still get paid for — working in the mountains. Then I remember hearing the distinctive voice of a woman over the two-way radio attached to the belt of the crew foreman just downhill from me on the fire line. The voice was memorable for its calm, soothing, faraway tone. Who was that? I wanted to know. It's Conrad Peak lookout, relaying some radio message from the ranger station in Red Ives, I was told. And what's her job, exactly? I asked. Well, she (many lookouts, I came to discover, are women) is supposed to spot and report fires and pass on radio messages to crews who can't reach the ranger station. That's it? And she gets paid for this? Yup.

Interesting.

Thus began my quest for a career as a fire watcher.

I became obsessed with the seasonal occupation of fire lookout. How did it originate? Why were there so few lookouts left? Why were there still so many (relatively speaking) in Idaho? I started visiting the few stations that remained erect and intact (though most were no longer staffed). Roundtop. Snow Peak. Middle Sister. Bald Mountain. I used my Forest Service key to open the padlocked doors and sneak into the cabins, take a look around, read (if any were available) notes or diaries kept by former lookouts, trying to imagine what it would be like to sit in a cabin surrounded by glass walls and get paid to watch cloud formations. I also came to discover there was a subgenre of literature written by and about fire lookouts, a very small body of writing by authors like Martha Hardy, Jack Kerouac, Gary Snyder, Edward Abbey, and Norman Maclean who waxed lyrical about the pleasures and delights of living alone on top of a mountain for months at a time.

As one might expect, there is a fair degree of competition for these kinds of jobs, especially nowadays as the budgets of the Forest Service (and nonmilitary government agencies in general) continue to be slashed. Lookouts have been phased out in favor of aerial detection, and more and more jobs go to volunteers (usually from the city) who think it's a wonderfully romantic existence to spend a summer living atop a mountain far from the maddening crowd.

I digress. As I said, usually it is not that easy to get a job as a lookout. But when I first applied for a lookout post in the spring of 1980, I was the sole applicant. That's right: an ex-law student with some experience as a surveyor and firefighter with no specific plans for the future — a person whom Erik Erikson would have said was in a state of moratorium in his life — was the only one to apply for the position of St. Joe Baldy lookout in northern Idaho. During the interview my prospective boss wanted to know: Could I read a map? Could I talk without embarrassing myself (and, more important, the agency) over the two-way radio? Would I maintain the lookout in good condition, keep it nice and tidy? Could I stay awake — and sane — while living on top of a mountain where I might not see or be able to talk to civilians for days at a time?

I answered yes to all the above questions, and got the job.

I worked that fire lookout, and five others, for twelve seasons. It was the best job I could ever hope to have.

This book is a memoir, an intellectual autobiography, and an environmental history. It is a memoir in that I offer a retrospective vision of a significant portion of my life. Author Patricia Hampl has claimed that "what is remembered is what becomes reality." In a way that is true. Through the art of memory we create and craft a life. But I would add that what becomes real is not only what is remembered but what gets written down, what an author chooses to include in a work, since what is recorded is what ultimately becomes real to writer and reader. I would also add that it is of course a great mark of our species' arrogance to think that the real world is constituted only by what we as humans perceive, remember, and record. Most of nature, the rest of the nonhuman environment besides human beings, exists whether we perceive it or not, acknowledge it or not.

It is an intellectual autobiography, a consideration of ideas and statements by authors whom I have read over the years and regard as having great significance. Some readers might object to the insertion of long quotations from various works scattered throughout this book. But ideas are part of the real world too and can have as much influence on each person's perception of reality as hard-rock reality itself. As an academic with a particular interest in environmental studies and as a lover of the outdoors — a lover of things as well as ideas — I aim to draw intellectual as well as spiritual sustenance from the relationship between humans and their environments.

Finally, this work is an environmental history of the Frank Church– River of No Return Wilderness in central Idaho, the area I have chosen to make the locus of my narrative. It is a selective natural and cultural history of the largest official wilderness area in the Lower Forty-eight states, a federal wilderness that is both vast and remote and which contains all sorts of evidence of past and present human occupation. As such, the River of No Return Wilderness serves as a paradigm of the intellectual and practical problems inherent in defining and managing wilderness. Examining these problems gives me ample opportunity to meditate on the meanings and values of wilderness at the turn of the twentieth century, at a time when so little official protected wilderness remains.

Like John Hanson Mitchell in *Ceremonial Time* and Dan Flores in *Caprock Canyonlands* and *Horizontal Yellow*, I combine environmental history and nature writing (the latter defined as a first-person narrative of one's direct experiences in the nonhuman environment) in my account of going native in a particular place. A word or two about what is meant by the phrase *going native.* I do not mean native in the literal sense of the term, as someone who is an original resident or a lifelong inhabitant of a place. Rather, I refer to the process by which a person becomes intimately familiar with a place by residing in it for a significant period of time and learning about its weather, geology, natural history, and various eras of human occupation. Ralph Waldo Emerson captured the essence of what it means to go native in this journal passage: "If life were long enough, among my thousand and one works should be a book of Nature. . . . It should contain the natural history of the woods around my shifting camp for every month of the year. It should tie their astronomy, botany, physiology, meteorology, picturesque, and poetry together. No bird, no bug, no bud, should be forgotten on his day and hour." Then, having once developed an intimate acquaintance with his/her personal landscape, the native comes to love and respect the place and fervently desires to protect it, to preserve its wild character while recognizing that natural change is integral to its biotic health.

In the name of creative license I have sometimes compressed time and transposed places to make it appear as if most of what follows took place in a single season at or near one particular lookout. I have fictionalized the story by changing names (to protect the guilty) and in some cases small details. Nonetheless, what I have written remains true to the spirit of my experiences. As Black Elk is supposed to have said, some things are true whether they really happened or not.

Although I have finally retired from lookout life, I still reflect on my experiences in the mountains of Idaho and think how lucky I was to be able to devote so much of my waking (and sleeping) life there, observing and participating in the spell of the alpine environment. As a species, for the most part we have found it hard to live in the mountains. I count myself among the fortunate few who have been able not merely to climb or to view mountains from afar, but actually to have had the privilege of dwelling in high lonely places above the trees for a few precious months at a time.

acknowledgments

An author is frequently asked, "How long did it take you to write your book?" In the case of writing this book I have usually replied, "Oh, about twenty years — since 1980, when I worked my first lookout and began keeping a journal." Over that time I have accumulated many debts. Intellectual debts I have acknowledged in the book itself. Here I wish to acknowledge debts of another kind.

The Idaho Department of Lands and the United States Forest Service employed me over the years as a fire lookout and, while I have occasionally been critical of government management of wilderness and wildfire, I wish to express my greatest respect for the field personnel of these agencies. There could not be a finer fire management officer than Jack Kirkendall, who embodies all that is good about the Forest Service.

I have been fortunate to teach at an institution that has valued my work in interdisciplinary studies. I thank the faculty in the departments of English and geography at Gustavus Adolphus College, and in the environmental studies program, for supporting my need to range far afield (literally as well as figuratively) in teaching courses and doing scholarship in nature writing and environmental history; and I thank the students in my courses over the years who helped me to formulate more precise questions about this project. The Faculty Development Committee awarded me a yearlong sabbatical and a summer research grant to begin and then continue working on *Mountains of Memory*. My research assistant, Sandra Valnes, provided valuable assistance during the copyediting and proofreading stages of the production process, and Megan McCready drew the maps for the book, for which (map freak that I am) I am most grateful.

Librarians and staff at Gustavus Adolphus College, the Idaho State Historical Library (especially Judith Austin), Boise State University, and the National Interagency Fire Center (NIFC) were unfailingly helpful and always cheerful in addressing my inquiries.

I presented portions of this manuscript in progress at various conferences sponsored by the Western Literature Association and the Association for the Study of Literature and the Environment. I appreciate the attention and feedback from the audiences over the years.

A crew from Action Whitewater Adventure, of Provo, Utah — Eric, Kathy, Crede, Mark, and Hattie — helped me negotiate an unforgettable five-day journey down the Middle Fork of the Salmon River in the summer of 1999.

Wayne Franklin has been working with me on this project, off and on, since the summers of 1985 and 1986, when he first agreed to direct my graduate school independent study projects on nature writing and natural history while I was working lookouts in Idaho. Over the years he encouraged me to continue working on what would become *Mountains of Memory*. I am deeply indebted to him, as editor of the American Land and Life series at the University of Iowa Press, for his trenchant criticism. While we did not always agree on matters of style and substance, this book is much better for his critical commentary. I am also much obliged to Holly Carver, director of the University of Iowa Press, for helping see this book through to publication, and to Charlotte Wright, managing editor, for her careful editorial eye.

Lookout life is solitary by nature, but various visitors over the years helped me to realize the absolute necessity of human company from time to time: George, Q-Ball, Cheryl and Blair, Ann Marie and Herb, Roach-Man, and the Vickster. I also wish to thank Larry Z (alias the Soup Nazi) for accompanying me on a final memorable visit to Ruffneck Peak in 1998, from which we spotted several fires (sadly, the lookout was not staffed at the time).

Finally, I thank Peg for understanding and respecting my love of and need for wilderness solitude and for spending a few weeks at a time with me on various lookouts (including our honeymoon). She may have been less enamored of lookout life than I, but I will never take for granted her friendship and love — not to mention patience while I continued to spend summers away on some distant mountaintop. I no longer desire to work lookouts, in part because I wish to spend more time at home. But I will always treasure our time together on the mountain, spent observing, reading, walking, talking — and even spotting a few fires.

spring

Frank Church - River of No Return Wilderness

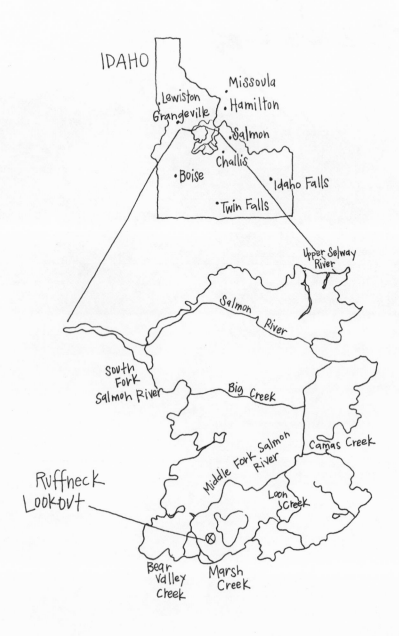

IDAHO

· Lewiston
Grangeville
· Missoula
· Hamilton
· Salmon
Challis
· Boise
· Idaho Falls
· Twin Falls

Upper Selway River

Salmon River

South Fork Salmon River

Big Creek

Camas Creek

Middle Fork Salmon River

Ruffneck Lookout

Loon Creek

Bear Valley Creek

Marsh Creek

North

1. Settling in

"How's our lookout doing?" asks Jack, the fire management officer (FMO) of the brush crew foreman, glancing my way. Jack is making the rounds of his fire crews out in the field in early June — the field being the two-million-acre Challis National Forest in south central Idaho. At the lower elevations in these parts (about six thousand feet above sea level) spring has arrived, but the mountains are still heavily draped in snow, the result of a wet, cold, *long* winter (the locals always emphasizing that last adjective). The crews get ready for fire season by working themselves into shape, repairing and replacing last season's equipment, and gathering slash from logging operations into piles to be burned in the fall when it's cold and wet.

Benny, the brush crew foreman, is an old-timer and short-timer — he's to retire at the end of this season. Although a veteran of many forest fires, he's well past the age when the FMO would actually assign him to active fire duty. So he bides his time, driving us to the many clearcut sites where we do our work and, more important, regaling us with stories about a bygone era when firefighters walked for at least a day to a fire (rather than be flown in by helicopter), fought it with only shovels and pulaskis, and lived on government C rations. Not surprisingly, Benny tolerates little whining about working conditions nowadays; if you moan about hard work his only response is, "You'd complain if they hung you with a good rope."

He responds to Jack's question by saying, "Well, we can't seem to get much work out of him 'cause he just keeps a-starin' up at the lookout." The crew members laugh and Benny's blue eyes twinkle as he looks over at me.

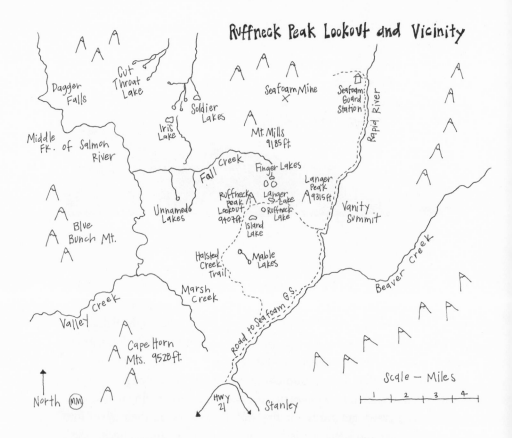

Ruffneck Peak Lookout and Vicinity

Cut Throat Lake
Dagger Falls
Soldier Lakes
Iris Lake
Seafoam Mine ✕
Seafoam Guard Station
Rapid River
Middle Fk. of Salmon River
Mt. Mills 9185 ft.
Fall Creek
Finger Lakes
Langer Peak
Langer Peak 9315 ft.
Vanity Summit
Ruffneck Peak Lookout, 9407 ft.
Langer S-Lake
Ruffneck Lake
Unnamed Lakes
Island Lake
Blue Bunch Mt.
Halsted Creek Trail
Mable Lakes
Marsh Creek
Beaver Creek
Valley Creek
Road to Seafoam
G.S.
Cape Horn Mts. 9528 ft.
Hwy 21
Stanley
North (MN)

Scale — Miles
1 2 3 4

These are the kinds of insults lookouts must suffer before they go up on the mountain for the season.

Actually I'm enjoying the (occasional) hard work and camaraderie of the brush crew this first week back on the job. After all, I'm in the mountains again, far from the flatlands of the Midwest where for the rest of the year I live in exile as an academic. I like the hard, simple, physical nature of piling logs after nine long months spent mostly indoors reading books, teaching classes, grading papers, and attending endless meetings. There are many worse things to be than a brush monkey, which is what higher-ups in the Forest Service call the people who perform this supposedly mindless labor.

Still, much as I enjoy being out in the woods again, I'm eager to get back up on the mountain and resume my job as fire lookout. So I ask Jack when he thinks I'll be heading up.

"Oh, I'm thinking maybe next week, when Ron the packer has a day or two open in his schedule," he replies. It's six miles and twenty-four-hundred-foot elevation gain from the trailhead to the lookout, a distance which will take Ron, his helper, Abe, and a six-mule team at least a full day ("from can't see, to can't see" as Ron says) to pack, climb to the summit, unload, and return to the trailhead. Since the trail is mainly south-facing, most of the snow along the route has melted by this time. But just below the summit there is a final set of switchbacks where snowdrifts often remain into early summer, and that keeps Ron worried. "It's his call," Jack says.

Looks like it'll be another week on the brush crew then. The forecast is favorable, with no precipitation expected the next week or so, and temperatures predicted to be in the eighties in the nearby Salmon River drainage by the weekend. So I'll spend my remaining time on the ground as a brush monkey, while reflecting on how much better life will be by next week. And every now and then I'll steal glances up towards Ruffneck Peak, elevation 9,407 feet, my soon-to-be-home in the mountains for the summer.

"Don't kick me, black mule," says Ron the packer. "It's too early in the morning to get kicked." We're outside with a blue day dawning above the Seafoam guard station, where the corral and bunkhouse for the brush crew are located deep in a tributary canyon of the Salmon River. Ron, Abe, and I are herding the mules and horses onto the stock truck to be transported ten or so miles by road to the trailhead.

I'm in awe as Ron methodically packs my stuff: boxes of groceries (enough to feed me for six weeks), books, and other personal items, plus eight cubies (five-gallon plastic containers enclosed in cardboard boxes) filled with drinking water. He places several of the boxes in mannies — six-foot-square canvas sheets—then wraps them in the canvas and secures the load with elaborate knots, to be balanced and tied on to the mules. Packing is a nearly lost art due to the rise of truck and helicopter transport in the modern era, and I feel like a character in Norman Maclean's story "USFS 1919." Because the lookout is in an official wilderness, the Frank Church–River of No Return, where federal law prohibits roads and motorized vehicles, the main mode of transport is still by horse and mule, so the artistry of a packer like Ron survives. One of the many benefits of wilderness is the preservation of cultural-historical values.

But Ron is too busy and too practical to be thinking in such esoteric ways. He's more interested in getting our collective butts in gear, as we have a full day ahead of us. So before too long we're in the truck and bouncing over Vanity Summit and down to the trailhead. Soon we're out of the vehicle, unloading the mules, then loading them down with gear and supplies.

Eight o'clock comes, time for an official government coffee break, but our boss gives no indication of stopping. As a practicing Mormon, Ron doesn't drink coffee and apparently sees no need for a coffee break. Nor does he swear or cuss. But he has no problem with off-color jokes. He assigns me Becky for the ride up to the lookout, a horse with the same name as the woman who is the recreation guard at Seafoam station. Ron tells me I'm gonna "ride Becky all the way up the mountain" and then laughs like hell.

The mules are strung up and ready to ride. Having ridden only twice before in my life, the last time being ten years ago, I'm understandably nervous. Abe offers reassurance, explaining that the horse assigned to me has been nicknamed Flatula because she farts so much and is really quite slow. But I keep thinking of a guy I encountered in Goat Rocks Wilderness in Washington state a decade ago who'd been crushed by his horse after it lost its footing and panicked, then fell back on him on a very steep slope. The National Guard was flown in for the rescue but the man died en route to the hospital. I still remember trying to console and keep him from lapsing into unconsciousness. Ever since, I've been leery of riding stock in the wilderness. And having seen on the topo maps of Ruffneck Peak how close the contour lines run together along the last mile or so of trail, I know we have some steep country to traverse. Maybe it'll be on foot for some of us.

The packer doesn't waste time with training sessions. Once Ron is on his horse and leading the mule train through the lower-elevation forest of lodgepole pine, it's up to me to keep up with him and Abe. Quickly I learn a few things: not to pull too tightly on the reins so as to avoid slowing the animal's gait and falling behind, and to lean backward when plunging down draws and forward when climbing. Occasionally Becky, sensing a greenhorn on her back, tries to rub me off by passing too closely to a tree, but Abe had warned me about this trick of hers so I come to learn how to steer her between trees with enough room to pass safely. We work our way around an occasional snowdrift until the timber thins out and eventually ascend above the Langer Lake basin where some deeper drifts remain and the trail starts to steepen. Ron suggests I get off and walk the horse on the steep slope where he plans to navigate around the snow-buried trail, and I happily comply. Then we're all riding again and in two hours are at the summit. We've had to walk only the last fifty feet of trail where the snow, several feet deep and softened by the morning sun, has Ron concerned about high-centering the stock. We dismount there and lug the cargo the rest of the way. The snow is firm enough to support human weight, so the going isn't too bad.

Langer Lake and Ruffneck Peak.

I've gained some valuable insight into horseback riding. Because you're higher off the ground on a horse, you have a better vantage point. Riding is also less strenuous than hiking with a heavy pack, so you can keep your head up and see more. And it's certainly faster than walking — not that speed is the ultimate goal of wilderness travel. There are legitimate ecological concerns over the impact of horses on the backcountry, of course, given the overgrazing that occurs around campsites and the increased erosion on trails resulting from stock use. But I now feel I could defend the use of these animals in the wilderness much better than I could have prior to the ride up. The horse, exotic species though it may have been (introduced by the Spanish conquistadors in the 1500s in the Southwest), is a venerable, practical, and relatively quiet form of transport in the wilderness, not to mention a historical and colorful part of the history of the American West. Its use ought therefore to be preserved, along with the woods and the mountains.

Ron wastes no time in unpacking. He grabs a bite to eat and points out a few of the local landmarks to help orient me to my new surroundings. Then, removing his work glove for a farewell handshake, he says very earnestly, "You have a good summer, hear?" I thank him for taking such

Ruffneck Peak lookout.

good care of me and my supplies. In keeping with the laconic male Western tradition, we have nothing more to say to each other.

I watch Ron and Abe ride down the trail till they disappear below the summit. Then I turn around to unbutton the lookout cabin.

Only then am I reminded of the powerful silence and solitude that come with living atop a mountain. It shouldn't take me by surprise, of course, since this is my tenth summer as a lookout. In fact, the absence of noise is one of the things I treasure most about this way of life. Yet the silence is also one of the hardest things to reaccustom myself to after spending the past nine months, and most of my life, in what Edward Abbey has called "syphilization." A life spent in places where dissonance is the rule, not the exception.

Actually, it's not so much silence I confront up here on the mountaintop, but stillness. For there *are* sounds: the occasional wind through the white-bark pines; the "phee-bee" of a mountain chickadee; the far-off roar of a creek. What is different, and so appealing, about life as a lookout is the absence for the most part of anthropogenic noise. Free of human-caused sounds, different landscapes produce different kinds of stillness, what environmental musicologists refer to as "the music of a place." R. Murray Schafer in *The Soundscape: Our Sonic Environment and the Tuning of the World* employs the term *keynote* to designate the "sonic ground" of a particular environment, its signature sounds. There is a certain sound to the prairie — say, wind passing through crinkly grasses, the intermittent, melodic call of a meadowlark. There is a different sound to the north woods — wind whooshing through the soft needles of a stand of white pines, the laving of lake water along a shore, the plaintive yodeling of a loon. There's yet another kind of stillness in the desert, where the sound of wind passing over rock and sand and expanses nearly empty of vegetation predominates. On alpine summits like this one, there's a sound having to do with mountains and trees and endless horizons — and the nearly ever-present wind. Looking up *stillness* in my *American Heritage Dictionary*, I read, along with the definition ("the state or an instance of being quiet or calm"), this accompanying statement by Barry Lopez: "The stillness that permeates the valleys is visual as well as acoustical." I glance up from the page and see in the basin below an immense carpet of conifers bending with the breeze. The wind then rushes up the slopes of the mountain and the trees sway gracefully around the lookout. I hear the elemental sound of wind whooshing in the pines. It is one of the keynotes of this place.

I should be unpacking gear and opening up the cabin, but I'm distracted by these sounds and thoughts. Save the practical, the quotidian, for later. First things first. Like the view: this cloud-free, early spring day in June, I can see a hundred miles in some directions. It's a mountain megalopolis: the Stanley Sawtooths and White Cloud ranges to the south, the Wallowas in Oregon to the northwest, the Bighorn Crags to the northeast, and the Lost River Range to the southeast. Plus many sub-ranges closer to home like yonder Tangos (a local appellation), peaking out at just over ten thousand feet. Mountains and more mountains, cut and carved by rivers over billions of years. Every man needs a horizon, said Emerson. Here, I have an abundant supply.

How often do we get to fulfill our dreams? It depends in part on the nature of our dreams, I suppose. For as long as I can recall I wanted to live in the mountains. Why? For the views; because the gods lived there in Greek and Roman mythology; because Indian braves fasted on them to have a vision; because Romantic writers like Thoreau climbed them for religious, intellectual, and aesthetic reasons; because it's a cool thing to do. Now that I've managed to arrange my life so that I can spend my summers on a mountaintop, I feel immensely gratified.

Stanley Basin and the Sawtooth Mountains.

Last week before coming up I had an interesting talk with Becky, the recreation guard who lives and works at Seafoam. A native Idahoan, born and raised in the mountains, she has worked for the Forest Service for a number of seasons. Somehow we got on the subject of free will versus determinism. She argued for the latter, claiming that mountains represented forces beyond human control that compelled people (like her) to come back to them again and again. Though a diehard proponent of free will, I had to see her point. After all, I myself was yet further proof of the lure of the mountains, just as some folks can't seem to leave the plains or desert or sea coast. Do people have innate preferences for certain types of landscapes? If so, why? There may be something to sociobiologist E. O. Wilson's theory of "biophilia" — literally, love of life. One aspect of Wilson's theory has to do with preferred landscapes. According to some psychological studies, the landscape of choice for many subjects is one with trees and open views from a promontory near water. Perhaps, Wilson has theorized, the desire for openness is traceable to our emergence as a species on the savannas of Africa several million years ago, where in order to survive we utilized our keen powers of vision and our ability to stand on hind legs in order to keep a wary eye out for predators. I have often wondered about humanity's love of prospects, the desire to see the world from the highest point around. Is our love of mountaintops a pre-Romantic phenomenon, an atavistic practical instinct?

The prospects up here are liberating and alluring, that much I know.

A snapping wind awakens me from my reveries. It's clear and sunny but at ninety-four hundred feet in June the temperature, with a brisk wind, must be in the fifties. I grab an anorak from my pack and pull it over my upper body. Much better. Now come the ritual moving-in chores: opening, cleaning, and stocking the cabin.

First I prop open the plywood shutters that protect the four walls of glass that make up the fourteen-by-fourteen-foot cabin. Next I slide open some windows — not an easy task since they have been shut for eight months — to ventilate my living space. What was just a dark cave becomes a well-lighted (if not yet clean) room: sunshine floods the cabin with all four shutters up. Already the space is feeling more comfortable, almost homey. I sweep the sills, shelves, and floor (lots of mouse turds), then empty part of one of the cubies into a galvanized bucket and mop the place clean with antiseptic. Between the fresh air, Lysol, and warm light the place becomes alive, vital. Once I've stocked the shelves and cabinets with canned and dry goods, stowed the perishables in a large metal garbage can in a nearby snowbank (my refrigerator), put my few articles of clothing and miscellaneous personals into the drawers beneath the bed, and placed my books and old typewriter on the table, the house has been transformed into my home.

I'm inhabiting the mountains again.

Evening. Another advantage of living on a mountaintop is that the days are prolonged, exaggerated in length because of the ample sky and space. Already I feel like I'm back on lookout time, when mechanical contrivances like clocks come to matter little and the days grow deliciously long and full. And since it's June and near the summer solstice, I'm enjoying daylight for sixteen to seventeen hours a day — from around 5 A.M. to 10 P.M. I fix a simple meal of a sandwich and pace around the cabin, gawking at the vistas, observing the pleasingly slow pageant of the sunset. Cumulus clouds to the west billow above the mountains, forming airy ramparts and ranges. The wind accelerates, rippling the U.S. flag I've hung from the pole at the southeast corner of the cabin. Each evening on clear nights this pattern will repeat itself: as the air along the ridges and peaks cools and becomes heavier it slides down the mountains and canyons, meeting the warmer air rising from the heated canyons below, and the merging winds cause the air currents to increase and swirl, until the air achieves a uniform temperature. Then, as the skies gradually darken, a calm ensues. Lookouts call this phenomenon a sunset wind.

I don a parka and step outside on the catwalk, standing on the lee side of the cabin. To the south, near the town of Stanley at the base of the Sawtooths, I can see the lights of an occasional car on the highway. Do these artifacts of civilization bother me? Hardly. The distant and fleeting headlights are but a reminder of how far I've come, literally and figuratively, from the industrialized world. There's no such thing as a pure wilderness existence anyway, in the sense that one can totally escape humanity. I use various gadgets up here that are constant reminders of civilization's presence: white gas stove, firefinder, binoculars, two-way radio, wood stove. The lookout itself is an artifact of civilization, as are the hiking trails leading up here constructed by the Civilian Conservation Corps (ccc) back in the 1930s. The federal wilderness I inhabit is also a creation of modern culture, the result of men and women of science, politics, and history coming together to decide where to draw arbitrary lines on a map. One experiences the wilderness not in absolutes but in terms of degrees of separation from the dominant industrial society. Spending three months up here on the mountain, encountering people only occasionally, witnessing nature uncontrolled (for the most part) on a daily basis, I feel I live as pure a wilderness life-style as one can achieve these days. The wilderness experience — as opposed to the wilderness itself — is, to a significant extent, a state of mind.

Venus appears in the southwestern sky, a dazzling orb pasted against the deep blue-mauve horizon. Soon the clouds dissipate, the sky blackens, and hundreds of stars emerge across the dark void. There are, I want to believe, more stars than I can recall ever seeing at one time. I'm reminded of how little in touch I am with basic elements like the night sky while living in the city for most of the year. Falling stars sputter across the sky. I make no wishes because I have none to make. It's my first night back on the mountain and it feels good to be home again, a native of this place.

A cloudy sunrise slowly unfolds behind Pinyon Peak. I awake blankbrained, very slowly emerging from my Polarguard sleeping bag. Stifflegged, I walk out onto the catwalk and piss off the porch, then return shivering to the cabin. I dress hurriedly, and fire up the Coleman stove in order to cook a huge cowboy breakfast: lots of coffee, hash browns, several eggs over easy, fried ham, and pan-fried toast. The radio is as quiet as a class-room after a tough question. Good — exactly the way I like to start the day.

Hungry after a hard first day on the job, I wolf down the food in the quiet cabin. Then, breakfast nearly over, I walk out on the front steps, facing south, and sit in the sun, sipping another cup of coffee. There's a light wind from the southwest, but in long pants and parka, absorbing the sun's rays, I'm quite cozy and content. Doing nothing. No thing. Well, if one wanted to dress it up a bit I guess we could call this activity meditation. But I don't chant or sit yogalike or close my eyes. I open myself up to the real world of the senses and delight in the sensations: the tang of hot coffee on the tongue, the trill of a rock wren down the slope, a sea of conifers surrounding the mountain. As my favorite poet, Wallace Stevens, said, the greatest poverty is not to live in the physical world. I think of previous lookouts and mountain ranges I have visited and books that I have read and people I have known and loved. I daydream and think of nothing at all.

One person's definition of leisure: the opportunity not to avoid respon-sibilities, but rather to redefine them so that work and play become one and the same thing.

What would my parents think of me now? Both of them have been dead for a decade or more. They never understood why I dropped out of law school to work for the Forest Service to live and play in the mountains. They thought I was still acting like the kid I was back in the Poconos, always walk-ing (and sometimes getting lost) in the woods behind our home. Back-packing in their eyes was "silly" and "not grown-up." But I continued to do it, determined to follow my own star rather than the course they charted for me, and so we drifted further apart, both physically and emotionally. Looking back, I realize now they simply wanted what they thought was best for me; they wanted me to succeed in their own prescribed way. My mother and father both came from coal-mining families, grew up during the De-pression, and were put to work at an early age to help make ends meet. My mother never got past the sixth grade, while my father, though a bright stu-dent and good athlete, went to work in the mines right after graduating from high school. I was the first member of my family to graduate from col-lege. So naturally they were disappointed when I chose to work in the woods rather than finish law school. "The point at which a society bears down on the individual is in the choice of vocation: here is the battlefield of values and the gamble for rewards," the late Sherman Paul, one of my graduate school mentors, wrote in a seminal study of Thoreau, *The Shores of Amer-ica.* As someone who struggled most of his life over the choice of a spiritual calling, Thoreau became one of my great heroes when I, too, confronted the unavoidable question of *what to do* at a critical time in my own life.

Then my parents died, and we never had the chance to reconcile. But a year before my father passed away, after I'd decided to go to graduate school with the hope of becoming a professor, I sent him a postcard with the following excerpt from Thoreau's essay "Life without Principle": "If a man walk in the woods for love of them half of each day, he is in danger of being regarded as a loafer; but if he spends his whole day as speculator, shearing off those woods and making earth bald before her time, he is esteemed an industrious and enterprising citizen." What I was trying to imply was that success is measured in different ways by different people and that I hoped he and my mother would accept a definition that differed from their own.

Though we never talked about it, I'd like to think my parents eventually came to understand my decision.

2. Working a lookout

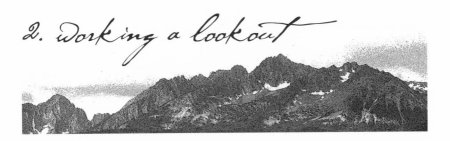

　　As B. Traven once said, this is the world, muchachos. This is the real world, and you are in it.

　It is a real world, all right, a world of rocks and ice, a tactile universe. Only rock is real, claimed Ed Abbey when he worked in Arches National Park in Utah, a desert consisting mainly of red slickrock sandstone sculpted by wind and water into fantastic shapes and sizes. Here in the wetter, colder mountains of Idaho, there are far more trees and the rock is of a different kind. Though none of the mountains within view is higher than distant 12,655-foot Mount Borah (the highest point in Idaho), they present rugged horizons in all directions, especially to the south where the White Clouds and Sawtooths top out at nearly twelve thousand and eleven thousand feet, respectively. Within the Frank Church–River of No Return Wilderness the mountains are not as high or as jagged; they resemble wave upon wave of rocky ridges cresting at their highest just above ten thousand feet.

　I have often wondered how the nearby Seafoam mine got its name. Could some poetic miner, having climbed one of the local ridges, looked out and thought of the ocean as he gazed upon the endless undulation of ridge-lines? During Precambrian times billions of years ago, this area was in fact under water, and on its ocean floor layers of fine sediments settled and accumulated. Then, from about 570 million years B.P. (before the present) to as recently as less than a million years B.P. there was significant volcanic activity, creating what is now known as the Idaho batholith, the largest body of exposed granite in the United States. This granite represents about one-third of the bare rock in the wilderness. How did there come to be so much exposed rock in this region? During the prolonged period of volcanic activ-

The General, part of the Tango Mountains.

ity millions of years ago, the land was also rising, the result of tectonic forces that literally pushed the land up out of the water. Small mountain ranges, such as the nearby Tangos (which includes the highest point in the River of No Return Wilderness, The General, at 10,329 feet), are a good example of this ancient volcanic activity with their striking red-and-white, pumiceous, cinder-covered slopes. Today, geologists identify the Tangos as part of the Challis Volcanics. As the land continued to rise, the pressure produced by the collision of plates and land surfaces created another kind of rock, metamorphic, which can be found in the lower reaches of the Middle Fork of the Salmon River canyon in the form of schist and gneiss. Then, during the last million years or so, a series of glaciers formed and disappeared, reshaping the land once again, though in this region only in a minor way since the mountains were not high enough nor the weather wet enough for large ice fields to form.

It's hard enough for me to think about rivers of ice carving out these V-shaped drainages and canyons, let alone comprehend the collision of massive plates beneath the surface of the earth occurring billions of years ago. If ever there were a science to prove the nonhuman reality of the world we live in, it would have to be geology. The relatively infinitesimal length of time humans have existed on the face of the earth, along with all the titanic geomorphology that occurred in our absence, mostly in infinitely small, incremental stages, conclusively demonstrates the geological insignificance of human existence.

Perhaps then it's partly out of egotism — the desire to believe that the human race does matter, has mattered — that I've always preferred relatively recent time, the human history of an area: the transformation of land into landscape. When I use the term *landscape* I have in mind a more specialized definition than the ordinary one of simply "the land out there" that we view at a particular time. I prefer the way the late cultural geographer J. B. Jackson defined landscape as "a synthetic space, a man-made system of spaces superimposed on the face of the land." In other words, landscape is human-modified space, usually the result of deliberate changes to the land made by people. And it's people, especially the various inhabitants of the Frank Church over millennia who have affected this land, who have left their cultural imprints on it, who interest me most.

Up here on the mountain, my thoughts wander through time, through human history and its vast prehuman background. That's why I return each summer to this job, this vocation: for the leisure it affords me to think at my own pace, about what I want to contemplate, if anything at all, the moments of reflective time we all find so rare down there in the so-called civilized world. Most people who visit me on the lookout inevitably say, "I'd go nuts in a place like this — it's too quiet, too lonely, too boring!" Perhaps they don't realize they're slowly but surely going insane Down Below, their senses assaulted by noise, their sanity at risk because of needless deadlines and pressures of job and family, all the everyday *shit* people think they have to put up with but don't.

But it's not all leisure up here. After a spell I realize I've got to return to the world of work after all. There are times, alas, when lookout time ends and clock time takes over. I'm actually getting paid to be a fire lookout (around eight bucks an hour, plus overtime), and one of my duties is to record weather observations. So each morning just before eight o'clock I walk to the weather station located about twenty feet from the lookout cabin and, using some basic instruments as well as my own senses, record a bunch of data: the degree of cloud cover, current as well as maximum and minimum relative humidity over the past twenty-four hours, wind speed and direction, fuel moisture, maximum and minimum temperatures, amount and duration of precipitation, and degree of lightning activity. I then report my observations to dispatch in the forest supervisor's office (SO) in Challis. This information is also turned in by other lookouts and personnel across the forest, as well as through automated RAWS (remote area weather stations), and duly recorded and compiled. It is all eventually interpreted by meteorologists who chart the weather patterns of the region.

Then there are the official duties of a fire lookout. My primary responsibilities, of course, are to watch for and report forest fires. The manual calls for me to do a check-look every fifteen minutes — a systematic visual sweep of all the terrain visible from the lookout. This being government work, there's a protocol: with the binoculars (my own Zeiss 10 × 40) I'm supposed to look up each and every drainage from bottom to top. But if I did this the recommended number of times during the daylight hours I'd probably give myself headaches and cause eyestrain, maybe even ruin my vision for the long term. So over the years I've worked out my own system. First I go about memorizing the terrain from the lookout, noting all the major landmarks: peaks, rivers, towns, roads, and any other marks of civilization. I become intimately familiar with the country so that if anything looks at all different — like wisps of drift smoke rising behind a ridge — it immediately catches my eye. As the day progresses the light changes and so does the appearance of the terrain, so this phenomenon has to be factored into what one sees as well. The time for greatest watchfulness comes after a lightning storm. Every year lightning triggers an estimated fifteen thousand wildfires in the U.S., and most of these occur west of the Rocky Mountains where it's drier. Fires are also caused by humans, of course, but in the relatively unpopulated West eighty percent of forest fires are ignited by lightning (though as the West continues to grow in population, the percentage of anthropogenic forest fires will continue to increase).

Given that it's June and still early spring in the mountains with cool and wet conditions prevailing, the fire danger is low and so is my degree of alertness. I do casual looks at this time, more for aesthetic and spiritual than occupational reasons. But it's important to be ready when a fire alert occurs. I wouldn't want to be scooped by the patrol plane, which usually flies every afternoon when the weather is good and sometimes several times a day following periods of intense lightning activity. I decide it's a good time to get the Osborne firefinder in shape for the season — one of the basic tools, along with binocs and two-way radio, of a modern-day fire lookout.

In the middle of the cabin, sitting on a five-foot-high wooden stand, is the firefinder. It's basically a giant compass (without the magnetized needle): a circular map, with a twenty-mile radius and one-inch-to-the-mile scale,

The Osborne firefinder.

oriented north, with the 360 degrees of the compass around the edge of the circle, engraved on a bronze base. In the center of the map is one's lookout. The firefinder rests on metal tracks a foot or so long to allow for sliding the base forward or backward. The lookout rotates the map until he/she is able to look through a set of crosshairs (like a rifle scope) at one end of the firefinder in order to sight in on a possible smoke. Once the fire is lined up, one simply takes a bearing — the location of the fire in relation to the fire lookout — reported in degrees, as in fifty-seven degrees (meaning in this case to the northeast of the lookout) with zero being north. The next, more challenging step is to coordinate the location of the fire that exists with the assumed location on the map. The map is divided up into townships and ranges and square miles, thirty-six square miles or sections to each township, and each section amounting to 640 acres. The key to being a successful lookout is to be able to locate the fire quickly within a quarter-mile of its actual location, so that when firefighters are dispatched (in a wilderness area, by plane or helicopter; outside a wilderness area, by vehicle) they can find the fire without delay. If the fire is near a major or easily identifiable landmark like a mountain peak or highway, there's no problem in locating it; if it's in flat country with lots of trees and no readily distinguishable landmarks, then it's a greater challenge in cartography.

One also has to be sure that what is being reported is in fact a real fire. In the vernacular of the fire lookout there is something known as a "false smoke." Sometimes in a certain light, a clearing on a steep slope, such as an avalanche chute, can look like a column of smoke. After a rainfall, wisps of ground fog (what lookouts call "waterdogs") can take on a remarkable resemblance to a smoking fire. Dust kicked up by a vehicle on a dirt road can also suggest smoke. Then there are the sources of real smoke, like mills or construction equipment, which a lookout should be notified about and whose locations he/she should have noted on a special form near the firefinder. A veteran lookout will usually watch a smoke for several minutes and check for the telltale signs: a blue-gray tint to the cloud, a persistent but changing column shape, perhaps even visible flame if the fire is close enough or viewed at night. Sometimes a fire will appear, then disappear and not show up again, depending on the temperature, humidity, winds, fuels, and topography. Other times it may not show up after the initial lightning strike until days later, becoming what lookouts refer to as a "sleeper." There is more to the job, and fires, than meets the eye.

Once the lookout has located the fire and verified it as a legitimate smoke, he/she calls it in to dispatch, reading off a standard form in which one notes the nearest landmark as well as the size, slope, fuels, and current wind direction and speed. A typical fire report goes something like this: "Challis Dispatch, I have a fire to report. It's on the southwest side of Langer Peak. My azimuth (bearing) is eighty degrees. The fire is located in the southeast corner of section 1, township 13 north, range 1 east. It's burning in some scattered timber. I can see the base of the smoke. The estimated size is a spot [involving only one or only a few trees]. The fire's rate of spread is slow at this time. It's burning near the top of a fairly steep, west-facing slope. The winds are light and out of the southwest at this time." The dispatcher then records the info and passes it on to the fire management officer of the ranger district, who in turn alerts an available crew.

Then comes an anxious game of holding out (and staying off the radio) till the firefighters are dispatched by either helicopter or plane and it's officially recognized by the firefighting personnel that the fire you've turned in actually exists. In the metaphysics of firefighting a fire does not become real until it has been seen and confirmed by others. Since lightning storms and resulting fires are impossible to predict from one year to the next — I've gone months, even an entire season, without spotting a single fire, as well as reporting over a hundred fires in another summer — reporting fires is an interesting, exciting, and rewarding aspect of the job. It's what we're paid for and expected to do. When we go weeks without a fire, the dispatch office and fire crews will often blame lookouts for the lack of activity. "Why don't you guys report a fire now and then?" someone from below will ask in a cranky (but joking) way. And I have heard stories, no doubt apocryphal, of a few dishonest lookouts who, maybe out of boredom, maybe out of greed, maybe for both reasons, decided to take matters in their own hands — deus ex machina — and start a forest fire, then report it to dispatch. But generally lookouts are honest and patiently wait for the arrival of storms.

As one who loves to pore over maps, I consider the job of looking for and reporting fires to be another inestimable perk. I get paid to read the landscape. There's a certain amount of solipsism and self-love that goes with this occupation. In certain ways being a fire lookout represents the epitome of the romantic artist's dream: living on a mountain, dwelling in rhapsodic ecstasy far from civilization, with the self as the center of the universe. But on a deeper level, if one is a fire lookout long enough, there comes the humbling recognition of how insignificant a role humans play in the grand scheme of things. "We rotate in the beneficent light of a minor star," once observed Loren Eiseley. Exactly. I mean, how long has that gnarly whitebark pine been around? How about the soil and rocks which form this mountaintop? The mountains and valleys shaped by fire and ice? Yes, everywhere there are signs of human presence: the lookout, the trails, the fires started and suppressed and allowed to burn. Yet, living here alone with just a handful of others in this vast expanse of wilderness, one cannot but help become aware of humanity's ultimately trivial presence.

Like a good government employee, I'm supposed to raise and lower the U.S. flag each day. Instead, I raise it on the first day and let it fly continuously the rest of the summer. I like to use it as a wind sock, to let me know which way the wind is blowing and roughly how fast. I like to hear it ripple in the wind. And I like to see it from afar — say from Langer Lake down below, with the binocs — as a reminder of the cabin's presence. The fact that I leave it up all the time has bothered some people. Unpatriotic, they say. But what is a patriot? I'm as proud to be an American as the next person — at least for certain reasons. I'm proud that we as a nation were the first to set aside nature as national parks and the first to preserve wilderness areas, and that we have been such staunch defenders of individual rights over a few centuries of political existence. But I'm also critical of our incestuous relationship with corporations, the greediness of politicians, the spinelessness of elected officials when it comes to making good, hard, tough decisions for the long term. Not my country right or wrong but right when I think it's right and wrong otherwise. Wendell Berry has defined patriotism as the responsibility to love and defend one's native ground. I like that definition very much — so long as it doesn't lapse into a dangerous provincialism — and think it applies to my position, my place, as a native of Ruffneck Peak. I'm proud and lucky to have the privilege of living on this mountain and want to learn as much as I can and make the best of this place, this country, while I'm here. And I'm grateful to my nation for giving me this opportunity to serve it, as a form of peacetime service to the landscape which is its foundation, and which is and has always been the basis of all cultures — a fundamental fact too often overlooked by most people, especially academics.

The Beat poet Gary Snyder, someone who has gone native in the northern Sierra Nevada, writes in "For All":

> I pledge allegiance to the soil
>   of Turtle Island
> and to the beings who thereon dwell
>   one ecosystem
>   in diversity
>   under the sun
> With joyful interpenetration for all.

Perhaps the wet weather has me in a feisty mood. Since it's still spring in the mountains, conditions are unstable and wildly unpredictable. Cloudless dawns are typical at this time of year, but by midmorning, as if by regular acts of magic, popcorn puffs of clouds appear low in the sky, roughly at eye level (nine thousand feet), forming flocks of fleecy sheep. Sometimes I feel as if I can simply reach out and grab some cloud as it passes by — a marvelous fantasy.

In every lookout cabin there is a chart explaining, with photographs, the seven stages of cloud development typical of summertime patterns in the West. Stage 1 clouds (altocumulus castellatus), ragged and fleeting, sometimes materialize early in the morning, signaling instability and presaging storm activity within forty-eight hours. Generally every day in the West fleets of cumulus clouds appear by late morning (Stage 2), and by mid-afternoon they've often piled up into towering cumulus (Stage 3), sometimes attaining a height of forty thousand feet. Anvil-headed cumulus or ice-top cumulus can form next (Stage 4). By then, shadows the size of western counties darken and float across the carpet of the national forest and the lower grasslands and meadows. Sometimes the dark bottoms of the clouds at the next stage (5) will produce curtains of rain not quite hitting the ground — what meteorologists identify as virga. Then a rainstorm may follow (Stage 6) with what all firefighting personnel, greedy for adventure and hazard pay, hope for — lightning and thunder (Stage 7). Better yet (for the purposes of fire ignition), there may not even be any rain, in which case the phenomenon is called dry lightning.

In June and early July, following a normal winter snowpack, the forests of the northern Rockies are usually still too wet and the air too moist with humidity for fires to start. And at higher elevations in the shade and on north-facing slopes there could be as much as ten feet of snow remaining. While it may be seventy degrees in the Stanley Basin at six thousand feet, at nine thousand feet it feels like the forties with the wind chill (subtract three to four degrees for every thousand feet of ascent). I sit in the cabin with all the windows and the door closed and let the occasional bursts of sun heat up the interior, while the wind blows through the treetops. But when it clouds up and begins to rain — maybe even sleet — then there's no choice but to fire up the wood stove with precious chunks of subalpine and white-bark fir that have been stockpiled the last couple of seasons.

As the day passes by seamlessly, I look up now and then from a novel, the quiet interrupted by the boom and roll of distant thunder and the ding of rain on the roof. Yes, more unwanted precip is falling, as we say in firefighting circles. I watch the storm track from Cape Horn Mountain northeast along Cape Horn Creek and then southeast down through the Stanley Basin (storm cells often follow drainages). When it passes and the rain relents, I walk out on the catwalk, ostensibly to do a check-look but really to dispel

The Cape Horn Mountain fire.

some cabin fever, take a break from reading, stretch my legs, and sniff some rain-cleansed mountain air.

Something catches my eye. Behind Cape Horn Mountain, I notice a different look to the landscape — can it be a smoke? I try to talk myself out of it. It's too wet, too cold, too early in the season. Nonetheless I run inside the cabin to grab the binocs (which I should have brought with me in the first place) and come back outside. Focusing in with the lenses, I confirm my initial suspicion: Fire! There's a steady, thick column, tinted gray-black, rising behind a ridgetop. The fire must be burning in the pitch of a fir or pine because of the dark smoke. There's little wind because the column is rising nearly straight up. I run back into the cabin and get to work.

No matter how many fires I've spotted, no matter how many smokes I've reported, the adrenaline always starts to flow whenever I see another fire. I wonder if any other lookouts have spotted it — not likely, because it's early in the season and some districts (to save money) may not even have sent up their lookouts yet. I line up the smoke on the Osborne firefinder, take a bearing, and work up a quick "legal" — what I think is the actual location of the fire. I can't see the base of it because the smoke is coming up behind the ridge and there's no telling just how far behind it is — the distances of objects in the landscape can be deceiving in that way, an example of what perceptual psychologists refer to as the moon illusion. But I'd seen the lightning cell develop over the area and heard the thunder, so I've got a good hunch the fire is in the vicinity of Cape Horn Mountain.

I note all the necessary data on the fire report. Then I take a deep breath to calm down before calling fire dispatch in Challis. As usual the voice in response is perfectly in control, unemotional, maybe at this time of year even a little skeptical. "Are you sure it's a fire, Ruffneck?" the dispatcher asks. I insist that it is. The dispatcher's skepticism is partly pecuniary. It costs thousands of dollars merely to put a plane or helicopter in the air with a half-dozen or so firefighters or smokejumpers plus pilot, all of whom are earning hazard pay (time-and-a-half) for their work. Understandably, the Forest Service wants to be sure they're responding to a real fire and spending precious fire management dollars wisely. But the supervisor is not likely to question the accuracy of a veteran lookout, so once I've reassured them that a fire is actually burning in the mountains the dispatcher says thanks and signs off. Silence descends on the radio once again, as well it should this early in the season.

My legal actually places the fire on the adjacent Boise National Forest. Our dispatcher on the Challis National Forest will call them on the phone to report my sighting, and it'll then be up to the Boise authorities to muster their personnel and respond. Since I don't have a Boise NF frequency on my radio (a blessing in disguise, for there's more than enough radio traffic on one national forest frequency come the peak of fire season to drive one batty), my only choice is to wait, keep looking for air traffic in the area, and hope that the Boise dispatcher will report back to the Challis dispatcher and that he in turn will let me know if in fact the fire's been confirmed and manned.

Nearly two hours pass. The whole time I'm pacing the catwalk, unable to do anything but keep glassing the area for signs of fire, and fire management, activity. The fire, meanwhile, varies in intensity; sometimes the smoke nearly disappears only to churn up again, a response to the changing fuel, air, and temperature conditions. Finally I see a midsized propeller plane circle the area several times, after which a number of parachutes open and descend on the ridgetop. Apparently, smokejumpers have been summoned from McCall, the closest base, about fifty miles north of the incident. Since the fire is over twenty miles away I can't make out much more. Nonetheless, my first fire of the season has been confirmed.

I celebrate with a pre-dinner cocktail — a precious can of beer I break from an even more precious six-pack, smuggled up with my groceries, un-beknownst to teetotaller Mormon Ron Hansen. Here's to you, Ron, I shout, and your sturdy mules and taut knots and my stealthiness. I also toast the Forest Service for a job well done (myself included) and try not to chug the brew all at once. One must savor all things precious and pleasing.

Gary Snyder, who (along with Jack Kerouac) worked several lookouts in the North Cascades of Washington in the 1950s, has written a wonderful poem about lookout life called "Things to Do Around a Lookout." This poem captures the poetic aspects of a lookout's day-to-day activities:

> Wrap up in a blanket in cold weather and just read.
> Practice writing Chinese characters with a brush
> Paint pictures of the mountains
> Put out salt for deer
> Bake coffee cake and biscuit in the iron oven,
> Hours off hunting twisty firewood, packing it all back up and
>   chopping.
> Rice out for the ptarmigan and the conies
> Mark well sunrise and sunset — drink lapsang soochong.
> Rolling smokes
> The flower book and the bird book and the star book
> Old Readers Digests left behind
> Bullshitting on the radio with a distant pinnacle, like you, hid in
>   clouds;
> Drawing little sexy sketches of bare girls
> Reading maps, checking on the weather, airing out musty Forest
>   Service sleeping bags and blankets
> Oil the saws, sharpen axes,
> Learn the names of all the peaks you see and which is the highest
>   there are hundreds —
> Learn by heart the drainages between.
> Go find a shallow pool of snowmelt on a good day, bathe in the
>   lukewarm water,
> Take off in foggy weather and go climbing all alone
> The rock book—strata, dip, and strike
> Get ready for the snow, get ready
> To go down.

3. visitors

Despite the fire I reported, human activity on the national forest is only just beginning at this early point in the season. The receding snows slowly open access to trails and roads in the high country. The warmer temperatures and spring rains melt the snow, increasing runoff and raising river levels — good for all the rafters on the world-class rapids of the Main and Middle Fork of the Salmon River, the longest undammed river system in the Lower Forty-eight states. Recreation guards and patrol rangers start their river-running season. Trail crews resume maintenance within the wilderness area. All of the seasonal staff has now returned to work, so, as far as the Forest Service is concerned, a new year has begun in the Frank Church Wilderness.

At this stage of the season, the workweek has become routine. My official hours (meaning the time for which I'm actually paid to work as a fire lookout) are 9 to 5, five days a week. My days off are Tuesday and Wednesday. Of course, given the fact that there is no clear distinction between where I live and where I work, between how I live and how I work, it's hard to tell when I'm working and when I'm not. I like to think I'm always working (better that than to think I'm always not working, i.e., loafing). It's a kind of subalpine, meditative, pure (as opposed to puritan) work ethic, if you will.

Once the fire season heats up, the regular schedule will vary. During off hours (other than 9 to 5, or on my days off) I get paid when storms are occurring and when I'm reporting fires, and when I'm needed to relay radio messages to and from crews isolated in the backcountry who are unable to go directly through dispatch. But in spring while it's still wet and cool I'm generally free to do as I please in the early mornings and evenings as well as on my days off. Like Gary Snyder I'll "wrap up in a blanket and just read," or bake cookies and bread, or gather firewood, or engage in some natural history study. I'm an amateur natural historian, so whenever I stray from the cabin I usually take along my binoculars and field guides to birds and flowers to check out the flora and fauna.

There are various ways of measuring time up here, and one of them is through phenology — the study of the seasonality of natural phenomena (when birds migrate, when flowers bloom, etc.). "But my friends ask what will I do when I get [to the pond]," wrote Thoreau in his journal prior to moving to Walden. "Will it not be employment enough to watch the progress of the seasons?" Most conscious, alert people, I would guess, are to some degree phenologists — students of the changing seasons, even if the change in the seasons is less dramatic in some regions than others. On this mountaintop, with no radio or TV, no cell phone or Internet, no bars, no shopping malls, and no movie theaters, there are few enough distractions of the kind one finds in society. Yet, if one is attentive enough, one discovers that there are in fact many diversions — and ones far more worthwhile than soap operas, e-mail, or sales of the latest gadget one doesn't need. Some days, especially during early spring when the snow has just melted, it's all I can do to make it down to the first bend in the trail, a mere twenty yards from the cabin, so many things are there to investigate.

To date I've seen or at least heard several mammals. Even before I was fully unpacked I had visitors — golden-mantled ground squirrels who audaciously scampered right into the cabin and began chewing open a bag of rice. Though tourists yell "Chipmunk!" when they see one scurrying around, it is, properly speaking, a squirrel (chipmunks have facial stripes, squirrels don't). About ten inches long, with golden brown neck, gray back and black-and-white stripes on the sides, they are the boldest, most approachable creatures in this subalpine environment. I try hard not to deliberately feed them (I've no desire to domesticate wild creatures), but I know they feast on the table scraps I occasionally throw over the catwalk. And I must confess that during rare lapses I've actually sunk to hand-feeding them a peanut or two when they come into the cabin begging. The tendency to find some (though not all) animals "cute" is one of our species' more regrettable traits.

A larger mammal hereabouts (twenty-five inches or so in length) is the yellow-bellied marmot. I notice them lumbering around the grasses and rocks on the summit, their rolls of fat and fur shimmering in the sun. When I approach too closely they'll stand on their hind legs and whistle, sounding out an alarm to other marmots, and the whistles recur like echoes down the mountainside. My Audubon guide to North American mammals tells me they're host to the tick that causes the deadly (but rare) Rocky Mountain spotted fever, so I'm happy they keep their distance — though, of course, I can easily pick up a tick by walking where the marmots have been. And, in fact, have. So far without disastrous consequences.

More elusive are conies—rock rabbits, or, as they're more properly called, pikas. Six to eight inches long, with oversized ears, they have a disproportionately loud bleat or distress call that they use to signal alarms to fellow members on rocky slopes. When I'm traipsing around the summit in mid-day to stretch my legs, I'll often hear but seldom see these diminutive fellows. There is a ventriloquial quality to their cry, for even when I think a pika sounds close by, I seldom spot it; instead, the rattling of rocks in another direction indicates it's somewhere else. I like pikas for their wildness, their refusal to submit to domestication, and find them just the kind of neighbors I desire: happy to keep an eye on your place and ready to sound the alarm when intruders come, but otherwise content to keep their distance. Comfortable distances make for good neighbors.

On the north ridge of the mountain, where the slope sheers off into a precipitous thousand-foot drop, I've seen half-moon-shaped tracks in the snow and mud. They could be the mark of deer, but in my desire for rarer sightings I prefer to think they've been left by a wilder, more circumspect mammal: mountain goats. I keep a perpetual sharp eye out for these noble, hirsute, mystical creatures.

I stray farther down the mountain in early morning and evening — the crepuscular hours. I have in mind physical as well as spiritual needs. I'm well stocked with water at the moment, with ten full cubies plus a few more I've filled with snow and placed in the sun on the south-facing side of the catwalk to melt into water. But one of the cardinal rules of lookout life is that one can never have enough water on hand. A storm could occur, bringing with it lots of lightning and fires, thus occupying the lookout for weeks on end and effectively pinning one down in the cabin. Friends visit and, of course, need to use water; occasional hikers come up, dehydrated, and ask for a drink. One grows conscious of just how much water one needs during an average day, and inevitably becomes a water conservationist in the arid West. It's a mile hike and a helluva drop — a little over eleven hundred feet, according to a USGS 7.5-minute topographical map — to Island Lake, the nearest water source. As I've mentioned, a cubie contains five gallons of water, which weighs about forty pounds. With the load strapped to a fairly comfortable packboard, I can get in some rigorous exercise every day or so, keeping me in decent shape and giving me the excuse to get away from work and home and see what's going on beyond the circumscribed radius of the summit. When a visitor to the lookout once asked me how I got my water and I explained the procedure to him, he chuckled and said, "Now I know how this lookout got its name. You have to be a ruffneck to survive here."

On the way down, cubie empty, unladen, I'm free to saunter. The first thing I notice are dogtooth violets (also called avalanche lilies), my favorite early spring flower, sprouting on wet slopes in the wake of melting snow. The many pendant yellow petals lend a delicate beauty to the otherwise stark subalpine environment of wind-blasted, stunted trees and jagged, chaotic rock and talus rubble. A friend startled me one time in the mountains by reaching down, yanking one of them out of the ground, and sticking it in his mouth. "Good greens and texture," he said as he munched away. Indeed, the Craighead brothers in their folklore-filled guide to Rocky Mountain wildflowers note that Indian tribes of the region used the leaves as edible greens and boiled and dried the bulbs for wintertime consumption. Bears feed on the bulbs, too, and deer, elk, and goat feast on the leaves.

Over the Langer Lakes basin I catch a glimpse of a large bird spiraling, higher and higher, till it soars above the ridgeline. Steadying my arms, I focus in with the binoculars, and confirm the sighting: a golden eagle. No mistaking that flat, immense wingspan. It climbs into the sky and I follow its flight until it dims with distance.

My two most regular avian neighbors (so far) are Clark's nutcrackers and Townsend's solitaires — like me, hardy inhabitors of the treeline environment. The nutcracker, with its long, pointed bill, is (as its name implies) fond of nuts, and feeds on the cones of the whitebark pines that dominate the tree cover at these higher elevations. Its jaylike, raucous calls break the silence as I tramp down the trail. The Townsend's solitaire is more melodic in its call, singing a kind of complex, extended warble as it takes wing. A member of the thrush family, it is (according to the Peterson guide) "among the finest singers." I can confirm this accolade, having heard at twilight its rarer cousin, the hermit thrush, fluting its ethereal song from the treetops. As Aldo Leopold has written, there is a peculiar virtue in the music of elusive birds. When I hear the thrush's call repeated on birdsong tapes in "nature stores" I am instantly transported back in time and space to the montane regions of the American West. Thoreau once referred to the song's "liquid coolness" and says that "this bird never fails to speak to me out of

Ruffneck Lake (left) and Island Lake (lower right).

an ether purer than that I breathe, of immortal beauty and vigor. . . . He sings to make men take higher and truer views of things."

I follow the switchbacks down to the trail junction, pause to admire the sweeping view of the lake basin, then turn left (east) and continue down more switchbacks until I'm as close to the lake as I can get before leaving the trail. From there it's a short, abrupt, cross-country drop through some scattered whitebark pines and wet meadow to the feeder stream of Island Lake. Where I doff the packboard and empty cubie I spot still more flowers: paintbrush, mountain bluebells, mule's ears. The still blue surface of the lake reflects the morning sky and small, soft puffs of clouds. I think about how lucky I am to be drinking water from this lake. Many cultures have a version of a sacred font; this is mine.

It takes little time to fill the cubie using a one-quart plastic bottle I've brought along for this purpose. Before heaving the pack on my back and strapping in, I sit for a while and contemplate the scene. The few sounds of the basin — rock wrens trilling, nuthatches horning, the spring burbling over the rocks into the lake — only emphasize all the more the stillness and solitude.

A sudden blast of wind up the basin blows across my sweaty body, chilling me. Time to head back up the mountain. From where I fill up back to the trail is about an eighth of a mile, nearly straight up. I remind myself to take small steps, very small steps, as I fall into a slow but comfortable hiking rhythm. The footing, in slick grasses and unstable rock, is dicey and there's no sense hurrying. Once I intersect with the trail I take a deep blow, then push onward and upward. No stopping for natural history now; I want to make it back to the cabin as efficiently as possible. My thoughts blur and focus on not much of anything. Mostly they have to do with an awareness of the tangible — the sweat dripping from my brow, the tension in my legs as I struggle against gravity, the purchase of my Vibram soles on the granite and gravel, the rhythmic sucking and blowing of air into and from my chest as I continue to push up the trail. It's a wonderful thing, to be reduced to a physical unthinking machine for a time, almost completely unself-conscious. And before I know it, I'm cresting the final switchback to the top and the cabin comes into view once again, the flag rippling in the interminable summit breeze.

The third week of the season I get a call from Jack, the FMO. "How would you like some company?" he wants to know. This is of course a rhetorical question; he's my boss, and while the cabin is my home and workplace it is, after all, owned by the government. Since I really have no choice, I might as well be congenial about the request. "Sure, why not?" I reply. Turns out that my guests are two college students from back East who are working for the Forest Service as volunteers for the season, doing trail and campsite reconnaissance. They'll be in the Langer Lakes area for a couple of days, a popular destination for backpackers and horse campers, and while they're in the neighborhood they'd like to visit the lookout.

All kinds of warning signs appear over this prospect.

First of all, I haven't yet had any visitors this season, which is exactly the way I like it. "It is very dissipating to be with people too much," as Thoreau, America's most famous misanthrope, once wrote in his journal. Indeed. The longest stretch I've gone on a lookout without seeing people has been three weeks — and now my chance at a new record is about to be lost. While up here it's impossible not to fall into comfortable routines, and visitors inevitably disrupt the rhythms of lookout life. Further, I'm suspicious of Easterners with their superior airs toward Westerners (I should know, being an ex-Easterner myself). Moreover, volunteers are held in suspicion by regular seasonal employees in the Forest Service because they're essentially doing work that used to be performed by paid laborers; they do receive a daily stipend for food but are otherwise not compensated, and in effect take away jobs from people who need the work and salary. Volunteers are really a form of scab labor — though they are hardly conscious of their exploitation, enjoying the privilege of working in the stupendous scenery of the American West. Finally, and quite frankly, after working with college students for nine months of the year, I need a significant respite from the irresponsibility and immaturity of young adults.

On the other hand . . .

Some conversation (with others besides myself) would be nice. And they will no doubt be bringing up my mail — always a highlight for a lookout seeking occasional written contact with the outside world. And these visitors are women, after all — young, fit, perhaps attractive members of the opposite sex. Not that I have any evil or untoward designs on them, mind you; but as an aesthete, one who is unusually sensitive to beauty in all its many forms, I see nothing wrong with a little aesthetic admiration. From a safe distance, of course.

So, one might as well make the best of an inevitable intrusion.

The visit goes fairly well. Despite my initial skepticism and reservations, I come to like Lisa and Christianne. They're both from Ivy League schools so, yes, they do indeed have a certain attitude, an air of superiority. But they're also open-minded, self-critical, and eager to learn. They arrive late in the afternoon, tired and sweaty after the long steep pull from the lake basin. Lisa is dark-haired, freckled, and solid; Christianne is blond, lean, athletic, a wry smile always on her face. We share a potluck dinner: my burritos and their "nature burger," some gawd-awful vegetarian soybean concoction that has the texture and taste of cardboard. Smothered in salsa, it's edible but not much more. I bring out some wine I've been saving for special occasions like this, and the meal is complete.

Lisa and Christianne are both well traveled; they've been to Europe, Nepal, India, as well as all over the American West. As fellow Eastern expatriates we share our views of Westerners and Easterners. We agree that in general the latter are ruder, more abrupt, impatient, blunter, more ambitious; the former more practical and down to earth, friendlier, more polite, and of course slower talking. Westerners seem to take for granted the sublimity of their surroundings, while Easterners are (ironically) more appreciative and protective of it — in part because as tourists they don't have to derive a material living directly from the wilderness by extracting its natural resources.

It's no surprise, then, that the two women are also diehard Sierra Club wilderness preservationists. So am I, but we have differing views of the role of people in the wilderness. Part of their job is to dismantle fire rings at popular campsites, largely for aesthetic reasons. According to the Forest Service, this strategy creates the illusion of a virgin campsite. I laugh at this particular practice of wilderness management. What about the trail you walked in on? The signs at trailheads and junctions? Why do preservationists insist on trying to eliminate all signs of homo sapiens from the wilderness? Why are preservationists so loathing of people in general? All species impact their environment in some way, I lecture (my tone taking on that of the omniscient professor). Granted, we as a species have had far greater impact than other species. But to deny that humans, especially modern humans, have played a role in the history of a particular wilderness is absurd; worse, it's dangerous and counterproductive. We manage wilderness as a cultural artifact, we have an impact on it simply because we (in effect) created it. For example: by drawing an arbitrary line on a map, designating it as a wilderness boundary, we allow trees to be logged on one side of it but not the other; fires to be suppressed on one side, but not the other; and so on.

To clinch my point I recite some elliptical lines from a Wallace Stevens poem:

> I placed a jar in Tennessee,
> And round it was, upon a hill.
> It made the slovenly wilderness
> Surround that hill.

> The wilderness rose up to it,
> And sprawled around, no longer wild.

My visitors are impressed neither with my lecture nor with my recitation of Stevens's poetry. They retort: So we shouldn't pick up and pack out trash either? What makes some signs of humanity acceptable and others not? If other animals, like beaver, can leave behind a littered landscape, why can't we?

These are good questions. But of course there is one important way we are different from other animals, I say — we make so much junk, so many *unnatural* things. So it's not a contradiction to pack out trash but leave fire rings in place. Paleolithic peoples made fires and left litter behind, but there was of course no official wilderness then. Now we have the power to discriminate, to make conscious choices about the kinds of impact we want to leave in official, capital *W* wilderness. The more important point, I argue, is to cultivate an ethical sensibility in the wilderness and take it home with you. Treat all places as sacred sites of sustainable existence, while realizing that we as a species — just like any other species — are always going to have some impact on the land and its resources.

The argument winds on, turns into a sermon (on each side), with no one's mind changed. Ah, the stubbornness and brashness of youth. Much better to be older and more mature but just as stubborn, brash, and foolish. I have to admit: it's interesting and engaging and actually fun to be talking with people again — really talking with them, by which I mean listening, considering, and responding in kind. Working a lookout all these years, I realize, has made me a better listener, because conversation with others is so rare you want to make it count when it does happen. I almost want to agree with Ed Abbey who as a ranger in a seldom-visited national park once said that the one thing better than solitude, the only thing better than solitude, is society. On occasion. In small doses.

We talk, we argue, into the night, pausing to take in the sunset — a phantasmagoric display of reds, yellows, oranges, even (I swear) greens, the kind of sunset a few nineteenth century landscape painters got down on canvas, when (they erroneously believed) the land was innocent and free. We walk out on the catwalk to admire the night sky. I quote Emerson: If a man would be alone, let him look at the stars. My guests are nonplussed, or indifferent. It's hard to read the youth of America nowadays. The wine is finished and we're all heady from the alcohol and maybe even the conversation. For a final treat we're witness to two nighthawks in flight, their silhouettes barely visible against the night sky, more audible than visible as they "bbblllrrrr" on their rapid descents. Bullbats, we used to call them in Pennsylvania. I've never seen or heard them here, in the mountains, this far from town. They bring a welcome bit of civilization to the wilderness.

Christianne and Lisa unroll their sleeping pads and bags out on the catwalk. We say goodnight and retire for the evening. It'll be a short night for me; it's late and usually I'm in bed long before this. I dream of wilderness, of wine, of women.

Morning: altocumulus castellatus. Ragged, fragmented (Stage 1) clouds across the sky. A sign of instability and incoming storms. On the Forest Service radio this morning the forecast calls for buildup later in the day. The predicted lightning activity level is two to three (on a scale of six). Because the visitors have more trail recon to do north of the lookout, in the Big Baldy area, they're off after a quick breakfast. I tell them I envy their mobility in the wilderness and invite them back if they're in the neighborhood again. As they depart I get in one last dig: leave some fire rings in place, think of future archaeologists and their work! They smirk and wave good-bye before disappearing below the summit plateau.

A lonely silence descends on the cabin.

Always, always, I'm overcome by melancholy after visitors take their leave. To dispel it I usually do household chores. Focus on the basic, the practical. Since it's likely I'll get some precip and maybe even some lightning today, I make sure the cabin and shutters are secure, enough wood is on hand for several days' worth of fires in the stove, and the firefinder is clean and ready to use. I wash the dishes from the meals of last night and this morning. I write in my journal. I begin reading another novel. And I fire up the wood stove to bake some goodies based on the recipes in the classic *Lookout Cookbook* (published by the Region One office in Missoula, Montana, in 1966, the cover photo depicting a crew-cut lookout flipping pancakes in his cabin). Whole wheat bread. Chocolate chip cookies. Corn muffins. As the temperature drops and the sky thickens with cumulonimbi, I forget all about firewatch duties and lapse comfortably into a Zen of home economics.

By midafternoon the baking is finished and I sit in a chair near the wood stove, the fire thumping within, sip tea strengthened by a jigger of whiskey, and munch cookies. The temperature has dropped into the forties, the sky has darkened significantly, the wind howls. I watch the storm clouds mushroom, come closer: twenty miles, ten miles, five miles. Squalls with curtains of rain are draped across the ridges, accompanied by occasional rumbles of thunder (but no lightning). Clouds drift past Ruffneck Peak, *below* me, at the eight thousand foot level. I hear rattling on the tin stovepipe atop the cabin. Rain? No, sleet. It piles up in windrows on the catwalk railing and the sills and weighs down the boughs of the pines around the cabin. Soon, visibility is reduced to twenty feet. By late afternoon I'm enveloped in a whiteout.

A winter whiteout. Snow, in the form of heavy wet flakes, falls on the summit. I hope there are no campers in the basin below or if there are that they've come well prepared, and I hope that Lisa and Christianne are holed up safely in their tent. I think back to the many times I've been backpacking and mountaineering, caught in a late spring or early fall storm, and remind myself how lucky I am to be snug and dry in this mountaintop cabin. Shelter from the storm.

Nightfall is a slow, nearly imperceptible transition from daylight to dark. The clouds are still thick, threatening more precip, though they've lifted a bit, to perhaps ten thousand feet. The uplifting curtain of clouds reveals a snowscape down to about eight thousand feet, a clearly delineated white line across the forested ridges indicating the break between freezing and thawing temperatures. I consider a nocturnal stroll down to the junction but can't seem to extract myself from this comfortable chair, this cozy cabin. Instead I continue to sip tea and whiskey and sit by the stove till it's completely dark and the fire in the stove has gone out and the clothes I'm wearing can't keep me warm anymore. Somehow I muster the energy and willpower to go outside and take a piss off the porch. A *long* piss, one which forces me to acknowledge the cold, raw aftermath of the storm. Then I return to the cabin and in the darkness undress hurriedly and slip naked into my sleeping bag. Soon I'm warm and toasty and the wind and rain lull me into a deep sleep.

The next morning I stay in my bag till what seems like long after first light. When I poke my head out I can see my breath. Finally I can hold it no longer and jump out of bed and, as is my custom, run out onto the catwalk to piss. I slowly open my eyes to take in the sky, the mountains, the forest. I check the thermometer — thirty-five degrees! Wet snow clings to and drips from the catwalk railing, the roof, the tree branches. Below, at around eight thousand feet, the world is blanketed by a thick cloud cover; above looms a delirious blue dome. It's gonna be a great day.

I fix a cup of Swiss mocha, bundle up, and sit on the steps of the southeast corner of the catwalk. Taking in the country. I remember a few years back when I heard I actually got the job on Ruffneck. I'd never been up here before, so I got out the maps and tried to imagine what the surrounding countryside looked like from the lookout. From the maps I could see that the Sawtooths were only thirty miles away, that I was near the headwaters of the Middle Fork of the Salmon River, and that the mountain I'd be working on was in the southwest corner of the River of No Return Wilderness, surrounded by ten thousand foot peaks. But once I got up here and could take in the countryside, I was reminded of the inadequacy of maps in representing the actual landscape. Despite recent technological developments in cartography like Geographic Information Systems and satellite imaging, the best way to know the land, to find out where one is, remains the basic, elemental, five-sense immersion in place. Nothing beats going native in coming to know the world, in discovering one's place on the earth.

By late morning the snow has mostly melted. I rejoice in the clarity of the air and scan the peaks and drainages with binoculars. The White Cloud Range, due south, is particularly striking at this time of day, with its exposed eleven thousand foot, barren granite summits shimmering in the morning light. Much closer to home I spot a Cassin's finch, red "as if dipped in raspberry juice" (according to one of my field guides), atop one of the snags on the summit, its lively warble a fine accompaniment to the heady morning feeling. From the lake basin below I then hear the plaintive call of a white-crowned sparrow, complexifying the mood of the day.

By noon it becomes so warm I eventually shed most of my clothes. I slap at a lone mosquito buzzing near my ear. Despite several cups of coffee I become drowsy from the heat and light, the somnolent stillness. There is the feel of seasonal movement in the air, the transition from spring to summer, in the high, clear, fresh air of the mountains.

summer

4. independence day

I'm sitting in the outhouse this morning reading the *New York Times Magazine* (part of a recent mail drop from a passing patrol plane), when my routine is interrupted by the unmistakable buzzing of a mosquito near my ear. Soon there's more buzzing, and I finish my duties in premature fashion, cursing the pests which will, for a brief time, render me a prisoner in my own house.

It's summertime in the Salmon River Mountains of central Idaho.

Generally summer begins about early July at this elevation. By then, most of the trails below ten thousand feet are snow-free, the Forest Service has put all of its seasonal crews back in the field, and the mosquitoes have emerged in full force as the snow recedes and the lakes and rivers reopen. I'm on the clock this fourth of July weekend (getting paid double-time to watch cloud formations), listening to the FS radio with all its chatter about "pilgrims" and "civilians" who have invaded the countryside for the long weekend. The two-way radio is my chief form of technological entertainment up here. There are many complaints about "cockleburs" (tourists who follow FS rigs too closely on the steep, twisty mountain roads) and "grousebrains" who either can't start their own fires without a gallon of Coleman fuel or who ignite fires that would warm a small army. Since the woods are still plenty wet and green this early in the season, the fire danger is low and the mood of the crews is relaxed and low-key. It should be an easy day of OT for all of us in and around the largest wilderness in the coterminous United States.

I brace myself for what seems to me, a mountain solitaire, a deluge of visitors the next few days. The Langer Lakes are a popular dayhiking and backpacking destination for Boise residents anxious to escape the heat of the desert for a weekend, in part because it's an easy three-mile hike in to the first lake. From there the climb steepens quite a bit from Langer Lake at 7,960 to Ruffneck Peak at 9,407 feet, so it's not likely that more than a half-dozen or so parties will actually trudge up to the lookout. The very nature of my workplace — the fact that where I work is also where I live — makes it hard, impossible, in fact, to become a total recluse. There is the private, solitary aspect of my job which I cherish — the primary reason I'm up here — as well as the public aspect of it, which requires me to be, at the very least, polite to the generally cheery, inquisitive citizens-at-large who visit. My home becomes my office, and thus is open to the public. On Independence Day I'm reminded of how dependent on the government I am in my mostly idyllic job.

Grumpily, I clean the dirty dishes which have accumulated over the last week, sweep the floors, and clean the windowpanes inside and out. I take my biweekly spit bath, then shave. I make my bed by unrolling my sleeping bag on top of the mattress. And I put on the official outfit on loan to me by my employer: a pair of green twill shorts and khaki shirt with the agency logo above the shirt pocket. I am grateful I've been given no Smokey the Bear ranger hat to wear as well.

As government organizations go, the Forest Service isn't all that bad. I like the people I work for in the local ranger station; the pay is decent, the working conditions splendid; and generally speaking I'm proud to be an employee of an agency charged with managing so much wild space. But the agency has long been an enemy of environmentalists, a not-so-green bu-reaucracy at least partly responsible for allowing some of the most egregious environmental sins in the country: massive clearcutting, severe overgraz-ing, and extensive open-pit mining. During its nearly one hundred years of existence, it has consistently demonstrated a preference for exploitation over recreation, in what are supposed to be multiple, not single use man-agement areas across the national forests of the country.

Take this national forest and wilderness in which I work and live. The clearcuts within sight are mercifully few and hard to detect from this par-ticular vantage point, but the boundaries of the River of No Return Wilder-ness, especially on this southwestern end, are largely determined by mining roads. Since there can be no roads in official wilderness, and since the roads were punched in during various mining booms in the nineteenth and twen-tieth centuries long before the wilderness was created in 1980, there was no choice but to draw the wilderness boundary around these incursions. Three miles north of the lookout, where there should be wilderness, are two mines, Silverbell and Seafoam, with roads leading right up to them, in a keyhole of officially sanctioned exploitation. And mining claims can continue to be filed and worked in the wilderness itself, under the provisions of an 1872 mining law — this, in spite of the 1964 Wilderness Act which was created to end such activities. There are two contrasting perceptions of the Forest Service: there is Smokey the Bear and the agency's long romantic history of fire suppression, and there is the "Forest Circus," a bungling, inept bureaucracy that functions (when it functions at all) mainly as a lackey of corporate exploiters. Like all histories, the history of the Forest Service is complex and ambiguous and has undergone significant revision over the years.

But for the moment I decide that it's too nice a day, and too early in the season, to be grousing about the government. Flotillas of fair-weather cumulus sail across the sky, the winds are light, and the temperatures are climbing into the sixties at this elevation. It's a perfect holiday weekend for outdoor recreation in the mountains.

My first visitors arrive around noon, a family of locals: a man in his sixties, his son in his thirties, and three Idaho towheads. They've come up to do some fishing, some camping, some mountain-gazing. Rather than sporting the latest trail fashions from REI, North Face, or Mountainsmith, they're campers of the old school, dressed in green and brown army fatigues, carrying Army-Navy store aluminum frame packs, with hatchets, big bowie knives, and bulky plastic canteens hanging from their belts. Undoubtedly they've carried in canned goods and fresh food to cook over an open fire. We talk of game ("Seen any elk?" is their first question), weather ("Hot as a pistol down in the canyon"), and the upcoming fire season ("Gonna be a busy one when the grasses finally cure in August"). The kids are so shy it's all grandpa can do to drag them into the lookout cabin to check out the firefinding equipment. When he (as an ex-Forest Service employee of the 1950s) shows them how the alidade works (the old-fashioned term for the earlier, more primitive version of the Osborne firefinder), they exclaim in genuine wonder — "Gosh! Wow!" — like it's the latest, slickest version of some computer game. I like them a lot and am genuinely sorry to see them leave after fifteen minutes of friendly conversation. They happily promise to mail my letters for me when they pass through Stanley on their way home.

I fix a quick lunch of a tuna sandwich and eat out on the steps, basking in the early afternoon sun. As always, I take in the tangible presence of things: the steepled forms of subalpine fir; the amoebae-like shape of the lakes below; the white stringy patches of snow lingering in the couloirs of the Sawtooths; the steady buzz of flies warming up in the sun; the glint of granite on yonder White Cloud Range; the faint exclamations of campers down in the basin. And, always, the ubiquitous wind in the trees on the summit. Henry Beston, in *The Outermost House*, a classic account of a year on Cape Cod, identified what he thought were the three elemental sounds of nature: "the sound of rain, the sound of wind in a primeval wood, and the sound of outer ocean on a beach." A coastal man, he preferred the sound of ocean waves; since I am a native of the mountains and forests, I prefer the music of wind in the trees — at altitude.

My reverie is interrupted by another visitor. A woman hiking with her dog strolls up the final switchback to the cabin. She seems surprised to see someone actually living here and confesses that she hadn't realized that lookouts were still staffed anymore, what with all the air patrol that is done these days. She's from Seattle, having come to visit after reading about the area in a hiking guidebook. I tell her that in the Cascades of Washington and Oregon, where there used to be hundreds of lookouts manned in the good old days of CCC, almost none are still in commission — casualties of progress and improved technology. But in these parts, people and institutions seem to take pride in doing things the old-fashioned way. There are certain benefits to conservatism, to honoring traditional ways of doing things.

We chat for a bit, but I sense that as a city woman she's not comfortable with the situation — alone in the wilderness with a strange man and only her dog to protect her — so she departs rather quickly. Or maybe she feels guilty, as some of the more sensitive visitors do, about interrupting my privacy. Or maybe she's a reticent person by nature. Whatever. I admire her for hiking alone in the woods and wonder what I'd do, irrepressible solitaire that I am, if I were a woman. Would I assume the greater risk of physical and mental harm by engaging in solo wilderness journeys? Would I carry a weapon for protection, thus contradicting my fundamental belief in the wilderness as a sanctuary from civilization? Or would I relinquish my love of solitude to some degree and travel only with others in the wild? I know women who've chosen all three options, none of which they're entirely happy with. There are (inevitably) gendered, and thus different, responses to the wilderness.

Late afternoon comes and what turns out to be my last visitors of the day. Two guys from Boise hoofing it up from their base camp in the basin, ex-

Californians who'd had it with the congestion and pollution and high prices of Silicon Valley. They got wind of some high-tech companies blooming in Boise, moved north, and found good jobs easily. They think they live in nirvana now and aren't eager for other exiles to discover Idaho's uncrowded spaces and relatively cheap cost of living. As an ex-Californian myself (having lived in the Bay Area for five years prior to moving to the Midwest), I like them immediately — find them hip and cool, interesting to talk with, being more worldly than most native Idahoans. They confess they'd been hoping that a woman was working the lookout, because it would have been nice to talk with a woman (preferably a good-looking one) working in the wilderness. Well, I say, I guess this just wasn't your lucky day — even though it seems, based on my experience, that more lookouts are staffed by women than men. I tell them about the solo hiker who'd just visited and we ponder the conundrum: a woman seeking solitary experience in the wilderness while guys are hoping to meet women in the wilderness. Where and how shall the twain meet? Or will they meet? We go on to talk of favorite places in the Bay Area: Telegraph Avenue in Berkeley, Point Reyes and Muir Woods in Marin County, Las Trampas Wilderness in the East Bay. The conversation reminds me of how much I miss the cultural and geographical diversity of the Golden State.

When they finally leave I'm lonesome for male companionship. Over the years, after many moves and the attrition in friendships that goes along with a peripatetic life, I'm down to a few friends whom I can genuinely call compadres. Men and women with whom I can drink beer and smoke cigars and talk of trails we have traveled and books we have read and people we have known and loved or wish wistfully we could have known and loved. I think of one friend in particular, my first climbing buddy in the West, whom I met while working for the Forest Service and who continued to visit me regularly each summer wherever I happened to be working a lookout — but with whom I have since lost touch. I get out a bottle and toast him, wherever he may be, hoping he's happy, fulfilled—and still climbing.

I continue to sip whiskey into the evening, humming one of my favorite Dylan songs, remembering especially its last two lines: "And many a road, taken by many a first friend, / and each one, I've never seen again."

Dusk. Near the shore of Langer Lake a campfire glows like a firefly through the cover of conifers.

5. eyes in the sky: a brief history of fire lookouts

The next day I find out that two other lookouts on the Challis National Forest are to begin working soon: Bernie on Little Soldier Mountain and Bobette on Pinyon Peak. Bernie, like me, is a veteran, having worked lookouts all over Idaho for many seasons. In the winter he retires to Boise, living off unemployment checks and money he's invested over the years, enjoying the comforts and ease of the simple, frugal life. Bobette is a local woman who wants to make some money to help put her through Idaho State University in Pocatello come fall. To spend the summer mostly alone on a mountaintop is a tall order for someone who's just graduated from high school, but Bobette seems ready for the challenge. I'd met her in Challis earlier in the season before I came up and was impressed with her direct, confident gaze and apparent maturity. At any rate it'll be good to have some (vocal) company the rest of the season. This is especially true during lightning storms when we can inform each other about blind spots around one's own lookout, as well as late in the evenings when lookouts are allowed to socialize for a bit on the radio, as Gary Snyder says, "bullshitting . . . with a distant pinnacle, like you, / hid in clouds."

Fire lookouts have enjoyed a long and storied history as part of the Forest Service. When civilians hear about working for the agency, it's the image of a fire lookout that often comes to mind. According to Ray Kresek in his wonderfully illustrated and colorfully written book, *Fire Lookouts of the Northwest*, the first lookout station was Bertha Hill, located in northern Idaho and staffed by the camp cook, Mable Gray, in 1903. By the turn of the century, national forest reserves were being established by the federal government in response to unregulated logging and unchecked forest fires.

During an unusually dry summer, with reports of large fires in other states, the manager of a timber company decided to post someone on top of a nearby mountain to keep an eye out for smoke. So twice each day, Gray rode by horseback to the summit of 5,520-foot Bertha Hill and climbed fifteen feet up a hemlock snag to sit in a perch constructed for her by camp laborers. There is no record of her reporting any fires.

From that humble origin, fire lookouts quickly evolved into mountaintop houses of varying designs. The architectural history of lookouts deserves its own study, as lookout construction went from the vernacular, pretty-much-anything-goes style in the early years to institutional, standardized, and prefabricated design by the 1940s. There are photographs of early twentieth-century lookouts that feature three floors: a storage space on bottom, living quarters on the middle floor, and a cupola (the actual working quarters) on top. In California by the 1920s, D-5 cabins appeared (named for the state's fifth district), with a twelve-by-twelve-foot lower cabin and cupola above. R-6 lookouts were built in the 1930s and 40s (so designated because they came from region six of the Forest Service, the Pacific Northwest). They were one-story affairs with peaked roofs and overhanging shutters that could be propped open during the fire season and then let down the rest of the year to seal up and protect the windows. The R-6 represents the classic era in lookout architectural history, the design which most readily comes to mind when people conjure the image of a lookout. Finally, the last major stage, what could be termed the modern era, came in the late 1940s, producing the flat top, which eliminated the peaked roof, thus earning the scorn of many lookout aficionados. Kresek, in his book on lookouts, sarcastically dismisses the flat-top design in this way: "USFS engineers everywhere agreed that the ideal way to shed the rain is with a flat roof. So, now we have the 'R-6 *flat*.' The tarpaper-topped cube is built out of plywood. Its window frames offer the poorest ventilation and more blind spots than any observatory yet designed."

Ruffneck Peak lookout, built in 1932, dates from the classic era with its signature peaked roof. Because of the high elevation of the mountain it rests atop, the lookout structure was set directly on the ground. But where lookouts were built on lower mountaintops at or below the tree line, towers had to be constructed so as to provide a view above the trees. Towers ranged anywhere in height from ten to one hundred feet, and the higher the tower the more likely that the glass house in which the lookout works consisted only of a six-by-six-foot room with glass walls all around, with a separate living cabin on the ground. I've worked on a lookout atop a forty-foot tower which, despite steel cable guy lines anchored in the ground, swayed in the wind during violent storms. That season of teetering in the treetops was enough to lead to my subsequent preference for ground-based structures. In this business, higher up does not necessarily mean better off.

Few people who visit lookouts think about the Herculean efforts required to transport the building materials up a mountain in the days before helicopters. (Today, most lookouts are "drive-ins," meaning there is road access to the top of a mountain; the few that are accessible only by foot are usually located in federal wilderness areas like Ruffneck Peak.) During the CCC era, when the majority of lookouts were constructed, the effort included the loading of lengthy pack trains of mules, the delicate handling of things like windows and instruments, and the tortuous negotiation of trails to the mountaintop. Occasionally a flat spot atop a rocky peak had to be created by dynamite blasting, and supplies had to be winched up the last stretch of the mountain because the slopes were precipitous. Perhaps the most challenging lookout construction site of all was on Three Fingers, a rocky 6,854-foot promontory in the North Cascades of Washington. Fifteen miles and four thousand feet in elevation gain by trail, with thousand-foot dropoffs on some sides, Three Fingers seemed an unlikely spot on which to try to construct a fire lookout. But not to several rangers of the Darrington district of the Mount Baker–Snoqualmie National Forest in the early 1930s. They climbed the mountain themselves, helped lay telephone cable (in the days before two-way radios), and had a blaster level off a portion of the summit in order to create a level foundation for the cabin. In 1933 the lookout structure was finished and ready for occupancy, the final fifty feet to the cabin ascendable via several sections of ladders anchored to solid rock. Although the lookout has long since been out of duty as a reporting station, it remains in use for visitors thanks to the preservation efforts of a Seattle-based group known as the Mountaineers.

As the architecture of lookouts evolved, so too did the technology. The early lookouts reported to their ranger stations via hand-crank telephone lines, and often a lookout had to go for a long hike down the mountain to repair a line snapped by a fallen tree. By 1945 more than sixty-three thousand miles of single wire telephone line had been strung throughout America's national forests to link lookouts to fire dispatch offices. The means of locating fires improved from the primitive alidade (basically a scope sight fixed on a rotating map standing on a crude post in the open air), with the lookout living in a nearby tent, to the standard Osborne Firefinder anchored on a wooden stand, complete with shelves for binoculars and fire lookout manual, within a fully enclosed, livable cabin. Eventually all lookouts were issued a set of 7 × 50 binoculars, quite clunky for general use in the woods but adequate for detecting smokes from the catwalk.

Lookouts even developed their own specialized set of furniture and interior design. In the standard fourteen-by-fourteen-foot cabin, the ceiling is typically seven feet high. All four walls feature windows that are usually four feet tall from the ceiling down. Only the firefinder, which stands five feet tall, could be higher than the bottom of the windows (to allow for sighting in on a fire). That means that all other furniture had to be lower than the bottom of the windows so as not to obstruct the view. A bed frame was usually placed in the southwest corner of the cabin, and a wood stove specially designed for lookouts in the northeast corner. Shelves and countertops were built into the east interior walls. A desk and chair completed the arrangement — except for one final piece of furniture, undoubtedly unique to lookouts. Because of the likelihood of the cabin being struck by lightning during a storm, a two-foot-high stool with glass insulators on the bottoms of the legs came standard with every lookout. According to the lookout manual, one is supposed to stand on the stool during a storm in case of a direct hit (the cabin is also grounded by brass cables running from the roof down the sides of the building to the ground). I was never struck directly in my twelve seasons as a lookout, but I always made it a practice to stand on the stool during every storm. As all lookouts come to know, lightning can and sometimes does strike the same spot more than once. One improvement in the overall interior design made over the years was to add a hanging map on the ceiling which could be let down to provide a larger perspective of the surroundings than that afforded by the twenty-mile radius of the firefinder. Overall, like Thoreau's hut at Walden Pond (coincidentally, about the same size), the lookout cabin imposed a simplicity of life-style upon the inhabitant.

As the Forest Service acquired more land, becoming a bigger and more important bureaucracy in the West in the early decades of the twentieth century mainly in response to devastating forest fires, lookouts assumed an increasingly prominent role in fire detection and suppression. The heyday of lookouts came during the Depression era when thousands of men were put to work to build trails, fight fires, and man fire lookouts. At their peak of popularity, more than five thousand lookouts across the country were in operation, and Idaho led the way with 966. During World War II, lookouts even became part of our national security system, as spotters worked year-round on mountaintops up and down the West Coast to detect the possible approach of Japanese bombers. And in wartime when many young men were conscripted or volunteered for the armed services, women often were given the opportunity to work as lookouts.

But it was also during WW II that new developments led to the eventual decline of fire lookouts. War-era technology was adopted for fire detection and firefighting during the 1950s: surveillance by airplanes and helicopters, smoke-jumping via parachute, fire-retardant bombs, infrared heat sensors, and communication via two-way radios. Even weather observations, the staple of a lookout's morning ritual, are mostly done automatically nowadays by RAWS. All these improvements led to the decommission, abandonment, and destruction of many lookout cabins. In the 1990s, when I visited the National Interagency Fire Center (NIFC) in Boise, Idaho, where all major fire operations are coordinated, officials there smiled condescendingly over the anachronistic role now held by lookouts in the fire management system. "We have RAWS to record the weather, LDS [lightning detection systems] to tell us where strikes occurred, and air patrol to report and locate fires," one higher-up at the center told me. "Why do we still need lookouts?"

One of the saddest ends of a fire lookout came over Memorial Day weekend in 1983 when the unmanned cabin atop Wylies Peak in the Selway-Bitterroot Wilderness was struck by lightning and burned to the ground. The event made front-page news in local newspapers. At seventy-eight hundred feet, situated in the heart of one of the largest wilderness areas in the country, Wylies Peak lookout was a fifty-eight-year-old, classic two-story log cabin with cupola that had been anchored to a granite dome summit blasted from twenty-five feet of rock. In 1976 the lookout was the first to be registered as a national historic site, saving it from destruction by the Forest Service, which had not manned it since 1954. Officials had discussed trying to preserve it prior to the lightning strike, but then adopted a "let it die" philosophy for lack of funds. Wylies Peak remains one of the most photographed sites in the Selway-Bitterroot Wilderness, and in many ranger district offices on the Bitterroot National Forest photos of the lookout hang on the walls. A color photograph of it graces the cover of Kresek's book.

Also contributing to the decline of lookouts was the passage of a federal law in 1965 that held the government liable for anyone suffering injuries, regardless of fault, while on government property. The result was the Forest Service's decision to destroy fire lookout structures no longer in use — which meant most of them, since many had been replaced by air patrol — so people wouldn't injure themselves visiting abandoned cabins. I witnessed some of this institutionalized vandalism while working for the Idaho Pan-handle National Forest in the late 1970s and made it a point to visit some remote stations that were on the hit list before they were leveled. Among my most treasured mementos are some lookout artifacts that I smuggled down from Snow Peak lookout in the Red Ives district south of the St. Joe River: maps dating back to the 1930s, some lookout dinner plates, and a journal kept by various lookouts over the years. Today, unfortunately, all that remains of many lookouts are their concrete foundations on the summits. In central Idaho, where there were once 128 lookouts in operation, only eight are still manned. On the Challis National Forest, only five are currently in operation (in addition to Ruffneck, Little Soldier, and Pinyon lookouts, Twin Peaks and Wildhorse lookouts remain active, though the latter is staffed mainly as a peregrine hack site through the Nature Conservancy).

Yet, lookouts are making something of a comeback these days. Because of budget cuts and because some fire management officers still believe in the efficacy of the lookout system (albeit on a greatly reduced scale), the Forest Service has come up with the idea of offering volunteer positions to those people interested in working a lookout for a summer. Not surprisingly, the response has been very positive: many a city slicker who's been raised watching "Lassie" and grown up with Smokey the Bear has been enticed by the romantic notion of living on top of a mountain for a while and helping save the woods from the ravages of forest fires. A number of national forests in the West have preserved lookout cabins and offered them as rental units for a weekend, a week, or even longer, to satisfy a similar kind of longing. (A book has recently been published on this subject, *How to Rent a Fire Lookout.*) Private groups and individuals have acted to preserve lookouts and their cultural history as well; groups like the Mountaineers and certain towns in Montana have established museums and worked to protect specific towers by securing national historic register status for them. The summer of 1998 I spent two weeks working as a (volunteer) lookout on 9,351-foot St. Mary Peak in the Selway-Bitterroot Wilderness, which is a two-story affair, the lower floor being completely built of native stone. Having recently obtained national historic register status for the cabin (built in 1953), the district ranger managed to acquire funds to renovate the lookout and keep it in operation. Now there's even an official organization, the Forest Fire Lookout Association (FFLA), which has been formed partly to preserve and staff as many lookouts as possible. The group has its own website: www.firetower.org, and its quarterly newsletter, *Lookout Network,* features news and updates on lookout preservation across America. Given this strong and wide-ranging show of support, it seems unlikely that lookouts will become extinct.

Thoughts of extinction are far from my mind this particular day in early July. Overconfidence? Indifference? Hardly. Rather, it's nice to reap the benefits of working for a less progressive national forest in backward Idaho, one not totally overtaken by the latest technological gadgets and fashionable trends. It's good to know that people still matter in the national forests. People have long mattered in these parts.

6. some former inhabitants

Whenever I become drawn to a particular landscape, one of the first questions that comes to mind is, Who were the first humans to inhabit this place? Answering it is part of the process of going native, satisfying one's curiosity about previous inhabitants. Despite a "cultural resource reconnaissance" of the Middle Fork of the Salmon River basin conducted by the Idaho State Historic Preservation Office in 1978, the answer to this question is uncertain. The earliest evidence of indigenous human inhabitation of the Salmon River Mountains appears to date back to about ten thousand years B.P. Compare this to the indisputably oldest confirmed place of human occupation in the Americas, the twelve thousand-year-old Clovis, New Mexico, site famous for spear points with fluted channels. Evidence of early humans' occupation of central Idaho has been found in the form of lithic scatters (stone arrowheads, scrapers, etc.), pithouse depressions, and rock art. A rock shelter excavated near Redfish Lake in the Sawtooth Range near Stanley contained scattered stone tools that date back to the end of the last Ice Age. Designated by archaeologists as part of the Big Game culture, the makers of these artifacts were probably seasonal inhabitants of the area who hunted large mammals such as *Bison antiquus*, a larger ancestor of the buffalo, as well as other megafauna like elephants and camels that eventually went extinct. Another rock shelter, eighty-two hundred years old, has been found near the town of Shoup, along the far eastern course of the Main Salmon close to the Idaho-Montana border, containing similar artifacts. These Paleolithic peoples undoubtedly ate plants to supplement their main diet of meat, but at present no evidence has been discovered to confirm this supposition.

I dislike the term *prehistoric* in attempting to categorize early humans. It is usually meant to indicate a people who existed prior to recorded, i.e., written or literate culture. But on the surface it suggests that somehow a group of people lived before history, or at least human history, which of course is absurd and contradictory. The term is also misleading in that it suggests that a group did not record its history, when in fact there is incontrovertible evidence that some early human cultures did just that — through rock art. There are at least twenty-six different pictograph sites along the Middle Fork of the Salmon River (not to mention both pictographs and petroglyphs throughout much of southern Idaho), all of which register various activities, real and imagined, of humans. I'll have more to say about these pictographs along the Middle Fork at a later point in the narrative.

The Big Game culture was followed by the people of the Archaic or Middle Salmon River Period, 7,800 to 1,200 years B.P. Material culture evidence from this period has been found at a seasonally occupied hunting and fishing camp at Dagger Falls, near the headwaters of the Middle Fork and only about ten air miles from Ruffneck Peak. Improvements in hunting technology distinguish the peoples of this period from the Big Game culture. The atlatl, a long, stone-tipped spear hurled at prey with the aid of a slinglike device, was developed, increasing both force and accuracy. The projectile point of the spear was made of obsidian taken from the Yellowstone area, which confirms that trading networks existed in the region. No doubt these people speared fish in the river and perhaps devised other means to capture fish such as with weirs. Based on the pithouse depressions dating back to this era, archaeologists speculate that the shelters of Archaic peoples consisted of shallow holes dug in the ground over which branches and perhaps animal hides were placed to keep out the elements. In addition to the atlatl, other improvements in the suite of technology found at the camp at Dagger Falls include woven baskets and milling stones for grinding seeds from wild plants. I try to imagine eking out an existence as a hunter-gatherer in these rugged mountains and valleys, concluding that I'd spend most of my time near the water where the greatest chance lies for capitalizing on food resources: fish in the river, berries and wild game along the banks. Hunting in the thick forest cover strikes me as a very long — and mostly obstructed — shot indeed.

During the late Salmon River Period, about twelve hundred years ago, the Shoshone and Nez Perce arrived in the area. These two linguistically different tribes were the last Native American inhabitants of the Salmon River

Mountains and represent two different culture areas (of thirteen covering North America) designated by anthropologists. Both of these culture areas, the Plateau and Great Basin, are partly in Idaho, divided by the Salmon River where it flows from east to west: the Plateau includes parts of Washington, Oregon, and Montana as well as northern Idaho; the Great Basin includes, in addition to southern Idaho, parts of Oregon, California, Nevada, Utah, Colorado, and Wyoming. In their material culture both the Nez Perce and Shoshone added the bow and arrow along with pottery to their complement of artifacts. Most of the archaeological sites and finds along the Salmon River and its tributaries are from this most recent period. Other than through the possible use of fire as a hunting tool (to herd or scare big game in a certain direction), it's hard to imagine these Native American tribes having much of an impact on the environment. However, some paleo-archaeologists have speculated, in a controversial theory known as the Overkill Hypothesis, that the Big Game culture helped cause the extinction of large mammals through overhunting. The theory goes something like this: These people had developed, for their time, rather sophisticated hunting technologies and techniques and preyed on species like the woolly mammoth which could not reproduce fast enough to make up for population declines due to hunting. So, also due in part to the climate change that occurred at the end of the last Ice Age some twelve thousand years B.P., the megafauna gradually disappeared. While the Overkill Hypothesis is plausible, it would seem that the impact of the native populations on the local environment remained minimal for two basic reasons: sparse population (only as many as several thousand in Idaho) up to the 1800s and relatively simple technology. As a former anthropology professor of mine was fond of saying, there's only so much damage one can do with a stone ax. The horse, after being introduced by the Spanish in the 1500s, spread to many different Western tribes and eventually did come to play a significant role in the Plains Indians' impact on the environment, but it was not utilized much by the Shoshone or Nez Perce in the high, steep, rugged terrain of central Idaho.

A sub-tribe of the Shoshone gradually inhabited the Salmon River Mountains when Euroamerican invasion began in the middle of the nineteenth century in Idaho. Called Sheepeaters by whites, which is what their Shoshone name, *Tukudeka*, means, this culture consisted of reclusive, scattered bands. The Sheepeaters were discovered quite late in the frontier history of the American West by fur trappers searching for beaver. The tribe lived primarily off big game in the mountains — elk, deer, bear, antelope, as well as bighorn sheep — in small bands of two or three families. They were said to be the best furriers in the mountain regions of the West and traded with other tribes (near the confluence of the Salmon and Snake rivers) for hard-to-obtain items like obsidian scrapers and shells. In the winter, when their furs served them well, they formed fishing villages along the river and ate the native salmon and steelhead. A nomadic people, traveling in the mountains wherever the hunting and fishing were good, they earned a reputation as a fiercely independent tribe. However, their independence was severely tested when the trade artifacts offered by whites started to become available in the nineteenth century. The only known portrait of wild Sheepeaters that exists is by the famous Western landscape photographer William Henry Jackson, taken along the Idaho-Montana border in 1871. A family of seven natives sits inside a skin teepee, its door slung open to reveal a group of dark, dispassionate faces staring at the lens. The photograph itself is a powerful emblem of the intrusion by Anglo-Americans upon the indigenous peoples of the region.

The Sheepeaters' territory was not seriously threatened by Americans until the second half of the nineteenth century. Because of the remoteness and ruggedness of the terrain, the only whites other than fur traders to venture into this inhospitable terrain were explorers. In 1805, the company of Meriwether Lewis and William Clark, having just crossed over what is now the Idaho-Montana divide via Lost Trail Pass on its epic journey to the Pacific, was warned by the Shoshone not to venture into the canyon of the Main Fork of the Salmon, which they called *tom-agip-paw*, meaning "Big-fish water" for the salmon and steelhead that thrived in the river. Captain Clark decided to see for himself how rugged the canyon was. After a brief reconnoiter involving a tortuous trip along the river's precipitous slopes, he readily confirmed their assessment of the Salmon River canyon as impassable. Some of Clark's original journal describing his exploration of the Salmon River (retaining his wildly erratic spelling and punctuation) is worth quoting:

[August 23rd, Friday, 1805] proceed on with great dificuelty as the rocks were So sharp large and unsettled and the hill sides Steep that the horses could with the greatest risque and dificulty get on. . . . The River from the place I left my party to this Creek is almost one continued rapid, five verry considerable rapids the passage of either with Canoes is entirely impossible, as the water is Confined between huge Rocks & the Current beeting from one against another for Some distance below &c. &c. . . . this river is about 100 yards wide and can be forded but in a few places. Below my [Shoshone] guide and maney other Indians tell me that the Mountains Close and is a perpendicular Clift on each Side, and Continues for a great distance and that the water runs with great violence from one rock to the other on each Side foaming & roreing thro rocks in every direction, So as to render the passage of any thing impossible. Those rapids which I had Seen he said was Small & trifleing in comparrison to the rocks & rapids below, at no great distance & The Hills or mountains were not like those I had Seen but like the Side of a tree Streight up.

At this point Clark judiciously decided to return with his party to the main force left behind with Lewis, which was camped on the Lemhi River to the southeast. After re-grouping they agreed to try another route to the Columbia River by following upstream what is now designated the North Fork of the Salmon River. Above its headwaters they managed to recross the Continental Divide via the Lolo Trail over the Bitterroot Mountains, led by Nez Perce guides.

Stanley Basin, which lies at the foot of the Sawtooth Range, about thirty air miles south of Ruffneck Peak and at six thousand feet above sea level, may well be my single most favorite *inhabited* place in the American West. Seen from the small town of Stanley (population around one hundred), the Sawtooths form a majestic, rugged backdrop of ten thousand-foot granite peaks seemingly within arm's reach. Stanley has been made somewhat famous through articles in *National Geographic* and the *New York Times*, but in contrast to a Western tourist trap like Jackson, Wyoming, it remains relatively undiscovered (though, ominously, espresso stands are sprouting like knapweed along the edge of town).

Stanley Basin was first entered by whites in 1824 when members of the Hudson Bay Company, engaged in fierce competition with other colonialist enterprises like the American Fur Company, were looking to expand territorial empire. The leader of the Hudson party was Alexander Ross, who kept a detailed journal and later published a book about the expedition, *The Fur Hunters of the Far West*. Ross's book makes for some great reading, especially for someone interested in the environmental history of central Idaho.

Ross and his company of trappers and various renegades of Native American tribes reached Galena Summit (8,752 feet) on September 18, 1824,

Stanley, Idaho, with Main Salmon River in the foreground and the Sawtooth Mountains in the background.

a pass ten miles north of present-day Sun Valley. Looking in that direction he declared that "no elevated height in this country can present a more interesting prospect. . . . It is of a highly picturesque character." What he saw was a broad grassy valley that formed the headwaters of the Main Salmon River, above which towered the Sawtooth Range (I look at a photo taken from near the pass of this same view as I write). As far as we know, no Euroamericans before Ross had ever seen this country. Ross went on to describe what he mistakenly assumed was virgin territory: "It appeared to us probably that no human being had ever trod in that path before; but we were soon undeceived, for we had not been many hours there before my people, going about their horses, found a pheasant with a fresh arrow stuck in it and not yet dead! So at the moment we were indulging in such an idea, the Indians might have been within fifty yards of us."

Ross's initial inaccurate observation of untrodden ground makes me wonder. Is the desire to explore terra incognita a human trait in general or is it specific to Euroamerican culture? Were the Tukudeka impelled by a similar urge, what one historian has termed "the Ulysses factor"? We will probably never know for certain, but my guess is that the seeker's instinct is fundamentally common to all cultures. Of course, humans explore for practical reasons — to find further sources of food and shelter, to claim new lands and people for economic expansion. But I like to think we also press on to satisfy a basic, fundamental sense of curiosity: What's around the next ridge? What lies beyond one more bend in the river?

Trying to satisfy all these urges, the party pressed on. As they descended into the Salmon River valley and Stanley Basin, Ross engaged in some hyperbole, claiming that "So high were the mountains on each side of us that in many places the view was so confined that we could see nothing but the sky above and the rocks around us." In fact, the headwaters area is a gently undulating meadow with scattered timber and was likely to have been so then, due to the burning practices of Native Americans, who periodically set fire to the grasses to keep the country open and to provide fodder for the buffalo and their horses, which fed on the revegetation. Not until the party entered the Main Salmon canyon east of the confluence with Valley Creek to the north (near the intersection of state highways 21 and 75 today) did the men encounter truly formidable going. Ross's writing at this point soars in pitch and quality to match the awful sublimity of the canyon: "We entered a narrow and gloomy defile, where mountains on each side closed in on the river, between which the river became confined like the water race of a mill and shot through the narrow channel in a white foaming cascade with the noise of thunder. Along the margin of the river in this dangerous place the rocks and precipices descended almost perpendicularly to the water's edge, affording only some fifty or sixty feet above the water, in the face of the precipice, a sort of zigging path."

Ross and company followed this "zigging path" for a while. Then the trail along the cliff petered out, and they were forced to turn their horses around on a narrow ledge and retrace their steps about a mile. They dropped to the river and tried to cross in several places, drowning one of the horses at one point. Somehow they managed to get through the canyon at river level. It took them eight days to traverse a stretch along the Salmon River that today can be traveled by car in less than an hour (though after heavy rains, landslides and rockfall still sometimes close Highway 75 through the canyon).

Inevitably, other whites followed in Ross's footsteps. Captain Benjamin Bonneville spent Christmas in 1832 in Stanley Basin, and Washington Irving wrote up the feast that Bonneville's party enjoyed in his account of the expedition. When gold was discovered along the Salmon River in 1862, the hordes of whites who followed quickly found reasons to persecute and dispossess the Sheepeaters, whom they branded "a constant menace to prospectors passing through or camping in their territory," according to Johnny Carrey and Cort Conley in *The Middle Fork & the Sheepeater War*. Soon, permanent towns appeared along the river where before there had existed seasonal fishing villages; in 1866, near another gold strike, the town of Leesburg quickly accumulated a population of three thousand. Tension between the Sheepeaters and miners was foreordained by the then-popular principle of Manifest Destiny as whites encroached on hunting and fishing territories of the natives, seeing Indians as obstacles in the pursuit of riches. In 1879, the murder of five Chinese laborers and then two whites near the town of Oro Grande (population fifteen thousand) on Loon Creek, a southern tributary of the Middle Fork, was blamed on the Sheepeaters. Several military detachments were sent into the Salmon River Mountains "to ascertain who the murderers were." The Sheepeater War followed.

The diaries of several soldiers that have survived the war contain a number of recurrent themes: the harshness of the topography and weather (it was June when they were first dispatched, a time of melting snow and spring rains, meaning high water in the creeks and rivers), scant rations (many provisions were lost during creek crossings, and game proved elusive in the canyons), and their evasive enemy, the Sheepeaters. What few trails existed were often buried in ten feet of snow or became goat trails scratched into cliff edges that climbed precipitously above the river, from which mules and rations often tumbled down mountainsides, never to be recovered. A general refrain in the journals of the soldiers goes something like this: "Curses loud on all sides on mules and this Godforsaken country." The white soldiers seemed utterly out of their element: "You people of low lands have no idea how loud thunder can roar or how bright flashing the lightning is on the mountain tops," one private wrote. "Mosquitoes as thick as redheaded children in Utah," he complained a few weeks later. "Wood ticks by the thousands are found everywhere and annoy men and horses very much," observed a captain. In making a descent from the ridgetops to the river, this same officer observed, "Within a distance of ten miles we have come from ten feet of snow to roses and rattlesnakes." The soldiers noted the remains of "wickiup skeletons" indicating a former Indian camp, but saw no natives during their search. Occasionally the troops came across the remains of miners' cabins, devouring the onions and potatoes growing in the tiny abandoned gardens. On July 3, 1879, one of the regiments declared itself lost. When scouts were sent out to reconnoiter the surroundings, they discovered "seven small lakes on a mountain" — possibly what are now known as Soldier Lakes, only three miles northwest of Ruffneck Peak as the crow flies. The names of Soldier Creek, Little Soldier Mountain, Artillery Dome, and so forth, which appear on maps of the area today, all derive their names from this woebegone military campaign.

Finally the troops encountered a band of Sheepeaters near Big Creek along the Middle Fork of the Salmon River. The soldiers were ambushed and barely escaped with their lives, nearly trapped by a fire deliberately set by the Indians in a canyon. But the army had seemingly infinite numbers of troops and supplies to draw on and patiently waited for reinforcements to arrive. Then in mid-August its scouts, mainly comprised of Umatillas (a tribe sympathetic to Anglo-Americans), surprised a band of encamped Sheepeaters, chased them off, and confiscated many of their supplies and artifacts. The next day a skirmish occurred in which one soldier, H. Eagan, was killed. One of his fellow soldiers observed: "He leaves a wife and daughter. We rolled his body in blankets and buried him. No shot was fired and no word was spoken, but he was left to rest as peacefully as if there had been pomp and ceremony. No more, old Comrade, will you be called to fat bacon and bean soup, to climb mountains nor damned by civilians for a lazy lout." Eagan Point and Eagan Creek now bear the deceased soldier's name south of Big Creek Gorge, and a monument marks the spot where he was buried.

Then the Sheepeaters simply disappeared for a time in the labyrinth of canyons and mountains. Often the only sight or trace of them was their signal fires, set high atop the peaks.

By the end of August, one of the regiments had exhausted its supplies as well as its mules and horses. The soldiers, having traveled over eleven hundred miles in two months in mountains and rivers without end, were spent too. Gratefully they returned to Boise to resupply and were replaced by another regiment. In mid-September the new soldiers succeeded in capturing a few women and children of the Sheepeaters. They subsequently came across another Sheepeater camp, and in the ensuing skirmish the Native American men escaped but left behind hundreds of pounds of wild meat set out to cure over a campfire. Eventually the tribe, like most other tribes of indigenous peoples in America, lost this war of attrition. By the end of September, fifty-one Sheepeaters had surrendered themselves. Thus the Sheepeater campaign of 1879 ended rather anticlimactically, if victoriously, for the United States. When questioned, the Indians denied having murdered the Chinese or the two miners. Nonetheless, they were all shipped to a reservation at Fort Hall in southern Idaho without benefit of a trial by jury.

Scattered bands of Sheepeaters continued to live in the Salmon River Mountains until the turn of the century. But apparently there was no anthropologist to record the extinction of this tribe, nor any lone surviving holdout like Ishi in California whose story could be recorded for posterity. Today, federal boundaries and regulations help to preserve the remnants of native cultures within the Frank Church, even as the modern legal definition of wilderness — a place "where man is but a visitor" — ignores their historic presence and denies the possibility of Indians reclaiming their lost land.

The miners whose cabins the soldiers discovered in the hinterlands had come in the 1860s after news of a big gold strike to the southwest near Atlanta in the Boise River drainage. Captain John Stanley, a Civil War veteran, traveled through the area south of Ruffneck in 1863 with a prospecting party. It was Stanley after whom the basin east of the Sawtooths was named. One of the more interesting mining stories of the region (reported by Cort Conley in his eminently readable *Idaho: A Guide for the Curious*) is associated with the Yankee Fork tributary of the Salmon River, about forty miles east of Ruffneck. A man named William Norton, drawn by earlier strikes along the Middle Fork in the 1860s, discovered in 1875 a vein of gold that produced $11,500 in thirty days' work; he named the mine the Charles Dickens. The next summer another party unearthed an even larger strike worth $60,000 in the first year of operation. This mine was called the General Custer and was subsequently sold for $285,000. Within a few years the towns of Bonanza and Custer appeared along the Yankee Fork, and as many as six hundred people lived in the former site before it suffered two disastrous fires in 1889 and 1897, when the remaining townsfolk relocated to Custer.

Bonanza retains an intriguing story of unrequited love, symbolized by several gravesites outside the town limits. The town's chief citizen was Charles Franklin, who laid out the town and ran the Franklin House Hotel. The summer of 1878, two English immigrants, Richard and Agnes Elizabeth King, relocated from Bodie, California, another mining town, to try their luck once again. While the husband prospected, his wife opened a saloon and dance hall; both proved to be profitable business ventures. Then one day, in an argument over ownership of a town lot, Richard King was shot in a saloon in Bonanza. Charles Franklin helped Elizabeth with the funeral arrangements, and gradually they evolved from friends into a couple. There was talk of a forthcoming marriage, but in 1880 a man named Robert

Remains of the mining town of Bonanza, Idaho.

Hawthorne stepped off the Bonanza stage, and the next summer he and Lizzie were married. A week after the wedding, tragedy struck: both were found shot dead in their log cabin at the north end of town. Neither the murderer nor the murderer's weapon was ever discovered. Franklin again helped with the funeral arrangements, and as Conley intriguingly observes, "The headboards [of the couple's gravesite] never mentioned Agnes Elizabeth Hawthorne's new surname." Distraught, Franklin let his business arrangements lapse and ten years later moved to prospect some claims in Stanley Basin, becoming yet one more wilderness recluse. Two years later, in 1892, prospectors discovered his decomposed body on the bed in his cabin, with his hands clutched around a locket in which was encased a photograph of Elizabeth King.

Who was it who said, of all kinds of love, unrequited is the cruelest?

Mining continued into the twentieth century in the Yankee Fork drainage. In the late 1930s, tests conducted by a mining company revealed that $16 million worth of gold was still recoverable through dredge mining, a complicated operation in which a steam-shovel-like device, anchored to a kind of large tugboat with legs, digs out a stream or river bottom. The dig-

The Yankee Fork dredge.

gings are then dumped into a hopper with a screen of three-quarter-inch perforations so that the smaller debris, which contains the gold, falls into sluices with mercury in them, thereby making it easy to remove the precious metal. To work the Yankee Fork, a monstrous dredge was constructed. Weighing twelve tons and floating on twenty-four steel pontoons each measuring ten by ten by twenty-seven feet, the whole machine was bolted together to form a hull 112 by 54 feet. All told, it cost $600,000 to build. The dredge continued to operate intermittently until 1952, when the gold in the creek was exhausted. It now rests at the confluence of Yankee Fork and Jordan Creek surviving as an in situ museum. Fascinated mining buffs and aficionados of Western history tour its rusting, grease-scented bowels. When I visited this site years after working the lookout, what was most striking was the stark incongruity of this colossal piece of modern technology anchored in a stream bed, surrounded by forest-clad ridges and the ten-thousand-foot peaks of the Tango Range. This artifact seemed the epitome of the Machine in the Garden. Yet, like Henry Adams when he encountered the dynamo at the turn of the twentieth century, I was spellbound for a time by this imposing feat of technology. Today its greatest, and saddest, legacy is a long pile of dredged debris running like a ghastly scar across some otherwise lovely mountain scenery.

Miners were the first whites to inhabit the region but, true to the boom-and-bust nature of extractive industries, their stay tended to be shorter than that of subsequent Anglo-American frontier residents. Longer-lasting human fixtures, perhaps with less devastating consequences in the long run, were settlers who attempted to farm and raise cattle and sheep in the valley bottoms (and try their luck at some prospecting in their spare time). It now seems incredible, in the face of numerous desiccated, abandoned, homesteader cabins along the Middle Fork, that people would actually try to grow crops in this inhospitable terrain, yet try to farm they did. Just south of the headwaters of the river, where Bear Valley and Marsh creeks join (about ten air miles northwest of Ruffneck), is a place on the river called Boundary Creek. Today Boundary Creek is where river runners usually begin their trips, and where the Forest Service operates a station to check permits and assign campsites downriver. At the turn of the century, Boundary Creek got its name because it marked the boundary between cattle and sheep range; the latter were not to be grazed south of the creek. Stanley Basin and the Middle Fork attracted settlers of all kinds: families, outlaws, and hermits. Where Sulfur Creek enters the Middle Fork, just a few miles downstream from Boundary Creek, a former Nebraskan named Jim Fuller staked a claim in the early 1900s after discovering the headwaters of the river while leading a grazing cattle train. So enamored was he of the setting that he brought his wife, Annazie, to the site, and together they homesteaded a quarter-mile claim in the 1920s a few miles up Sulphur Creek from its confluence with the Middle Fork. Photographs in *Idaho for the Curious* reveal three log cabins with shake roofs — one to live in, another a bath house built over a hot spring, and a third for storage — against a backdrop of a V-shaped gorge and forested ridgelines, with fleecy cumulus hovering in a summer sky. It was seemingly an idyllic pioneer homestead. The Fullers and their four daughters and son were part-time residents only; they grazed cattle in the creek bottom come snowmelt in the spring, stayed for the summer, and trailed out again in the fall before the next onset of winter. They lived out this happy arrangement until the 1940s. A commercial ranch and airstrip have since replaced the cabins where they first homesteaded.

Permanent, year-round residents were fewer but perhaps even more colorful. Joe Bump (as in bump on a log — a photo shows him in exactly that position) was a packer who tried his luck at prospecting along the Middle

Fork near its confluence with Soldier Creek. He added on to a cabin built by two previous prospectors in the 1930s who packed and rafted in twelve-inch diameter pipe to construct a diversion ditch to work their placer claim. The claim never amounted to much for either the original prospectors or Joe Bump. Eventually he was forced to leave his homestead after getting caught in a blizzard and suffering frostbite and blood poisoning in his toes. The cabins remain, however, and represent one of the more interesting archaeological features along the river. When I hiked by the cabin in the late 1990s on a backpacking exploration of the upper Middle Fork, I found to my surprise that it had been "wrapped" by the Forest Service in fire-resistant foil, to prevent its possible burning from nearby forest fires. The agency was acting according to law in trying to preserve historical artifacts within the wilderness, but I was sure that Joe Bump would have been astounded by the efforts to save his cabin.

Though nowadays mention of solitary backcountry residents may conjure images of the Unabomber in some minds, at the turn of the century these recluses of the wilderness were generally admirable, an ingenious and determined lot. Bear hunter Charlie Norton of Custer was an unfortunate soul whose face was clawed and crushed by a grizzly but who lived to tell about it, though he had to endure countless operations to re-open his mouth when his scars healed and the skin contracted. Then there was Cougar Dave Lewis of Big Creek, a Civil War veteran who decided to come West for more wartime activity. Lewis was not disappointed, as he became one of the scouts for the Army during the Sheepeater campaign. When he was eighty years old he retired to become a bounty hunter of lions in the backcountry, and earned enough to buy his staples with the cougar pelts he cashed in. He lived in Big Creek Gorge, at the beginning of Impassable Canyon, until he was ninety-three. Then, in an ironic turn of events, his land was eventually sold to the University of Idaho, on which the famous wildlife biologist Maurice Hornocker conducted his studies of mountain lion. After years of investigation Hornocker concluded that these predators had only an inconsequential effect on elk populations in the area. Lions, one of the chief nemeses of the pioneer era in which Dave Lewis thrived, were thus removed from the bounty category and reclassified as big game. To see one now in the wild is truly a privilege.

My favorite former resident of the Middle Fork was the famous hermit of Impassable Canyon, Earl Parrott. Cort Conley tells his story well in *Idaho Loners*. Parrott entered the canyon around 1917, ten miles upriver from the confluence of the Middle and Main Salmon rivers, where the granite walls are nearly perpendicular. Having tried his luck in Alaska during the Yukon gold rush, having been rejected by a woman, and having lost the money he made prospecting because of a bank failure, he decided to put behind him once and for all society with all of its untrustworthy institutions and relationships. He built two cabins, one a crude shelter on the beach of the Middle Fork, the other a larger, more livable dugout structure two thousand feet above on the canyon rim, accessible only via a series of Anasazi-like ladders up the cliff faces. There Parrott cultivated a beautiful garden in which he raised many kinds of vegetables and delicious strawberries. He dried all his produce and shot an occasional deer to meet his food needs. Once a year he floated downriver seventy miles to the town of Shoup on the Main Salmon for salt, matches, tea, and bullets purchased with gold dust he panned from the creeks. His existence was not discovered until 1923 by a Forest Service survey party. He lived in the canyon until 1942, at which time he had to come out because of a prostate gland problem. He chose to vote against FDR in 1936 because, he said, ccc crews were beginning to intrude on his privacy. Alas, the modern world was making inroads, even in the canyon of the Middle Fork. Parrott spent the remaining two years of his life in the river town of Salmon, Idaho — no doubt forlornly gazing back towards the mountains, thinking of more solitary, peaceful times.

I love the hermit life I live in the mountains, but it's a far cry from the independence from society that Earl Parrott enjoyed. And I admire the works of nature writers like Thoreau and John Muir who lived, for a time, by themselves in nature. But Thoreau lived only a mile from Concord and was known to raid his mother's cookie jar at home, and even Muir had to return to civilization after his tea and bread ran out in the high Sierra. Few people know of the true self-sufficient hermits like Parrott, and fewer admire them. They're written off as cranks, misanthropes, the flotsam and jetsam of society, although they're the ones who have actually lived a life of wilderness solitaire, in their own quiet fashion. They represent the real Anglo natives of this place — readers and writers, not of textbooks, but of the primary book of nature, students and shapers of the Earth itself.

The federal government which Parrott opposed in the 1930s had entrenched itself in the region by the second decade of the twentieth century. With what Frederick Jackson Turner termed the official closing of the frontier in 1890 and widespread concern about the profligate waste of our natural resources, the federal government acted to preserve and manage the remaining forests in America. First came a law in 1891 giving the president the authority to set aside "public lands wholly or in part covered with timber or under-growth . . . as public reservations." Then in 1897 the Forest Management Act established the goals of aiding water flow, furnishing lumber, and protecting timber in what would become the national forests. It was during the administration of Teddy Roosevelt (1901–09) that the largest amounts of forest lands were initially added to the federal domain. Gifford Pinchot, head of the Forest Service during TR's presidency, convinced Roosevelt to set aside over 148 million acres of national forest, mostly in the West. It was also under Pinchot that the Forest Service formulated its multiple use policy. The national parks (first set aside in 1872 in Yellowstone and later administered by the Park Service, which was not created until 1916) were managed as single use — primarily for recreation. The Forest Service, on the other hand, followed a utilitarian philosophy of providing for a variety of uses in the national forests — the greatest good for the greatest number of people — which included logging, mining, grazing, water control, as well as recreation.

The national forests were also created to facilitate fire prevention and management. In addition to being logged off, forests in the West were being devastated by fires both wild and human-caused in the early 1900s. The worst year for wildfires in the twentieth century in America was 1910, when a single fire — the Great Burn of August 20–24 — consumed an estimated three million acres of forest in northern Idaho, western Washington, and northwestern Montana. (The Forest Service has produced an anecdotal pamphlet history of this fire, appropriately titled "When the Mountains Roared.") That year more than five million acres burned because of wild-fires, causing the Forest Service to declare the equivalent of a holy war against fire and galvanizing the nascent agency into standardizing its fire-fighting techniques and resources. According to Steve Pyne in his epic history, *Fire in America*, foresters in the northern Rockies dated their lives according to major fire years: 1910, 1917, 1919, 1926, 1931. Through innovations in technology, increased funding, and greater cooperation between the federal and state governments, the amount of land burned by wildfires in a decade has been reduced from over thirty-nine million acres in the 1930s to less than five million by the 1960s. It is largely through its firefighting efforts that the Forest Service developed its heroic persona and won widespread kudos as a federal agency.

The Challis National Forest was created in 1908 for several reasons: to protect the forests from fire, to prevent erosion along drainways due to overgrazing by cattle and sheep, to regulate the extensive prospecting and mining operations which had already taken place, and (the lowest priority of the time) to provide for human recreation in the forest — mainly fishing, hunting, camping, and hiking. The Challis is now one of the larger national forests in the country, amounting to over 2.5 million acres, much of it official wilderness. Its forests were never heavily logged, mainly due to the extreme remoteness and ruggedness of the area and the relatively small girth of its trees because of the land's high elevation and aridity. Not until the 1970s, with the advent of helicopter logging, would such remote timber become more accessible. But by that time the push for preservation of the Salmon River drainage had become too strong. It is mainly in the northern part of the state, a region of greater precipitation and lower elevations, where the colorful history of logging the tall timber of Idaho was played out.

In spite of the relatively restricted logging that has taken place over the years on the Challis National Forest, the Forest Service has had a tremendous impact on the environmental history of the region by dictating both the kind and degree of uses on its lands. It has exerted both a visible and an invisible hand by building trails in the mountains and along the creeks and rivers and by suppressing fires that once burned uncontrollably. After the Yellowstone fires of 1988, of course, there has been considerable discussion about the ecological harms of suppressing fires as well as the dangers of allowing them to burn uncontrolled. But even before then, the Forest Service (as well as the Park Service) had established a let-burn policy in certain areas, authorizing what it called Prescribed Natural Fires (PNFs). The agency designated certain parameters in which prescribed natural fires would be allowed to burn depending on whether they were burning in a wilderness area, whether they threatened private property, human lives, and/or historic structures, and whether, given climatological and topographical conditions, they were burning beyond a designated area. Not surprisingly, given the uncertainties inherent in some of these parameters, the agency has received much criticism for its decisions in fire management policy.

The inexactitudes of fire management policy were exemplified in July 1979 when the Mortar Creek fire erupted in the Middle Fork canyon. It began as a campfire along the river that was not totally extinguished by a party of horse campers. Hot and dry winds, along with the cumulative effects of several successive drought years, led to the blow-up of a minuscule campfire. Although the Forest Service acted as quickly as it could in attempting to put out the fire by dropping in a helitack crew and bombarding the fire with retardant loads, the steep terrain and dry, hot conditions defeated its initial efforts. Soon twenty-five hundred acres had been consumed. Only a week later, after six hundred firefighters were flown in, did the blaze appear to be under control. The critical word, unfortunately, is *appear*. The Forest Service then made a terrible strategic error in declaring the fire ready to be mopped up and pulled all but fifty of its firefighters. The next day a hot spot developed outside the fire line and, fanned by intense and searing winds, the fire blew up once again. This time, as Conley observes, the Forest Service "had more problems than a one-legged man at an ass-kicking contest." Aerial photos of the Mortar Creek fire at this stage suggest the dropping of a nuclear weapon. Surveillance flights were canceled because at thirty thousand feet — the height of the convection caused by the mushroom clouds of smoke, which was also the elevation at which the photos needed to be taken — the air was too turbulent. In two days the fire grew by twenty thousand acres. Like all major blazes, it created its own microclimate. Temperatures soared to eighteen hundred degrees, sucking in superheated air into convection columns, with updrafts of seventy-five miles per hour. These winds in turn preheated fuels on chimney-like slopes ahead of the fire's path. Conifers full of sap and pitch exploded, igniting more spot fires across canyons and creating whirlwinds that knocked down entire ridgelines of trees. It was finally the weather, not human agency, which put the fire out, as a cold front moved in bringing heavy rains and plunging temperatures. "A change in the weather / has been known to be extreme," Bob Dylan once observed, a point underscored when a firefighter on what was left of the Mortar fire had to be evacuated for hypothermia in the final stages of mop-up. All told, the Mortar Creek fire consumed over sixty-five thousand acres and cost $5.7 million to suppress.

Amazingly enough, during the fire river runners continued to float down the Middle Fork below the fire — a testament to the determination and resilience of river rats, not to mention their insanity. No one knows for sure if the Sheepeaters ever attempted to float the Middle Fork, but the lack of any type of watercraft among their archaeological remains suggests they didn't. And recall that the Shoshone advised Captain Clark in 1805 against running the Main Salmon. So, as usual, it was not the natives but foolish, imperialistic white men who dared to do what the indigenes knew was an affront to the gods. The Main Salmon was successfully run by two French trappers in 1832 (though two others in their party drowned in one of the many rapids). The river received its famous nickname in 1904 when a newspaper reporter who had accompanied famed river pilot Harry Guleke down the Main Salmon subsequently stated, "I recommend this river of no return as a hair-raiser."

There are unconfirmed stories that this same Captain Guleke floated down the Middle Fork to its confluence with the Main Fork of the Salmon around the turn of the century. But the first documented report of a successful run of the Middle Fork came some thirty years later by a party of boatmen with previous experience on the Colorado River. Johnny Carrey and Cort Conley tell the story in *The Middle Fork and Sheepeater War*. In July 1936 a group of seven men, led by Doc Frazier of Bingham, Utah, started near the true headwaters of the river, where Marsh and Bear Valley creeks come together (named Cape Horn by some imaginative cartographer because of the big swing Highway 21 makes around the northern end of the Sawtooths). They made the run in several lightweight, wooden, fourteen-foot boats with the bottoms reinforced with the rubber strips of conveyor belts (the granite of the Idaho batholith, they had learned from an aborted attempt on the river in 1935, was significantly harder than Utah sandstone). The Frazier party portaged around rapids only once, at Sulphur Falls on the upper river, and occasionally stopped at a rancher's place to resupply and make inquiries. They even visited Earl Parrott, the hermit of Impassable Canyon; one wonders in what mood he greeted these intruders. Apparently the party had a whale of a time. Of all the photos of the trip that Conley and Carrey include in their account, my favorite is of the *Lota Ve* (named after one of the party's daughters) nearly enveloped in white turbulence, one crew member having just lost an oar, the other crawling on the deck of the stern to get back into his seat — an image that wonderfully captures the exhilaration and the terror of river-running! Only after the party passed the confluence with the Main Salmon did they experience the more serious misfortune of having a crew member break a leg as his boat flipped in a rapid. Since Doc Frazier was a medical doctor they managed to care for the patient as best they could, though the plaster of paris brought along for just this kind of emergency got wet in the flipover so the broken bone could not be set. Three days later they drifted into Riggins and traded one of their boats for some beer. They'd earned it.

According to the Forest Service, more than eleven thousand people ran the Middle Fork in 1998.

It may have been river-running more than any other form of recreation that led to the creation in 1980 of the River of No Return Wilderness. (Nearly coterminous with the Selway-Bitterroot and Gospel Hump wilderness areas, this immense tract of wildland amounts to nearly four million acres of official wilderness.) The River of No Return Wilderness includes parts of six national forests: the Challis, Salmon, Bitterroot, Nez Perce, Payette, and Boise. Since the turn of the century, this area has been the focus of four major management preservation efforts. In 1925 a relatively small part of the central Middle Fork canyon was set aside as a federal game preserve. In 1931, one million acres, including most of the Middle Fork basin, was set aside as the Idaho Primitive Area, a development that came at a time when the concept of wilderness was making headway in the Forest Service, thanks to the efforts of Aldo Leopold and Bob Marshall. In 1968, with the creation of the National Wild and Scenic Rivers Act, the Middle Fork of the Salmon River, from Boundary Creek to the confluence of the Main Salmon, became one of the original eight rivers in the United States to be designated as a wild river for its "outstandingly remarkable scenic, recreational, geologic, fish and wildlife, historic, cultural or other similar values." Finally, the passage in 1980 of the Central Idaho Wilderness Act, which included the creation of the River of No Return Wilderness, led to the most recent, and most important, stage of federal protection.

In the late 1970s, when the political battle was being waged over whether and how much of the area should be preserved as wilderness, I was living in northern Idaho and about to enter graduate school at the University of Idaho in Moscow, one of a few remote islands of liberalism in a very conservative state. I recall vividly the involvement of students and professors in the campaign conducted by the ad hoc River of No Return Wilderness Council, the long speeches in behalf of wilderness preservation, the door-to-door canvassing for contributions and signatures on petitions to be sent to Idaho state and federal representatives. (A free poster of the wilderness area that I picked up at a table of preservationist literature still adorns a wall in my study.) The preservationists argued that we had to protect the native salmon and steelhead populations of the Columbia River system (the Salmon flows into the Snake which in turn flows into the Columbia) by ensuring that the Salmon River would remain the last major undammed river in the Lower Forty-eight. They argued that we had to protect the over 190 species of wildlife which lived in the proposed wilderness. They argued that the Main Salmon deserved wild-river status (the same as the Middle Fork) in order to ensure that the river-running tourist industry stayed profitable. And they argued that the timber values of the forest that remained in the proposed wilderness were minimal compared to the land's recreational value.

Across the state, public hearings were held to discuss the wilderness bill, and many heated debates occurred. In Salmon more than five hundred people came to represent the logging, mining, and recreation industries, and 160 speakers testified in over eight hours. Anti-wilderness representatives pointed out that most of the supporters of the River of No Return Wilderness bill were not from Salmon; but then neither were those representing the logging industry. Few minds were changed by the testimony, the local paper reported. It turned out to be a typically democratic gathering in a bureaucratic age: with no clear consensus emerging among the populace, a government agency is forced to make a decision on its own.

Somehow, in the end, the preservationists won. In the waning months of the Carter administration, on the eve of the Reagan revolution, in the last year of Idaho Senator Frank Church's long tenure as a great, eloquent, liberal spokesman of the West, the bill establishing the River of No Return Wilderness was signed into law. The files on Church's involvement in the political fight to pass the Central Idaho Wilderness Act, now housed at Boise State University, reveal the passion the senator held for wilderness as well as the clear-headed realism it required to pass such legislation in a state and Congress skeptical of locking up natural resources. In January 1980, just after Senate passage of his wilderness bill, Church reported to his constituents on the balanced compromise the legislation embodied. While the bill helped protect over two million acres as federal wilderness, it also freed up 915,000 acres adjacent to the wilderness boundaries for logging. "By drawing the boundaries [of the wilderness] with care, we [he and fellow Idaho Senator James McClure] were able to provide for *both* more wood and more wilderness," Church claimed. He also noted that a special mining management zone in the wilderness was created to allow for valuable deposits of cobalt to be extracted; but in the same area a major drainage was preserved as wilderness because it was one of the most productive bighorn sheep ranges in the state. Church concluded his report by stating, "This region is what Idahoans mean when they refer to our state as 'God's Country.' It is a place of rare beauty and quiet solitude, a jewel in the crown of Idaho's natural splendor." Church knew this firsthand from backpacking and fishing trips in the primitive area.

In a letter to a constituent in which he discusses the Forest Service's compliance with certain provisions of the proposed legislation, Church revealed his pragmatism, a trait for which he was often praised: "If the agency does not comply with the letter and spirit of the law, they will hear from me as well as — I'm sure — from you. Past experience indicates that the Forest Service performs best when they are being watched closely by those people with an interest in their programs. So the answer to your question is, keep an eye on what they're doing."

The River of No Return Wilderness was later renamed the Frank Church–River of No Return Wilderness after Church died (of cancer) in 1984. While I generally object to parks and wilderness areas being named after politicians, in this case I make an exception. In Idaho, most folks now refer to the wilderness simply as the Frank Church.

The controversy over wilderness in central Idaho continues. In fact, attention is shifting from wilderness *preservation* to wilderness *restoration*. Among the species that disappeared in Idaho in the twentieth century due to the encroachment and depredations of modern society was the gray wolf, Canis lupus. In 1987 the u.s. Fish and Wildlife Service designated the River of No Return Wilderness as part of a Northern Rockies Recovery Area, a proposed sanctuary in which the wolf would be reintroduced as part of an effort to restore certain indigenous animal species to the bioregion. Consequently, thirty-five wolves were captured in Canada and transported and released in different locations in the wilderness in 1995 and 1996. While environmentalists were thrilled at the possibility of hearing wolves howl in the canyons of the Middle Fork, ranchers were outraged over the prospect that their livestock grazing along the edges of the wilderness boundary might be killed and eaten by the very varmints they and the government had worked so hard to extirpate from the West in the past one hundred years. The wolves were radio-collared to enable wildlife biologists to track their movements. Of the thirty-five wolves released, four have died, several under suspicious circumstances (two other wolves have been lost from radio contact for an extended time and are presumed dead as well).

While visiting a lookout in northern Idaho in the summer of 1998, I ran into wolf trackers from the Nez Perce, the Indian tribe which, having subcontracted with Fish and Wildlife, has taken on the responsibility of wolf recovery and management in Idaho. They told me they were following a pack of wolves in the Clearwater Mountains but had lost track of them in the labyrinth of creeks and rivers. They were now waiting for a helicopter to fly them over the terrain in the hope of re-establishing contact. The goal of the wolf recovery program, they said, is to develop a sustained population of ten breeding pairs (approximately one hundred wolves) for at least three consecutive years in the next ten years.

When the Nez Perce trackers told me about the wolves, I looked out over the countless forested ridges, trying to conjure an image of the animals loping through the tangled woods. I have seen timber wolves in the wilds of northern Minnesota, but never in Idaho. Surely, I thought, if wolves could survive and even flourish in the upper Midwest, they could do so here, in the 2.4-million-acre River of No Return Wilderness.

With the help of homo sapiens, that is. "Man always kills the thing he loves, and so we the pioneers have killed our wilderness," wrote Aldo Leopold in *A Sand County Almanac*. Perhaps, in our species' curious love-hate relationship with the wild, we also have it in our power to restore some things which we, blinded by hate, might too have actually loved — or, at the least, respected. It is good that the history of wilderness preservation now also entails efforts at restoration. At least in the case of the timber wolf, there is still time to make amends.

So much for the human history of the wilderness and the efforts to preserve and restore it. Isn't the concept of a peopled wilderness an oxymoron? So the conventional wisdom of wilderness preservation would have it. Preservationists traditionally describe wilderness as natural, pristine, and untouched. The text of the Forest Service map of the Challis National Forest describes it as "rugged and unconquered." The Wilderness Act of 1964 defines official federal wilderness as a place "where man is but a visitor."

But here I am, a resident, a self-proclaimed native, in the largest federal wilderness in the Lower Forty-eight. Moreover, it's clear that I'm only one in a long history of inhabitants of the Frank Church — the latter far more legitimate and longer-term residents than I am. Environmental historians such as William Cronon have helped make us realize that the old classifications and definitions of wilderness are oversimplified and inaccurate. For millions of years the human species has made an impact on the land — just like every other species. Granted, humans have had far greater effects on the planet than any other creatures, and there are few places on earth that haven't been affected by human actions in some way. We need to rethink our conception of wilderness as virgin land. It's not. Why can't wilderness and humans coexist? Why can't wilderness refer to land that is/was inhabited by humans at some time, including the present? Properly speaking, Thoreau once said, there can be no history but natural history. Meaning that we can't and shouldn't try to separate nature and culture.

However, because wilderness has been inhabited by people does not mean that we should do away with federal wilderness. We still need Wilderness with a capital *W*, as defined in the 1964 Wilderness Act. We need it as land that for the most part suggests the appearance of pristineness and remains valuable to us for precisely that reason: as a sanctuary for human sanity and serenity in a world fouled by overcrowding and too much technology and pollution. "Of what avail are forty freedoms without a blank spot on the map?" Aldo Leopold once asked. We also need to preserve wilderness as a laboratory of biotic health for creatures such as wolves that have nowhere else to live relatively free of human interference. Wilderness with a capital *W* is still eminently worth preserving for precisely these reasons. In fact, we need far more of it than we now have: only one hundred million acres or so of federally protected wildlands currently exists, and more than half of that is in Alaska. Those one hundred million acres amount to only about a paltry four percent of America's total land mass. It's been said before — by wilderness visionaries like Thoreau, Muir, Leopold, and Abbey — but the truth is worth repeating: civilization couldn't exist without wilderness. Not spiritually, or materially. Wilderness is the foundation of culture.

7. running the river

During the summer that I worked Ruffneck lookout I heard the expression "running the Middle Fork" so many times — over the Forest Service radio as well as from visitors — that I vowed I would run the river myself someday. A decade later I did, and what follows is an account of that mythic journey.

Seventeen middle-class Americans, ranging in age from ten to seventy-seven, gather outside a motel at sunrise one early summer day in 1999 in the small mountain town of Stanley, Idaho, wondering what the hell they've gotten themselves into.

I am one of these seventeen strangers.

We are about to embark on a voyage of exploration down the Middle Fork of the Salmon, the premier whitewater rafting river in the Lower Forty-eight. Of the five guides who will lead us, two of them are now herding the reluctant passengers and their duffel bags into a school bus to drive up the washboard road to the airport, a rutted clearing in a meadow below the Sawtooth Range. By the time we get out of the bus, it is clear from the looks of some of the clients that they harbor grave misgivings about the adventure for which they have paid $1,300 each.

Nevertheless, we all file obediently into the three small prop planes that will fly us from Stanley to the airstrip at Indian Creek guard station, where we'll meet the other three guides who have deadheaded (i.e., floated the rafts, gear, and food sans paying passengers) the first twenty-five miles of the river from the put-in at Boundary Creek. We're not floating the upper portion of the river because in late July there is too little water flow, and too

Middle Fk. of the Salmon River

Cache Bar

Impassable Canyon

Main Salmon River

• Parrott Placer Camp

Big Creek

• Wilson Cr. Camp

Camas Creek

Flying B Ranch

Marble Creek

• Lower Grouse Cr. Camp

Indian Creek

• put-in

Pine Cr. Flat Camp

• Middle Fk. Lodge

Rapid River

Loon Creek

Dagger Falls

⌂ Ruffneck Peak Lookout

21

21

```
0        5        10
|--------|--------|
Scale in Miles
```

North (MM)

many exposed rocks, for the heavily laden rafts to pass over without difficulty. I have mixed feelings about not running the first twenty-five miles: I'm sorry to be missing the narrower, perhaps wilder upper river, but am grateful for the opportunity to fly over and see from the air a significant portion of the River of No Return Wilderness. Soon my own misgivings about running the river are forgotten because I'm enraptured by the view of the Salmon River Mountains. We're flying at around ten thousand feet over the Rapid River drainage, and to the west I can make out the profile of Ruffneck Peak and even pick out the white lookout cabin on top of the mountain. The flight is smooth, the view tremendous, and before long we're making the steep descent into the Middle Fork canyon and taxiing across the gravel airstrip.

After another duffel-shuffle organized by the guides, we lug the gear down the steps and landing ramp to the sandy beach, along which flow the emerald waters of the Middle Fork. I pause to take in my first view of the waters of the river, a waterway long considered sacred to wilderness aficionados because its entire corridor is protected by federal wilderness, all of it within the Frank Church. There may be deeper canyons; there may be more ferocious rapids; but there is no more pristine runnable river in the United States outside of Alaska. We are about to float on sacred waters.

But one of the things that concerns me is that some members of this commercial trip may not be aware of the significance of the journey. I know none of them and the only reason I am on this trip is because it's the only way for me, a novice whitewater adventurer whose only experience on rivers has been in canoes on relatively tame Class II waters of the upper Midwest, to do a trip on the Middle Fork. (Class I are the easiest, Class VI the most difficult.) The teenagers and some of the adults I've chatted with so far give no indication they know of the river's fabled wilderness status. For them this is something of a waterpark adventure with guides steering their rafts and cooking their meals and helping them set up their camps at night. In other words it's a controlled wilderness experience, and I am all too aware of the contradictions inherent in this oxymoron.

But at least a ranger is here to help them appreciate the privilege of wilderness travel a bit more. Part of the orientation for the trip involves a mandatory talk given by an official of the Forest Service, the agency which regulates the river and wilderness. Rick Piva — Ranger Rick, as he likes to be called — is a tall, lean, sinewy guy in his late thirties who begins his talk by telling us that last year more than eleven thousand people were allowed to run the river. With most of those people on the river in a sixty-day span,

Middle Fork of the Salmon River.

there's a great potential for overcrowding and human impact. The Forest Service is trying to balance access to the river with impact on the river, Rick says. To do this they allow no more than six parties a day (three commercial and three private parties each), with a maximum of thirty people in a party. There are preservationists who claim that this amounts to too many people for a true wilderness experience — solitude being a key ingredient of a bona fide wilderness journey — and Rick tells us that the Forest Service is currently re-examining the amount of usage it allows on the river. The agency may well lower the number of parties and people beginning next year — an ominous development for the whitewater rafting companies who herd approximately half of the people down the river each summer.

In the meantime we're to pack out everything, ranging from the trash we generate to the human waste we produce. Among the gear stored in the three large rafts is a chemical potty, which will be set up at each camp for the four nights we're on the river. Look for and pick up all signs of human presence before you leave a spot after stopping on the river, admonishes Rick, especially things like lint from fleece garments and twisty-ties from packaged food. He wants us to preserve the pristine appearance of the river as much as we can. At the conclusion of his fifteen-minute talk he implores us to take a bit of the wilderness back to civilization, figuratively speaking, by treating our homes, wherever they may be, as wild and sacred too. He finishes with two short poems by Wendell Berry and Gary Snyder, and then we file out to the rafts. Before I leave I thank him for the talk, especially its literary aspect, and mention that I used to work Ruffneck lookout. We swap a few quick names and stories.

The guides begin their instructions. Eric, the lead guide, gives us pointers and warnings about handling the two smaller rafts we'll be paddling as well as the two inflatable kayaks available to whoever wants to use them. Paddle when and how the guides tell you to. Never get ahead of the lead raft. If you spill, try to stay with the watercraft. If in the kayak, keep it pointed downstream and don't get caught sideways in a rapid. And always, always wear your lifejacket when on the river.

By this time it's 10 A.M. The rafts are fully loaded with food, gear, and people for a five-day trip. We have eighteen miles to go to our first campsite. I'm alone in one of the kayaks as we shove off into the purling waters of the Middle Fork, the canyon still shaded and cool but with the sky promising a warm clear day.

The adventure begins.

Fortunately for me and my fellow rafters the river is comparatively tame the first seven miles or so. At this point it's an intimate mountain waterway, perhaps one hundred feet across. The river corridor is just beginning to make the transition in vegetation from the lodgepole pine and subalpine fir of the upper elevations to the scattered ponderosa pine, Douglas fir, and open grasslands found from Indian Creek downriver. Our starting elevation is just under five thousand feet. Rocky fins protrude in spots along the banks as well as in the river, evidence of the Idaho batholith that we will be encountering with greater frequency the deeper we descend into the canyon.

I'm enjoying the mobility and relative solitude immensely. While my fellow party members chat in the rafts with the guides and each other, mostly oblivious to the passing scenery, I can study it in relative quiet. Rounded-off, pine-studded, grassy hills, rising to seven thousand feet, form my immediate horizons. Overhead looms a cerulean blue Western sky. There is only the sound of the river as I float downstream.

Always keeping a ready eye out for rocks as well as holes and waves, I seem to have little trouble negotiating the kayak around and through the Class I rapids. The first real challenge comes at mile 31, where Marble Creek Rapid, a Class II, has formed below the mouth of the stream by that name coming in from the left. The rapids have been created by debris pouring down from the creek into the river during flood stages to form standing waves as the water passes over the boulders. The guides advise me to stay about thirty feet from the left bank and take the rapids head-on. I watch several of the rafts proceed first, hear the whoops and hollering of the passengers, then run it myself. The troughs between the waves are deeper than I thought, the waves much more powerful, and initially I have trouble keeping the kayak straight. But with some power strokes I wrestle it into position and ride the waves like a cowboy on a bucking bronco. Near the top of one of the last waves the water smashes into my face, quite cold and bracing. I ride it, spin around to look upstream to appreciate the view of the rapid, and let out a holler myself. Damn that was fun! I've been baptized by my first real rapid on the Middle Fork.

At mile 32 we stop for lunch at Sunflower Flat Hot Springs. Here an enterprising pioneer earlier in the century improved the site by fashioning a shower of sorts, placing a trough on a ledge over which the hot waters flow. A few of the party bathe and soak in the shallow pools above while the crew sets up tables and prepares lunch: cold cuts and cheeses, several kinds of bread, fruit, vegetables, cookies, sugary drinks. Though I've mainly been sitting for several hours, I'm famished and wolf down lots of marvelous-tasting food, which I find infinitely better than backpacking or lookout cuisine. I also mingle a bit with the passengers, chatting with a petite woman from Pennsylvania, Mary Ann, and her ten-year-old son, Jonathan. They're here because they won a trip through a charity auction. Having never been

West before, they're awed by the surrounding scenery. It's so postcard-perfect it almost seems unreal, Mary Ann says. Indeed it does.

In an hour we're off. We see no other parties on this day but there are signs of civilization. Just downriver from the hot springs we pass under a pack bridge which spans the waterway, then float by a series of cabins which constitute the fabled Middle Fork Lodge, complete with airstrip. This is, according to Cort Conley in *The Middle Fork: A Guide*, "the most celebrated natural sanctuary and vintage guest ranch on any fork of the Salmon River." The first white man to come to the area was a miner who worked the nearby tributaries looking for gold in the 1880s. Then an Englishman in 1889 established a homestead and farmed the river terraces with irrigated water for several decades. In the 1940s, Tom McCall developed the property into a sportsman's lodge, one of the key attractions being a splendid natural hot springs. Given the ranch's isolation — accessed only by tortuous trails and airplanes — this was no easy feat. In the 1960s Harrah's of Reno and Lake Tahoe bought the property and transformed the Middle Fork Lodge into a famous resort, visited by numerous celebrities, including Presidents Jimmy Carter and George Bush. Finally in 1990 the Nature Conservancy bought the property and placed some restrictive covenants on the development to scale down the more civilized accouterments, such as automobiles and the fenced-in tennis court.

I feel ambivalent about the lodge's existence within the Frank Church. On the one hand I'm appalled by the very thought of this kind of development in a wilderness celebrated for its pristine qualities. The notion that an easily accessed resort can coexist with a heavily restricted wilderness waterway seems absurd on the face of it. On the other hand I recognize that the lodge property is aesthetically pleasing and occupies but an infinitesimally small fraction of the 2.4-million-acre wilderness. In a way its existence for us is a moot point, for we quickly pass by. Soon we come to the next bend in the river and the lodge is lost to sight and thought. To float is to forget.

There are further signs of human presence six miles downriver. At Cameron Creek, where a major stream debouches into the river, we take out and trudge up an eighth of a mile onto a hot sunny open terrace. Along a rock face, Eric, the lead guide, points out a panel of pictographs painted by the Sheepeater tribe several hundred years ago. My pamphlet on the geology of the Middle Fork reports that "the paint was made from iron oxide, a chemical compound that forms readily at the surface of the earth — you know it as rust! Yellow pigment, which is not very common along the Middle Fork, was made from another iron-bearing mineral called limonite. Black pigment was made from carbon or soot from fires. Pigments were mixed with animal fats, blood or urine, which is one reason they have survived the elements for such a long time."

We study the images: there are several animals resembling bighorn sheep, along with a group of anthropomorphic stick figures, wielding bows and arrows. It is estimated that these images were painted between two and three hundred years ago. Did the artists draw these images to commemorate a successful hunt? Or to ensure success in a future hunt? Or to represent a dream of a successful hunt? The possible interpretations are numerous. We are riveted by these primitive yet beautiful images, wondering at the presence of peoples who were so much more intimately connected to the natural environment than we are. Most Americans, most first world residents, would not and could not relinquish their hold on all the necessities and conveniences of modern civilization. So we only dream of a deeper bond to nature, all the while drifting further away from the possibility of reconnection.

After eighteen miles on the river we take out at mile 43 at Pine Creek Flat Camp. To provide adequate spacing between parties and to avoid competition over campsites, the Forest Service assigns campsites the entire length of the river to each of the six parties allowed to enter the river at Boundary Creek every day. Cort Conley in his guide to the Middle Fork describes Pine Creek Flat as a "sage splashed bench." Along with the sage, scattered ponderosa pines create some much-needed shade in the heat of late afternoon. We unload the gear then quickly, expertly — as if we've been doing this for weeks — make camp. I choose a clearing amidst the sage and pines farthest from the main camp and set up my cot and unroll my sleeping bag. No tent for me — the few fair-weather clouds are rapidly dissipating in the late afternoon heat, so with the threat of storms diminishing I opt for a clear, unimpeded view of the night sky. From the ammo box issued to me for personal items I pull out a flask of whiskey and toast the purling river from a granite ledge just above a graceful rapid. Long may you flow.

Dinner is embarrassingly sumptuous — salad followed by steaks smothered with onions and mushrooms, baked potatoes with sour cream and chives, rolls, corn on the cob, strawberry shortcake. I chat with Stanley, a seventy-seven-year-old Asian-American from Washington, D.C. He's an interesting guy, a retired journalist on his first river trip. First time he's ever been camping. All day he sat on the huge gear raft piloted by Eric, implacable, looking like a lean Buddha. He talks of the "choreography" of the rapids and river-running, watching how Eric maneuvers the craft perfectly into each route above the rapids and obstructions.

Early in the evening I take a solo hike down the trail which runs along much of the Middle Fork. The rest of the guests are content to putz around and perhaps are even a little intimidated by exploring beyond the boundaries of camp. Just above our encampment I encounter more evidence of the human past: a well-preserved log cabin dating back to the early 1900s. It was built (so reports Cort Conley) by Fred Paulsen, whose feats of strength were legendary. I wonder if he constructed this cabin by himself, and why. Prospecting, no doubt. He stayed many years, never got rich on gold, but discovered a valuable vein of solitude.

Beyond the cabin I spook a coyote above the trail, then a blue grouse. The river purls below. As much as I enjoyed being on the water, it's good to plant my feet on terra firma once again and walk this blessed earth. As far as my primary choice of outdoor recreation goes, I guess I'll always be a hiker as opposed to a river runner; perhaps it has something to do with growing up in mountains with no major navigable river nearby.

Back at camp at 10 P.M., there's still twilight in the sky. I scribble by headlamp in my journal, then drift off to sleep under a twinkly dome. I see — or dream about — a falling star streaking from one end of the canyon to the other in the deepening night sky. No matter. Whether dream or reality, the image is as powerful and tangible as the river and rock.

I awaken to the predawn smell of sagebrush and pine. Sagebrush and pine and cowboy coffee. The guides are making breakfast. I sit up in my sleeping bag and take in the scene as my senses liven to the surroundings: the canyon still dark in the half-light of early morning, the river running smoothly below, the sky turning roseate. A good day beckons.

Breakfast is as sumptuous as dinner. In addition to lots of pungent coffee, there are several kinds of juices, along with pancakes, eggs, sausages, muffins, fruit salad, and yogurt. A backpacking minimalist for most of my outdoor life, I can't help but feel guilty for this spread of delicious food. But, hey — we're paying for it, right? The sauce of guilt somehow makes the food taste all the better.

By 9 A.M. we're floating in the shadows, the air still chilly. The water feels all the colder as it splashes over the bow of the kayak. I'm paddling solo again, but the other kayak is also in use this morning, piloted by two other guests. Good for them. No major rapids await us today on this stretch of the river, just lots of Class II challenges mainly involving some obvious rock-dodging.

Our first stop is not too far downriver at mile 46, the site of Whitey Cox's camp. On a bench above the river is a hot springs and an incongruous marble white headstone marking the grave of Cox, who died in a rockfall while prospecting nearby in 1954. Around the headstone lie numerous to-kens left by sympathetic visitors: a u.s. flag (Cox was a veteran of WWII), dried wildflowers, several elk racks. I test the water of the hot springs — not scalding, just right for a soak. This sunny bench above a bend in the river was indeed a good place to live, and to die.

Lunch is staged where Loon Creek joins the Middle Fork. Loon Creek, along with Big Creek (farther downriver), is one of the most historic and peopled drainages in the Middle Fork basin. Here in 1869 a gold rush began, bringing some twenty-five hundred prospectors to work the snaky tributary, which runs southward forty miles from its headwaters in the Tango Mountains. Several years later the gold panned out, leaving only a few Chinese workers. Their mysterious murder in 1879 triggered the Sheep-eater War.

A half-mile up the creek is a hot springs that all of us visit. A rectangular pool rimmed with finished lumber has been constructed, one more amenity in this pristine wilderness. I continue to learn that the Frank Church is a complex place, celebrated as immense, remote, and pristine — yet featuring all kinds of evidence of a long-inhabited landscape: pictographs, miners' cabins, ranches, pack bridges, airstrips. As a lookout, because I could never see down into the canyon from where I was stationed, I always wondered: What was the river corridor itself like? It seemed infinitely remote and un-touched: the mysterious Middle Fork. Now that I'm on the river, seeing it firsthand, I recognize that it too — like every other place — has a cultural history. We need a different, a more accurate term than pristine to describe even this wild and scenic river, one that denotes its privileged status as the premier wilderness waterway yet acknowledges that people have long lived and visited virtually all parts of its main corridor and side canyons.

Farther down we see a band of bighorn sheep drinking along the river at the base of a rock slide. In this peaceable kingdom they seem unperturbed by our passing. One is a young ram with the makings of a big curl. The an-imals are both symbols and living examples of wildness in a heavily regu-lated wilderness.

At our camp at the mouth of Grouse Creek, mile 56, elevation four thousand feet, I talk with Jerry from Pittsburgh (one of several people among the group who come from my home state). Jerry has brought his sixteen-year-old son John along as a way to "get to know him better." A nice gesture, so far largely lost on John. I hear him giving his dad a hard time about everything, from the red sweatsuit he "looks too fat in" to the lack of luck he's had while fishing. The youth of affluent America: no one is more resentful, and no one is easier to resent. Jerry, a corporate executive with a chemical company, has moved around a lot, but prefers the Pennsylvania Dutch work ethic — no better worker or craft is produced than out of that region and culture, he claims. I rather like his hard-boiled, skeptical eastern attitude; when I ask him if he's having a good time so far he simply replies, "Guess I can't kick too much."

After yet another lavish meal (grilled salmon with all the trimmings), I feel the need to go on another solitary walk. Once again I head downstream, to scout out our future route. Immediately I encounter a well-preserved structure — Tappan cabin, it's called, for the Tappan family, Fred and Daisy, who settled here in the 1930s as cattle ranchers. They lived self-sufficiently for many years, raising fruit trees and garden vegetables on irrigation water, running cattle on the range until forced to move when the Forest Service reduced their rangeland allotment. Daisy had a difficult transition to more civilized country, reporting that "it was three years before I could sleep without the sound of that river and creek. It was just too darned quiet." Standing outside the cabin now kept up by an outfitter, listening to the plashing of Grouse Creek filter through the tangle of vegetation along its banks, I think I know what she means.

I climb a sagebrush steppe a couple of hundred feet above the river, trying to glimpse a series of rapids, Tappan I, II, III, and IV, which will confront us almost immediately after we put in tomorrow morning. But the canyon is too deep and twisty from where I stand to see down into it. There is only the rather unnerving noise of whitewater seeming to increase as the river cuts through the gorge.

The massive cliffs across the river from camp tower to more than 8,600 feet. They're part of the Caston Pluton, granite formed from magma that has consolidated beneath the earth's surface and been pushed upward by millions of years of tectonic pressure. Back at camp, I sit in one of the plastic lawn chairs and watch Hattie, one of the guides, emerge from the river in her polka-dot bikini. She tells Jerry and me about her life as a river guide in the summer and ski instructor at Jackson Hole, Wyoming, in the winter. And about her boyfriend, who surprised her the previous river trip by back-

Tappan cabin.

packing into the canyon and showing up at one of their camps. Invoking a rather fetching metaphor, she says, "I was the ice cream at the end of the hike." Jerry and I look at each other, each of us thinking: I hate beautiful women who talk about their boyfriends.

I retreat far from everyone else to camp in the twilight on the sandy beach beneath some pretty ponderosa pines. Just above the silhouette of the canyon rim, the Big Dipper, distinct in the night sky, seems immeasurably close — and far away.

I'm not quite ready for the rapids as we set off the next morning at 9 A.M. for a long day on the river, despite having had several cups of cowboy coffee to accompany my hearty breakfast. But then again, neither is my partner John, Jerry's sixteen-year-old son. Bored by the rapids so far, he's looking for some action, albeit not quite so early in the morning. Just a mile downstream from where we put in, the river widens and pools before narrowing into a slot canyon. I can see lots of foamy whitewater ahead. That must be the first in a series of Class III–IV drops and chutes and waves that make up Tappan Falls. Kate, the most experienced guide of the crew after Eric, tells us emphatically to watch and follow the route of the rafts which precede us. "You'll have a fun ride in the kayak," she says, with a smile that may be envious or devilish.

She's right about the fun, in any case. The Tappan rapids, spread over a mile or so of river, blur together in my mind afterwards. What stands out most prominently in recollection is Tappan II, a significant drop over a ledge running all the way across the river. We take the right side as instructed, the safest route, and are practically swallowed up in the waves and reversals of the rapid. "Keep paddling!" I shout to John, to maintain our momentum through the maelstrom. We emerge soaked but still buoyant, the self-draining feature of the "rubber ducky" (what kayakers of hard-bodied craft disdainfully call these inflatables) working to perfection. "Now *that* was a fun ride," says John. Good thing he and I are wearing polypropylene long underwear, as for the next couple hours we're still in the shadows, and the water feels numbingly cold.

Finally we emerge into the sun by late morning near Camas Creek. In fact, it seems hardly canyonlike along this stretch as the walls disappear, the slopes become less steep, and the valley widens. Gently undulating hills become our horizons. It was here in 1931 that Zane Grey, the best-selling writer of the pulp Western, undertook a two-month pack trip for material that figured in one of his novels, *Thunder Mountain*. We can see farther than at any point previous to entering the Middle Fork corridor. Soon after passing the mouth of Camas Creek, I spot Middle Fork Peak lookout to the east as the river courses due north. Nice to have a view of the mountains and the river, I think.

The Flying B Ranch, our next stop this morning, is jointly owned now by 150 families that use it as a vacation spot and guest ranch. There's a store of sorts which sells candy bars, pop, and ice cream to fat- and sugar-craving river runners, among them most of our own group. I prefer to bask in the sun on the beach and watch the world float by. The river's getting crowded at this point; more than fifty people pass by in all sorts of watercraft — rafts, sweep boats, dories, duckies, decked canoes, and kayaks. Few of them bother to give the standard hand wave or nod of hello in acknowledgment of a fellow river runner, so accustomed are they to the presence of humans. Here, at this time, it would be impossible to describe the river trip as a wilderness experience. I turn my attention to Colleen, a sixteen-year-old Californian from our group who's sucking on a popsickle. "Are you having fun?" I ask. Sort of, she replies. Later I tell her parents that she'll be thanking them in years hence for taking her on this unforgettable journey. They're not so sure. To tell the truth, neither am I.

Haystack Rapids.

Soon we set off for a lunch spot just upstream from Haystack Rapids, our next major obstacle. Haystack is a technical challenge, involving a lot of maneuvering through a veritable boulder garden. As we eat lunch we watch the flotilla of watercraft negotiate the rapids. Most vessels make it through OK, though several kayakers get overturned in some tricky spots; eventually they manage to spill out downstream with their boats. It seems there are two choices: carefully cross the river diagonally from right to left, the route of the larger rafts and sweep boats, or stay on the right, being sure to thread the needle between two boulders at right center near the bottom of the rapids, the route of the kayaks and canoes. John and I opt for the latter, and the tension builds as we begin our run downstream after the rest of our party makes it through successfully. What is surprising, despite what Eric the lead guide had warned everyone about, is the deceptively strong undertow beneath the seemingly slow-moving surface water. I can feel this undertow pulling ferociously on my kayak paddle as we make one turn after another to pick our way through. The final challenge comes up on us much faster than I anticipated as we slam into the side of the boulder on the left at the bottom of the run yet somehow slide through the eye of the needle on the right. "I didn't think we were gonna make that last turn," says my partner John afterward. "Had it all the way," I lie in response.

I now better appreciate the technical skills necessary for whitewater kayaking, which I recognize involves a great deal of risk and adventure. While backpacking is physically more challenging and provides for a slower, more thoughtful, meditative passage through the wilderness, kayaking has its moments of oneness with nature too. They may come on a calm stretch of river as you're allowed to sweep your senses over the surroundings, or while you're running a rapid just right, merging with the current and waves around rocks and slipping down a tongue of water. It's a moment of fluid grace for which there may be no equally satisfying equivalent while hiking.

The canyon walls become higher, with black belts of basalt streaked across the solid formations of the Idaho batholith into which we plunge ever deeper. At our third camp near the mouth of Wilson Creek, we've dropped to thirty-eight hundred feet, far below the nearby ridges that top out at seventy-eight hundred. We set up camp on a sandy beach beneath towering ponderosas as the winds begin to swirl underneath darkening skies. A thunderstorm is brewing, and everyone except me scrambles to set up their tents.

As usual, I head for the farthest spot from base camp to set out my bag and cot, choosing a sheltered bench beneath a pine that must be five feet in girth; I'm well-protected under its massive limbs. Here I engage in my daily toast of the river with a sip of whiskey and wait out the storm. Lightning flashes upcanyon, followed by thunder, then sprinkles of rain and cool winds. In half an hour the storm passes, and the canyon heats up again in the afternoon sun.

I opt for a pre-dinner hike downstream to Rattlesnake Cave, where more pictographs are to be found. Jonathan, the ten-year-old prodigy and son of Mary Ann, accompanies me. He is a mature, articulate, and cute kid — writes an environmental newsletter for his private school back near Detroit, Michigan, plays the violin and sings in the choir, reads voraciously. His only fault is that he's much too serious and obedient for his age. But as I recall, rebelliousness will come later.

Around a bend, with Jonathan leading the way, we come to a rocky spot beneath a cliff wall. Suddenly, he pauses. "What's up?" I ask. "Oh, just a rattlesnake." Yes it is — I see the rattled tail just before it disappears in the crevices. Must have been sunning itself after the cooling storm. I lead the hike from then on, after fashioning a combination walking stick and snake poker from a broken branch. Wouldn't want to have to explain to his mother how I managed to get her son snake-bit on a little nature walk.

Once we reach the creek that marks the turnoff to the cave, I see it's an ugly, steep, talus-strewn slide to the pictos from the main trail. I make it alone, advising Jonathan that it's probably not a good idea for him to try it in sandals. Besides, I'd like to see and appreciate the rock art by myself for a bit; he'll see them when we stop here tomorrow morning to check them out as a group. Under a massive granite overhang I make out moose and sheep figures, stars, suns, and what I can only describe as paleolithic doodling. It's a good campsite, with plenty of shelter and only a short distance from the river. Unfortunately, in modern times this advantage was recognized by too many river-running parties and the site got trashed. Some of the pictos became obscured by the smoke of campfires. So the Forest Service has rightly closed this site to camping.

After a dinner of spaghetti and salad, Hattie serves a tasty dessert of blueberry pie. How much better could it get than this? Well, slightly better. I retire shortly after dessert to write ruefully in my journal.

The next morning I lie in my bag in the predawn stillness and take in the elemental sounds and smells. I listen to the white noise of the rapids, the keynote of the canyon. Yesterday after the storm I was refreshed by the bracing bouquet of the sage-scented air after the thunderstorm. Later in the morning when it gets warmer I'll get a whiff of the aroma of pine duff warmed by the sun.

Blue grouse hunt and peck around my campsite this morning, and several mule deer browse the heavy vegetation along Wilson Creek. They stir hardly at all when I walk past them towards the main camp and the smell of morning coffee.

I chat with Mark, another of the guides, as the crew prepares breakfast. In his late twenties, model-handsome, he'd struck me initially as a pretty boy without much substance. But I'm impressed now as he talks about how long it takes to acquire the skill needed to read the river. This is his third summer on the Middle Fork, and he feels he's just getting to know it intimately, able to sense its moods and adapt to its seasons. A good guide, he explains, instinctively, inevitably draws a mental map of the river as he/she continues to float it, until at some point when experience matches the challenge of the riverscape you begin to do things unconsciously, by second nature. "But you should never get cocky, never think that you know all the river knows," he says. "The river is always changing, its volume is never the same. So it's never totally predictable." He walks over to his duffel bag near the shore and extracts a battered paperback entitled *An Innocent on the Middle Fork: A Whitewater Adventure in Idaho's Wilderness* by Eliot DuBois. Read this, he offers, it's a classic of river-running in these parts.

Four miles downriver we make a lengthy stop at Waterfall Creek Falls, where a tributary creek cascades down a long slope of boulders. Part of its appeal for me comes from the knowledge that its water originates in the mythic range known as the Bighorn Crags, the most impressive peaks in all the Salmon River Mountains. This is a range that I could just barely descry from my lookout atop Ruffneck Peak some fifty miles away. We climb out of our boats and carefully scramble up the boulders to the Middle Fork trail. Shortly downstream, across from the mouth of Big Creek, the trail is forced to leave the river because of the high, nearly vertical walls that form the lower stretch of the gorge known as Impassable Canyon. The path switchbacks up to the alpine lakes for which the Crags are famous. I vow someday to hike up there.

After we regroup and resume our float, I spin the kayak around to glimpse the side canyon of Big Creek. This famous tributary has cut an imposing defile, and it's a challenging river to run in its own right in spring when water levels are higher. At Last Chance camp, across from the confluence of Big Creek and the Middle Fork, pithouse depressions have been discovered containing projectile points dating back seven thousand years. Just a few miles upstream on Big Creek is where Dave "Cougar" Lewis lived from the 1870s to the 1930s, winning a reputation as a top-notch hunter of mountain lion, earning a $50 bounty for each one he killed. As I mentioned in the previous chapter, he sold his property in 1934 and eventually it became the Taylor Ranch, another in a series of famous primitive resorts in the Middle Fork country. Pat Peek, a retired teacher and freelance writer, recently wrote a memorable account of living at the Taylor Ranch with her husband, a professor of wildlife management at the University of Idaho, called *One Winter in the Wilderness.* The stories about the wilderness accumulate like the sand of the river banks. They too are part of the natural history of this place.

Our next stop is three miles downriver at Veil Falls. One of the guidebooks to the Middle Fork states simply that "Veil Cave gives one the feeling of being in a cathedral." I would agree. After a hot quarter-mile scramble up a steep rocky slope, we enter a huge amphitheater in the cliff wall. A stream runs down the face of the overhang, becoming a fine mist before it reaches the ground 150 feet below. Rainbows form in the air as the sun strikes the slope; people shower and laugh in the spray. The guides tell me about some

The beginning of Impassable Canyon.

more pictographs near the ceiling of the overhang, maybe another fifty feet of tricky scrambling and climbing upward. I make my way up to view some of the best Sheepeater images I've seen yet: deep ochre-red paintings of bighorns carefully dabbed onto a solid granite panel. I am all alone at this sacred site, the laughter and voices of rafters fading to silence as I take in the images.

Bighorn pictographs in Veil Cave.

Hattie pays me quite a compliment when I return. "Don's a Middle Fork man," she says, nodding approvingly in my direction to the other guides who are clustered in the shade, trading stories while the paying guests play in the water. I feel the pleasure of kindred spirits uniting, if only temporarily. After an hour or so we file downslope and resume the journey.

Hot blasts of upcanyon wind slow our progress on the river in the afternoon. The guess among our group is that the temperature is easily in the nineties today, maybe even approaching one hundred degrees. The cold water of the river has become a tonic as we make it through the most challenging series of rapids yet, Class III to IV: Porcupine, Redside, and Weber. I find Redside the most fearsome, with a tricky hard left after our kayak negotiates some ferocious reversals and dodges a boulder that suddenly emerges from the foaming whitewater just as John and I plunge into the cataract. Barely after that is Weber rapids, with more obstacle courses of boulders to run.

It was at Weber, I read later, that Eliot DuBois had his closest call with the Middle Fork. DuBois, an undergraduate at Yale in 1942 with lots of whitewater experience on rivers in New England, decided to try to run the Middle

Fork with a folding kayak. He hadn't planned to run it solo, but his two other companions had to pull out for various reasons shortly after they started near the headwaters at Marsh Creek. Things went fairly well for DuBois until he came to Weber. He had just had a clean run down Redside, and by his own account was feeling confident, maybe even cocky about being able to make it through the rest of Impassable Canyon to the confluence with the Main Salmon. He didn't scout Weber as he had done above earlier major rapids, and as a result paid the consequences of a major upset: damage to his boat, a loss of some valuable supplies and gear, and a bruised leg. But he managed to retrieve his kayak, fashion a crude flotation device of sorts by stuffing an air mattress inside the craft, and set out again. Before doing so he wrote a note explaining what had happened and, should he not make it out, where he would make his final run, then deposited the note in a metal Band-Aid box in a cairn above the high-water mark on the river bank. Years later the box was recovered and the note miraculously returned to DuBois by a fellow river rat. Obviously, DuBois did make it downriver safely, and his tale stands as one of the great accounts of whitewater kayaking: he was the first person we know to make a solo run of the mighty Middle Fork.

In 1970 two rafters drowned when their raft upset on Weber Rapids. They were part of a party which included TV anchorman Tom Brokaw. I didn't know any of this until after having run Weber, which is probably just as well. (Brokaw's account of the tragic trip, "That River Swallows People," can be found in Verne Huser's anthology *River Reflections*).

As we pass the narrow slot canyons of Papoose and Ship Island creeks, plunging deeper into Impassable Canyon, I feel we are finally in a bona fide wilderness: there are no trails or bridges to suggest the passage of previous humans. Impassable Canyon: it has a wild sound, suggesting no man's land. Although thousands of people have floated this river since the advent of the twentieth century, the canyon looks unmolested. Descending into the depths of the Idaho batholith, I realize that geology, not anthropology or cultural history, is the dominant mode of interpretation here. Above (though we can't see them) are the Crags, the mysterious mountains.

Finally, our longest day on the river nearly over, we arrive at Parrot Placer, our campsite for the night, a narrow strip of sandy beach where the walls soar steeply from the water at thirty-four hundred feet to over eighty-seven hundred feet above. As I set up my camp I hear the most plaintive of birdcalls, the song of the canyon wren. Now I feel like I'm in the desert, the most spare and spartan of landscapes. As Paul Shepard says in *Man in the*

Landscape, "The desert is the environment of revelation . . . sensorily austere, esthetically abstract, historically inimical. . . . It brings introversion, contemplation, hallucination. . . . To the desert go prophets and hermits; through deserts go pilgrims and exiles."

Am I hallucinating? There is petite Mary Ann in a blue-and-red bikini, emerging from the cold water on this searing day. From my isolated campsite beneath a juniper I toast the river again and its mighty rapids. I toast beautiful women in the wilderness. I toast the wilderness itself and all its liberating effects.

There is yet more anthropology and cultural history to be fathomed along this stretch of river. Parrot Placer is named after Earl Parrot, the famous hermit of Impassable Canyon, who lived just downstream from 1917 until 1942, proving that the simple self-reliant life in nature was still possible in the twentieth century. Also evident are the scars from the Ship Island fire, started by lightning, which burned over ten thousand acres in this vicinity in 1979. As a result the slopes are even starker than normal, devoid of large trees, the blackened snags of ponderosa serving as stark monuments to a former life. This stretch of desert canyon is hot enough without trying to imagine wildfire baking its walls.

I linger around the campfire well into the night, trading stories with Crede, another of the guides, who goes to school at Utah State University. Like me, he's an Edward Abbey devotee and an aficionado of wilderness literature. We quote *The Monkey Wrench Gang* from memory and confide in each other about illicit acts of monkey-wrenching we've committed in the past. He tells me of a monthlong adventure in Patagonia. At one point, hitchhiking through the region to get near some peaks he and his two climbing buddies wanted to ascend, they experienced some bad luck and couldn't get a ride for over a day on the sparsely traveled roads. Out of desperation they blockaded the road, forcing any vehicles that might pass by to halt. A Volkswagen bus stopped five minutes later. The driver was a Californian who told them he would have picked them up without the barricade. When they finally got close enough by road to start their ascent, one of his friends decided he really didn't want to climb the mountain anyway. So they had to abort the expedition. As Crede says, in the wilderness you find out what people are really made of. The trail tells no lies.

Tipsy from a cigar and shots of whiskey, I only dimly remember the sight of the big *W* of Cassiopeia downcanyon from camp before falling asleep.

The next morning I am awakened by the call of a canyon wren. A descending series of clear, whistled notes, decelerating in tempo: "tee-tee-tee-

tee-tee-tee-tee-teer teer teer." No better alarm clock exists. In fact, the call awakens me without an alarm. Ah, to be soothed awake. I sit up in my bag and slowly take in the still dark canyon. There is only the sound of the wren, and the ever-purling water of the Middle Fork.

When I come to base camp to fill up my mug with coffee, Eric greets me with a sinister grin and these words: "Today, my friend, we run the biggest whitewater of the river." I turn to Mark for solace. But, given the faraway look on his face, I gather that mentally he's in another place, already off the river and fulfilling his fantasy of being served fine food in a fancy restaurant by beautiful waitresses in miniskirts. Crede, who's married, recognizes the look and just shakes his head. As do Kate and Hattie.

No choice then but to read the text of the river as we begin our final day's float down the Middle Fork. "Along this final stretch," reads my geology guidebook,

> the river cuts through Precambrian gneisses that have been intruded by granite dikes. The beauty of this section lies in the color and textures of the rock. Look for folded layers in the gneisses along the canyon walls. The evidence that water is a sculptor can be seen along canyon walls and on large boulders in the middle of the river such as "clam shell" rock. In many places the difference in hardness of rock layers can be seen as running water erodes soft layers to leave small scale valleys and ridges on rock faces.
>
> The steep narrow canyon wall along this section formed because the river is eroding down at a much faster rate than sheetwash and mass wasting are removing material from the canyon wall [where it then falls to the river bottom]. The shape of this river channel indicates that the region is undergoing rapid rates of uplift, which in the framework of geologic time could be at a rate of millimeters per year.

I think of John Wesley Powell running the Colorado River through the Grand Canyon in the 1860s and expatiating on its sublime geology. The Middle Fork has not been anywhere near as celebrated a river as the Colorado, because it wasn't discovered until early in the twentieth century, well after the heroic age of exploration in America had passed. Nor was it ever run and written about by a literary explorer like Powell. And its geology, I guess some would argue, is not as stupendous as that of the Grand Canyon. As a result, far fewer people know about and have experienced the Middle Fork, and so running it provides for a wilder experience. I'll take it over the Colorado any day. Not that one should have to choose. As Eric said to me during the trip, these two rivers provide the greatest whitewater runs of any two in the country outside Alaska.

Not quite three miles downriver is the first set of major rapids, at Upper Cliffside, a Class III. Here the river makes a right turn, smashing into cliffs on the left and shallowing out on the right. John and I chat with Crede in one of the big gear-rafts before we run it. "If you want a good ride, stay left. Watch out for the big hole part way down," Crede advises. "And if you want a *really* good ride, stay far left, as close to the cliff face as you can." Naturally, John says in response, "Let's go far left." So we do.

Folks in the rafts behind us said later that it appeared as if we stalled out on top of one of the larger standing waves in the middle of the rapid. I distinctly remember that moment — pausing in midair, on the crest of the wave, then getting knocked out of the kayak by a vicious lateral wave. Given our location so (too) close to the wall, there was absolutely nothing we could do to prevent from capsizing, once we had committed to the far left. I recall seeing John swept up in washing-machine turbulence, then me next, riding the waves, getting taken under, emerging momentarily, flailing and grabbing onto the kayak for buoyancy as we spilled out at the bottom of the rapid at the end of the cliff face. Where we were retrieved by Eric wearing a malicious smile in his gear raft. "You guys ok? That's good. There goes your perfect run of the river. Now you'll have to come back and try her again."

Nobody else dumped on Upper Cliffside, which infuriates John and me all the more. We stomp and curse on shore as all the rafts and the other kayak, piloted by a couple from South Dakota, run it cleanly. I'm thoroughly soaked and chilled, not to mention well hydrated. There are high clouds, and I'm ruing every bit of sun that is blocked by them on this cool morning.

Here is what Eliot DuBois wrote of Upper Cliffside when he ran it in 1942:

> Most of the current was on the left, passing close to a cliff that finally hooked to the right so that the current plowed full force into the rock face. The water at that point seemed to turn under and then deflect to the right. The left side of the river would have been an unhealthy place to be in a boat, but on the right I had a smooth and fast ride. As I came abreast of the cliff with its curling wave, I shot over a gravel bar which was a few feet under water. The bank fell away on the right, revealing a giant eddy — more a whirlpool than an eddy because it was rotating fast enough for the center to be visibly lower than the perimeter. Just

to my left was a train of standing waves, but I was on an undisturbed filament of water.

This rapid, which I realized would be much more of a hazard at low water, is now called Upper Cliffside. The new name is very descriptive of the place. . . .

"Much more of a hazard at low water." I agree. DuBois ran the river in June, nearly at flood stage, which of course poses its own set of dangers. In late July, the Middle Fork was definitely at low water stage, when some rapids become more challenging. Like Upper Cliffside.

Although a bit rattled and certainly chilled, John and I have no choice but to get back in the kayak and run the rest of the rapids, some of them reportedly much more imposing than Upper Cliffside. No more gonzo stuff, I tell John sternly; we are going to run the rest of the rapids conservatively, cleanly, and successfully. I've had enough of challenging the river.

The rest of the runs go beautifully. In fact, the rest of the short day goes beautifully: Lower Cliffside (Class III), Rubber (IV), Hancock (III), Devil's Tooth (III), House Rock (III), Jump Off Joe (III). They come so quickly in succession that we (fortunately) don't have time to dwell on our earlier spill, are forced by circumstances to concentrate only on the wildly dancing waters ahead. I recall, vaguely, the ferocious waves of Rubber; the maneuvering required to pick our way through the exposed rocks of Hancock; the calls of canyon wrens serenading us all the way downriver; an ouzel bobbing beneath and above the water at, appropriately enough, Ouzel Rapid; and the clamshell smoothness of some of the house-sized boulders polished by thousands of years and pounds of water flow in the lower reaches, where the river narrowed to an incredibly small slot beneath towering canyon walls and bighorn sheep drank from the edge of talus slopes, peering curiously at the strange, multicolored watercraft passing by.

For a spell, as time and place become one and the same thing, it is only us and the river, the confluence of when and where.

Then we come up on the Main Salmon, a murky green, wider flow, with a gravel road running along its bank. Here the trip on the Middle Fork ends, at least figuratively, though in truth we have a few more miles to go before taking out at Cache Bar.

After unloading and deflating the rafts and kayaks we have an all-American picnic consisting of 3.2 Budweiser, fried chicken, potato salad, chips, and chocolate cake. Then we board an old school bus for a teeth-rattling ride back to Salmon, Idaho. I sit in the back of the bus by myself, alternating glances out the window through the roiling dust at what I can glimpse of the Main Salmon, and at Hattie, who is reading a well-thumbed copy of *Catcher in the Rye*. She'd earlier mentioned she had been an English major in college. A beautiful, sweet, outdoorsy, literate woman: she meets all the major criteria. Life, with all its bends and confluences, rapids and obstructions, takes us on some interesting runs.

The bus driver is nice enough to point out "the place where William Clark turned back" on the 1805 Lewis and Clark expedition through Idaho en route to the Pacific. According to the guidebook to the Main Salmon, "Hoping to find a westward passage through the canyon for his canoe party, Clark climbed to a high vantage point to see if the country opened up. Upon seeing Pine Creek Rapids [Class III–IV] and the sheer rock cliffs, Clark was convinced that they would have to find a different route west." I wonder, as many historians have no doubt wondered: if the expedition had attempted to run the Main Salmon, would it have been successful? Certainly the Lewis and Clark party would have faced greater river-running challenges on this river than on the wider, tamer Columbia, which gave them few problems as they negotiated or portaged around its rapids. What they feared, rightfully so, was having no choice but to run the river through life-threatening rapids where portaging and lining their craft would have been impossible — something which Powell and his crew were forced to do on occasion on the Colorado. Perhaps they might not have made it, altering the course of American history in profound ways. Like all heroic and smart explorers, they knew when to risk it and when not to take the dare.

Dinner that night is served by lovely waitresses in miniskirts in a fine restaurant in Salmon. Mark is all smiles, and so am I.

Afterwards, camped along the Main Salmon a few miles upriver from town, far enough from the maddening crowd, I finish reading *An Innocent on the Middle Fork*. Like any good nature writer, Eliot DuBois reflects on the significance of his experience in the wilderness once it has ended:

> Two days later I was on the eastbound train, sitting beside an attractive ballet dancer who lived on Long Island. I had come full circle; I had made the transition back to my own familiar world. The Middle Fork was receding into the past, but at the same time it was still with me. I was on my way home, not just after an exciting vacation adventure, a hare-brained enterprise, somehow survived, but after a rite of passage, a loss of innocence. I was changed. I knew that the experience might not convey wisdom in all matters, nor bravery at all times, nor

guarantee any other virtue, but it would make a difference for as long as I lived.

How had the experience on the Middle Fork changed my life? I had fulfilled my dream of seeing the Frank Church from the bottom up, so to speak — from the river's perspective, for which this largest wilderness in the Lower Forty-eight is most famous. I had seen a different kind of wilderness: one more crowded than I realized, more peopled in the long run, yet certainly as interesting and in some respects as wild if not wilder than the wilderness of the subalpine environment in which I had lived as a fire lookout for several months. There is no single Frank Church Wilderness, I realized; there is a great diversity of wilderness, biological and cultural, within its 2.4 million acres. Even in the Middle Fork canyon itself, which begins in high subalpine fir and lodgepole pine and terminates in juniper and cactus and sage and contains all kinds of evidence of human occupation over thousands of years. The Wilderness Act has preserved this diversity even as it has changed our perception and use of the river corridor — made it more popular, managed the traffic on it, prohibited further homesteading while allowing residence and visitation at its many dude ranches and regulating recreation on the river itself.

Edward Abbey ran the Main Salmon in the 1980s (with Cort Conley, river guide as well as author). He had this to say at the end of the trip:

> What is it, exactly, that makes this forested mountain valley different from almost any other that I've seen in the West? After a minute the answer comes: this valley has never been logged. The forest that we see from the Salmon is a virgin forest, too rough and remote for the timber industry to get a handle on by its old techniques. Now the region could be logged, new methods are available, but fortunately and just in time the place was saved by the Wilderness Preservation Act. We Americans have done some things right.

Of course Abbey was wrong in describing the forest as virgin; the woods in these parts had been affected by fires set by Indians and Euroamerican pioneers for hundreds of years. Nonetheless, he got it absolutely right in identifying the Wilderness Act as the savior of this bioregion.

8. midsummer musings and field notes

One morning in mid-July, back on the lookout, I'm awakened early by high winds, shuddering the shutters and rippling the flag. There's no drawing of the curtains or shades in this cabin because there are none. So at sunrise (at this time of year around 6 A.M.) the light is inescapable no matter how hard I try to burrow down inside my sleeping bag. Finally I give up and struggle out of bed to make some coffee.

Groggily, I fire up the Coleman stove and slowly come to my senses. After making many hot meals in the lookout I have come to tolerate, maybe even appreciate, the smell of white gas, especially in the morning, because it means that coffee is imminent. In minutes the water is boiling. I spoon several generous servings of instant coffee into a giant thermal mug then pour the hot water into the cup. As I raise the mug to my lips I think of that famous scene in *The Graduate* and thank the mad scientists who invented plastic. Then I go out and sit on the front steps of the cabin, sipping my mocha. Though it's windy I find the temperature tolerable in the sun with a wind jacket on, and know that since it's midsummer the day is likely to get warmer. I revel in the quiet and take in the views, which are always changing with the altering light. At this time of day it's a pleasure to look to the south and see the many ridges of forest and drainages unfold, as it were, as the morning progresses. The stony buttresses of the Langer basin protrude from the forested valley, convenient landmarks in an otherwise difficult to read, gently undulating terrain of unbroken woods. If there were a smoke in that flat country, it wouldn't be easy to pinpoint on the firefinder map, I think.

My priority this morning is not fires, however, but hawks. Raptors. I've seen ten different kinds up here and I know from experience that this kind of windy day is conducive to their aerial acrobatics. Sure enough, before long I spot an osprey rising out of the Finger Lake basin over my left shoulder, easily identifiable by the gull-like crook in its wings and its plaintive cry, a piercing "keeer keeer keeer." It's fishing for cutthroat trout in these alpine lakes, no doubt. The osprey spirals from seventy-eight hundred to ten thousand feet in a matter of seconds and soon disappears into the distance. A bit later I hear one of the marmots whistle from the talus below and look up to see a prairie falcon circling the lookout, fold its wings and drop like a feathered bomb into the Fall Creek drainage. I get a good look through my 10 × 40 Zeiss of (as Robinson Jeffers once put it) "the intrepid readiness, the terrible eyes." Not to be outdone, a golden eagle soars high above Langer Peak an hour later, it too eventually disappearing in the blue wild. I sit and watch these raptors soar for hours. What else is there to do? What better thing is there to do?

Since I have a couple of days off and know from experience that I'm not likely to have another pair of days free until late in the season because of increasing fire danger and lightning storms, I take advantage of the leisure time available. I still keep an eye out for smokes, of course, since I'm up here anyhow and since spotting a fire would put me instantly on the clock and on overtime pay to boot. But in lieu of fire detection I decide to read for a bit, then have some lunch, and afterwards mosey about the summit in the afternoon to check out the latest bloom of wildflowers.

I'm only about ten pages or so into another novel when I hear rockfall on the north side of the cabin. Marmot, I think, and return to my reading. I hear rocks falling again. A big marmot, I reckon. When I hear the noise a third time, I'm finally intrigued enough to leave my chair and walk out on the north side of the catwalk. But from there I can see nothing. So I return to the cabin and grab my camera and anorak (kind of windy out there still) with the vague idea of walking out the knife-edge ridge to the north, maybe getting a good photo of a marmot for the scrapbook. The ridge is now barren of snow, which is a mixed blessing. On the one hand, the moisture on the summit is disappearing, which means the mosquitoes will soon be gone; on the other hand, along with the disappearing snow goes my source of refrigeration. To revise an old saying, it is a rare wind which doesn't bring any harm.

At the northern edge of the summit plateau, before it drops vertiginously into Fall Creek, a hogback ridge runs northeast more gradually. There I see the source of the noise — and it's no marmot. It's three goats! A big billy, appearing as old and hoary as Methuselah, a smaller nanny, and an adorable kid. They are grazing their way up the rocky chute from the Finger Lakes basin, feeding on the sparse vegetation that survives among the talus. The two adults look rather scraggly as they're shedding their winter coats in patches, the whiter new coat in contrast to the grayer, shaggier older fur. I stay where I am, about fifty feet away, so as not to make any noise and risk scaring them off. But it's obvious the billy is aware of me, for he's peering up to the ridge-top with those black, implacable, seemingly omniscient eyes. Yet the three of them continue to calmly and slowly ascend the ridge until they're perhaps thirty feet away. Only then do they angle off out of sight down the other side of the hogback.

The entire scene has lasted maybe fifteen minutes. I've managed to get a number of good shots with a telephoto lens to capture a historic personal moment: this is my first sighting of goat while on the lookout. For me it represents an unadulterated encounter with the wild. Maybe it's not a pure encounter (for all I know these goats could have been transplanted here from somewhere else, as they have been in other mountain ranges in the West), but I have had an experience involving a creature beyond human ken and (at least immediate) control. For an enchanted moment the billy goat and I looked into each other's eyes and saw . . . each other. Call it a memorable exchange (at least from my perspective), however fleeting, between two mammalian members of the local biota.

In one of my favorite works of travel literature, *Notes from the Century Before*, Edward Hoagland writes of his visit to the Stikine River of British Columbia in the 1960s after witnessing sumptuous numbers of game and exploring unending mountain ranges with only traces of a heroic pioneer culture:

And why am I so elated? Am I an antiquarian? It all adds up to whatever you make of it. I'm elated because I respond as I did on my first ocean voyage. It's as though the last bit of ocean were about to become more dry land, planted and paved. The loss would not be to us who have already sailed it, who have no wish to be [a] seaman, and who can always go back and relive in our minds what we've experienced. The loss is to people unborn who might have turned into seamen, or who might have seen it and loved it as we, alive now and not seamen, have seen it and loved it.

This kind of celebratory lament in nature writing has been labeled "creative grieving."

Although I live atop a heap of volcanic and metamorphic rubble, I realize I live in a garden myself — a wildflower garden. Having been oblivious to the blooms of wildflowers around me for what seems like weeks, I'm suddenly conscious of being surrounded by colors. On the summit alone I discover mountain heather, penstemon, moss campion, paintbrush, arrowleaf, alpine aster, cutleaf daisy, sego lily, plus a few other species I can't readily identify.

The most profuse and colorful are the bush penstemon. The lavender, tube-shaped flowers occur in sprays less than a foot tall, surmounting a bushy cluster of lustrous green leaves. The bush penstemon can often be found between rocks, and I'm delighted when scrambling along the talus slope to encounter them between the hard gray granite chunks which make up the mountain. When I descended the long, steep, east face of the summit the other day to retrieve a pot that had fallen from the catwalk railing (I'd put it there to dry in the wind), I came across literally hundreds of clumps of mountain penstemon, basking in the morning sun, reminding me of Tennyson's "flower in the crannied wall." The flowers in bloom all over the east face gave me plenty of reasons to pause as I made my way back up the precipitous slope to the cabin.

Another early summer bloomer on the summit is the sego lily. Although the Craigheads' *Field Guide to Rocky Mountain Wildflowers* states that it grows at low elevations, I've found the sego lily at nine thousand feet in these parts. Like the mountain penstemon, it prefers dry, well-drained slopes. On top of a single slender stem about a foot high is a showy, cup-shaped, creamy white flower with a purple spot towards the bottom of each petal. Its bulbous root is edible and was eaten no doubt by the Sheepeaters (*Sego* has a Shoshonean etymology). Bighorn as well as domestic sheep feed on the plant. The Craigheads, in some wonderfully poetic phenology, report that sego lilies bloom "in June and early July, first appearing when young golden eagles are feathering and their parents are busy hunting rodents, and prairie falcons are fledgling." I think of sego lilies as the tulip of the alpine environment.

Probably the easiest flower to identify, and one of the most widespread, is Indian paintbrush. I love this flower for several reasons: its fiery red color, its abundance, and its name. The flower's bristlelike bracts appear as if they were dipped in brilliant red paint. Virtually anyone who has hiked in the mountains of the West knows, or ought to know, paintbrush because it is so common. Like the robin, perhaps its loveliness is overlooked because of its very omnipresence. Call it a democratic beauty. Paintbrush begins to bloom "when young magpies leave [their] nest."

Sulphurflower is, as its name implies, a bright yellow. Its tiny flowers grow in umbels atop a slender six-inch stem, above basal leaves that form green mats on the ground. Sulphurflower, too, likes the dry, open slopes of Ruffneck's summit plateau.

All these flowers, and many more, are perfectly observable to the naked, wandering, inquisitive eye. As Annie Dillard writes in *Pilgrim at Tinker Creek*, we are here to witness. Seeing can, or should, be an active mode of vision, a conscious investigation of the external landscape, the world confronting the senses. For many years I hiked in the mountains and saw only peaks and summits, not flowers or trees or birds. It was a kind of macho, myopic vision: the only things worth noticing, I felt then, were the mountains that I planned to conquer. How did my vision change focus, sharpen, zoom in on the undiscovered country of the nearby as well? It was as a result of becoming a fire lookout, of going native in the mountains, when I was required to remain in one place for several months. I have traveled a good deal in Concord, said Thoreau when accused of provincialism. He counseled everyone to live at home like a traveler, to behold one's own environment with fresh eyes. As a lookout I'm paid to watch for fires, yet I have come to realize over the years that I want to do much more than look; I want to see.

Midafternoon. Through convection, the clouds build into mountainous masses of condensation. Though I'm a terrible artist, I sketch these airy ramparts in my journal, thinking of the great cloud studies done by nineteenth century landscape artists like Turner and Ruskin. The clouds seem to be following the textbook explanation of a developing thunderstorm. At this point they have metamorphosed into Stage 3: towering cumulus: masses of water droplets, caused by the heating of the forest and all those suspirating trees, forming twenty thousand-foot cloud banks. Next, they build into Stage 4: the tops of the cloud banks flatten out into anvil heads, while the bottoms of the clouds start to darken. Then Stage 5: some premonitory grumbling from above. To the south and east, curtains of virga — Stage 6 — drape from the cloud bottoms. In fact, an incredible scene unfolds to the south where the eleven thousand-foot granite summits of the White Clouds glisten in a momentary burst of sun, while dark, forty thousand-foot cloud-mountains billow above, mimicking the peaks below: like corresponding terrestrial and celestial ranges.

But for whatever reasons the clouds don't evolve into Stage 7, lightning storm. Instead, the towering cumulus dissipate and drift eastward along the Main Salmon River, leaving in their wake a rainbow that arcs from Finger Lake to Langer Lake. The excesses of God, Robinson Jeffers called such phenomena. A paraphrase of a Wallace Stevens poem comes to mind: The sublime comes down to spirit and place. The empty spirit in vacant space.

More often than not, the clouds are not transformed into storm-makers. But occasionally they are, producing lots of downstrikes, what we in the firefighting trade call lightning busts. And sometimes the lightning comes with no rain at all. Then it's dry lightning, a firefighter's fantasy.

9. fire on the mountain,
lightning in the air

The next morning I again awaken to howling winds, along with a dark-red sky, the clouds stretched like taffy. Lightning to the far southeast struck late last night, and over the radio I heard that the Lost River Ranger District on the Challis picked up a couple of fires.

It's my second day off in a row, and since I'm told by the office this morning that I won't be on the clock today — this in spite of the ominous sky and predictions of stormy weather — I decide to walk down the Halstead Trail in the early afternoon for a hike and a swim. I want to check out the Mable Lakes, a cluster of pothole ponds about two miles south of the lookout, where I can get in some R&R as well as stay within a reasonable distance of the lookout in case we get some lightning (and thus pick up some OT after all).

The Mable Lakes are at eight thousand feet, which means more than a quarter-mile drop from the lookout. I pack a lunch of cheese and crackers, water, and an apple, then saunter down the trail. The first part of the hike I keep an eye out for smokes because after so many seasons as a lookout, fire-watching has become an ingrained habit. But soon I'm in the trees and so my vision refocuses on the nearby — the dark brooding greens of the sub-alpine fir, Engelmann spruce, and whitebark pine. I'm enveloped in the soft dark arms of the woods.

The Halstead Trail, because it's longer by a couple miles than the Langer Lakes trail, is not as heavily used and maintained and therefore harder to negotiate because of all the blowdowns over the years. That's good: the more solitary a hike, the more interesting it is. Today there's a particularly eerie feeling about being out in the wilderness, with little wind, the air close and sticky, and the sky having an unreadable gray, flat look, with no corrugations or breaks — as if this part of Idaho were underneath one gigantic, brooding thunderhead. I don't have a good feeling about the weather but press on anyway, trying to think how nice a dip in the lake will feel.

Within an hour I'm at the first of the lakes. I find a good drop-off not too far from the trail where the water appears deep enough and jump in. It's surprisingly warm — this lake in the Mable Lakes chain isn't very big, and in fact it appears to be shrinking, turning over to meadow judging by the grasses sprouting at its northwestern edge. Vague, troubling thoughts of global warming drift through the back of my mind, but lying on a rock on a warm (if cloudy) day dispels the problems of the wider world easily enough, for a time. I muse over the virtues and vices of the pastoral escape.

After lunch on the rock and another dip, then a nap, I overcome the inertia of a lethargic mood and trudge back up the path. By the time I reach the junction of the lookout trail, where the view opens up again, I notice curtains of virga sweeping across the Knapp Creek drainage to the southeast. The winds have picked up too, swaying the tops of the conifers on the ridgelines. I then hear loud grumbling. Suddenly there's a flash in the sky. Seconds later I'm practically knocked off my feet by a boom and crash: KAPOW! Now, more than anything else, I want to get back to the shelter and security of the lookout cabin.

I have less than a half-mile to go, back up the two long switchbacks and then the final leg over the hump to the summit. Bolts of lightning flash and crash, followed by a brief shower then high winds. Practically running through the ghost forest of silver snags on the west face of the mountain, I'm reminded of how close lightning has struck near Ruffneck lookout. Then the cabin appears as I ascend the summit, and I leap up the steps of the porch and at last find shelter from the storm.

Even before I can catch my breath I spot several fires, two burning directly below in the Fall Creek drainage above the Finger Lakes. My adrenaline starts to race. Time to follow procedure! I sight in on each smoke with the firefinder, noting the azimuth, location, and conditions, then jot down the info on the lookout report. Only one of the five fires I can see appears to be troublesome — on Blue Bunch Mountain to the west, as it takes off in an old snag which topples and then spreads the fire further. I report all the information to Challis Dispatch, then wait and listen for the smokejumpers and helitack crews to respond.

Within half an hour the jumper plane is flying over the Blue Bunch fires, testing and judging the direction of the winds. Then four smokejumpers tumble out of 4-0 Zulu in succession as it makes several passes over the fire. South of Ruffneck a helicopter is dropping off firefighters at the closest accessible spots to the Langer Lakes, in forest clearings or on open, relatively flat spots along the ridgetops. The helicopter then makes return trips to the helibase for more firefighters to be dropped off on the Finger Lakes fires. My job at this point is to make contact with the firefighters once they're on the fire, to relay between them and dispatch if necessary and to generally keep an ear open if they need anything. The firefighters' job is first to assess the fire, reporting its size, fuel, and conditions as they appear on the ground, then get to work. Often this will involve dropping a tree with a chainsaw or bow saw (in the wilderness, chainsaws, because they're motorized equipment, are generally not allowed). Then they will cut up the tree into manageable chunks, trying to eliminate all ladder fuels like tree branches that can transform a more manageable ground fire into a much more dangerous crown fire which spreads rapidly from treetop to treetop. The last stage of their work involves extinguishing the fire with available water and dirt. It's hard, dirty, dangerous duty, and will take at least a day to do it properly; among the gear dropped off with a smokejumper or helitack firefighter is a sleeping bag, food and water to last forty-eight hours. It's a true wilderness experience, much wilder than hiking in the woods on a well-maintained trail with signs and bridges and established campsites.

For the next couple of days I'm a prisoner in the lookout, relaying radio calls, listening to the chatter between fire crews and dispatch, keeping track of which fires are demobed (demobilized) and which are still manned. I'm also watching for more fires that might still appear following the lightning bust, since little moisture fell with the storm. My job of radio relaying is alleviated by the technicians who fly up to the summit of Ruffneck Peak in helicopter 2-9 Juliet to set up a temporary radio repeater from which the fire crews down in the nearby drainages can bounce their message to dispatch on a separate, less-used channel (so as not to clog up the regular channels with fire traffic). Even though I'm an avowed techno-primitive, I have great respect for these technicians, people who by definition are good with their hands and heads. In no time at all the repeater is set up and the helicopter is on its way — but not before one of the radio techs drops off a Pepsi and candy bar for me as a thank you for a job well done on the recent lightning bust. I wave as they take off, then devour the exotic sweets.

A crew of twenty now works to contain and then suppress the messy Blue Bunch fire on a steep, heavily forested slope. A Sikorsky, an enormous industrial helicopter, is contracted by the Forest Service to make water drops on the fire, which it does after making runs from a nearby alpine lake. Retardant planes are also called into action and they periodically paint the perimeter of the fire (now at five acres) with pink-red loads of ammonia phosphate to prevent it from spreading. By the time the fire is suppressed, the Forest Service will have spent tens of thousands of dollars putting out a couple of fires in the middle of nowhere, in the River of No Return Wilderness.

Why? Why not just let them burn themselves out? Isn't that what happened before the days of Smokey the Bear? Isn't lightning-caused fire a natural occurrence, an act of God, and good for the forest anyhow? Isn't this a wilderness area, where the forces of nature are supposed to prevail? Why not declare it a PNF (prescribed natural fire) and let it burn while monitoring it?

Trying to answer these kinds of questions forces one to address larger issues of the role of government in managing natural resource policy as well as to confront the metaphysical implications of the terms *Nature* and *natural*. Since natural resource policy is inextricably linked to definitions of what is natural, it's important to consider a variety of perspectives on this issue. Humans, like every other species, have always affected the larger environment around them, for the subsistence needs of food, shelter, clothing, and transportation. As environmental historians now know, Native American tribes deliberately set fires on the plains and in the woods to hunt and practice horticulture. Fire was used as a herding device to drive bison where they wanted them to go. They also noticed that after a fire, shrubs like huckleberries thrived, so they intentionally started fires to grow and harvest berries. Anglo-Americans cleared the forests for farms and used the timber for their cabins and to build railroads. But fire was also a great scourge and source of fear to the pioneers who lived in the woods, and fire protection was one of the chief priorities of the Forest Service when it was created early in the twentieth century. Thus, by suppressing wildfires we inevitably reshaped the forests and the natural environment of the West. Complicating fire management policy has been the growing trend in the West in the last twenty to thirty years toward building homes in the woods that lie within reasonable commuting distances of small cities like Missoula, Montana. These houses — often constructed of flammable materials like raw logs — are being located where fires have periodically raged, creating a new kind of fire management consideration: urban-wildland "interface fires," fires which burn along the ever-shifting border separating forests from modern civilization. Saving private property has thus become one of the highest priorities in the once sparsely populated intermountain areas of the Rocky Mountains, an area known for its conflagrations of apocalyptic proportions.

The Forest Service, caught between environmentalists who say they want fires to burn because it's natural and good for forests, and property owners who understandably want to protect and save their holdings, must make a judgment each time a fire starts — and there are thousands of ignitions each summer in the West in a typical fire season — as to whether a fire will burn itself out or burn out of control. Mostly the agency errs on the side of caution. Of course one could say that this is done to line the pockets of FMOs and firefighters and pilots of planes and helicopters — the formidable bureaucracy that has emerged as a result of expanding firefighting in the West. But it's also true that for reasons of aesthetics, recreation, and livability (not to mention liability), it seems wise to put out many wildfires. The truth is there is no neat line to be drawn between the natural and the man-made, between nature and culture. We're all implicated in the mix of human and nonhuman, culture and wilderness. Wildfire management thus provides a revealing look into the current debates over natural resource policies and definitions of wilderness.

Fire management has become all the more complicated since the Yellowstone fires of 1988. Although some of those fires were caused by people and others by lightning, the public's collective memory of the Yellowstone inferno, thanks to distortions of the story by the mass media, is of naturally caused forest fires that the Park Service let burn to the point that they eventually got out of control and torched nearly one million of the park's 2.2 million acres. Whatever the exact numbers, the public perception of the Yellowstone fires was of a policy that had backfired on Smokey the Bear. The let-burn philosophy that had come to prevail in some (but certainly not all) national parks and wilderness areas in order to replicate natural or wilderness conditions came under attack in the wake of the loss of thousands of acres of trees and private property and of threats to human lives. Regardless of the accuracy of this perception, fire management officials in both the national parks and national forests have been much more conservative in their implementation of the let-burn policy since 1988. As a result, more money is now spent on wildfire suppression, and bigger paychecks are issued to firefighting personnel.

Smokey the Bear has been politicized. Then again, maybe he always was.

At the same time, during a severe drought when lots of lightning is followed by high winds and little moisture, big fires will inevitably occur, no matter what measures we take to prevent them. The statistics of the 1988 fire season bear this out: that year over seven million acres burned across the country, more than any year since the 1950s (in 1950 more than seventeen million acres were lost due to wildfires, the worst year ever since such data was recorded beginning in 1919). It was only after WW II that fire management agencies finally began to get a handle on wildland fires through improved technologies. Although it is true that we have been able to control nature in many ways — genetically modified organisms (GMOs) being the most recent, spectacular example of this feat — the fact remains that humans cannot prevent large-scale natural disasters like earthquakes, hurricanes, tornadoes. Or wildfires.

The truth of these claims is being verified as I write the final draft of this book in the fall of 2000. After decades of near-total fire suppression and years of drought in the American West (perhaps related to global warming), wildfires, most of them ignited by lightning, raged across the region in August. As of September 30, 2000, fires have burned more than 6.8 million acres nationwide, most in the arid West. In August 2000 more than one million acres were burning in eleven Western states, the most land on fire at any one time in the United States since the great 1910 fire. Particularly hard-hit has been the Bitterroot Valley in northwestern Montana, where along U.S. Highway 93 south of Missoula a number of residents have lost their homes in the surrounding woods. The entire state of Montana was declared a federal disaster area. In Idaho, the Frank Church Wilderness was closed for several weeks due to uncontrolled wildfires. One of them, the Clear Creek fire near the Bighorn Crags, alone consumed more than two hundred thousand acres. Idaho had the dubious distinction of leading the nation in number of acres burned in 2000 with over 1.2 million.

With wilderness comes wildfire. What will the fires next time be like?

Cooped up in the lookout for four days straight because of the fire bust, I notice that I'm running precariously low on water — down to three cubies. Since all the fires have been demobed by now and the sky looks clear, I feel it's safe to make a water run this evening. I call Bernie on Little Soldier and let him know I'll be gone for a couple of hours; besides the walk for water I simply want to get out and stretch my legs, check out the trails, see what's been going on around the lakes.

I'm in somewhat of a funk as I start down the trail. Part of it has to do with the inevitable lassitude of summer setting in. My melancholy is also related to the natural let-down that comes following the flurry of activity and rush of adrenaline from reporting all the fires after the recent lightning bust. The peaks and valleys of the surrounding countryside stand as a metaphor for a lookout's moods around this time of the season: when there's lightning and fire activity and lots of radio traffic, the time seems to fly by; but when there are no fires the days seem endless and sometimes, frankly, quite boring. With all the windows cranked open and flies buzzing interminably and only a slight breeze blowing, it's easy to lapse into a state of somnolence and hard to break out of it. So my solution is to go for long hard walks at the end of the day after dinner, in the cool, refreshing, arctic half-light of dusk.

For the umpteenth time, down, down, down the trail I go. I drop off the pack and empty cubie at Island Lake and head east to a smaller unnamed lake in the basin I've come to call Bufflehead Pond after the ducks I saw breeding there earlier this summer. Sure enough they're there again, floating warily on the surface as I approach. I give them ample room so as not to disturb them into flight. I'm then distracted by giant splinters of a subalpine fir near shore, easily noticed because of the fresh, yellow-white inner wood. What happened here? Apparently during the most recent thunderstorm, lightning struck this tree, splintering and scattering it. What's more, its top half — about thirty feet long — was spiked into the ground, as if thrown down by some giant of incredible strength. One of Thoreau's favorite adjectives for this kind of circumstance comes to mind: *titanic*.

Back at my watering hole I notice new flowers in bloom: red monkeyflower and elephanthead. The former is about a foot high, with rose-red flowers and two yellow patches in a funnel-like throat, and grows only in wet places in the mountains. The Latin name, *mimulus lewisii*, links it with Captain Meriwether Lewis, who discovered it on the 1804–06 expedition. As always, the Craigheads provide some wonderfully poetic natural history: "Toward the end of the flowering season, the pink corollas dropping into the water of streams and ponds paint their surfaces with solid layers of colorful blooms. Smaller pockets make natural fingerbowls, outrivaling the rose-petaled ones at court banquets." Here the season is not so late that the flowers are dropping their petals, so I can appreciate their beauty just as they are.

Another bloomer in wet high places is elephanthead. On stalks one to two feet high are thirty to fifty pink flowers resembling an elephant's trunk curving out and up, a reminder that a close examination of a flower is always worth the effort. In the meadow above Island Lake there are hundreds of these flowers now in bloom, as well as paintbrush, arnica, bluebells, penstemon, buttercup, valerian, hawkweed, and too many others for me to readily identify. And who needs to know all the names anyway? The colors alone are enough to satisfy any aesthete.

It takes longer now to fill up the cubie with water since the spring isn't running as fast with the melting of the snow. In the relaxed, upbeat mood I've achieved since I left the cabin, however, I readily recognize that there's no hurry. I have plenty of time to get back up to the summit before it gets completely dark. Besides, who cares about walking in the dark in the woods? I've done that before and have grown comfortable with the surroundings by this time. As long as one knows the terrain and is confident — but not cocky — about where to go, a nocturnal walk in the forest can be, despite what all the German folktales suggest, a therapeutic, calming experience.

I hear the cubie gurgling, overflowing with water. I pull it away from the spring and strap it into the packframe and onto my back, then trudge cross-country up to the trail. As I return to the lookout I hear faintly in the distance one of the loveliest of noises, the sound of mountain water.

10. society

Despite my love of lookout life and its delicious isolation, I occasionally get the urge to check up on the rest of humanity and see how it's faring.

It's time to do some anthropological fieldwork on small-town Western culture.

A week after the lightning bust I get another day off. This time the predicted LAL is one to two, which means there's little chance of lightning. The sky in midmorning confirms the forecast: only a few fair-weather clouds are starting to form. I call Jack the FMO and he gives me the OK to come down off the mountain for a day or two. I then call Becky, the recreation guard at Seafoam, to catch a ride into town. It's her day off too, and she plans to drive home to Salmon so she agrees to meet me at the Langer Lake trailhead at noon. I take a spit bath and shave, then quickly stuff a few things into a daypack — a novel, two full water bottles, gorp, jerky, hat, raingear (you never know). Before locking up the cabin I do one last check-look of the surrounding country — all clear! — then practically run down the first series of switchbacks. Like a farmer heading into town after a hard week of work, like a GI heading to the big city for a weekend of leave, I can't wait to have a beer, wolf down some greasy food cooked by someone else, admire some lovely women from a discreet distance, spend some cash on a few needless items, rub elbows with some members of my own species. To repeat what Ed Abbey once said, the one thing better than solitude, the only thing better than solitude, is society.

On occasion. In moderation.

The trail winds through the ghost forest just below the summit — a stand of whitebark pine snags weathered silver-gray from many years of exposure at high elevation. I'm told there was a fire near the summit some twenty years ago, the result of a lightning strike. Fanned by hot winds, it quickly ran up the mountainside, threatening the lookout cabin itself. The lookout had to be evacuated by helicopter but the cabin was saved by a retardant drop. When the fire reached the other (east) side, rocky and barren, it quickly flared out for lack of fuel. An old joke about the Ruffneck Peak blaze is that the lookout had no trouble locating *that* particular fire.

The snow has disappeared from the high country except in the north-facing couloirs and remnant snowfields of the distant Sawtooths. There's even a tint of brown in the meadows of Stanley Basin, where temperatures have reached the eighties for the last couple weeks. Rooster tails of dust rise behind rigs traveling the many dirt roads in the national forests. And even though I'm tromping downhill high in the mountains, I'm already breaking a sweat. I can't wait to gulp that first cold beer.

There appears to be no one camped in the Langer Lakes as I walk by, which makes them all the more delightful. I stop at the southeast shore to take some photos of the lake with Ruffneck Peak in the background against a cloudless azure dome. Aside from the twittering of a few chickadees and nuthatches, all's quiet in the basin.

The final two miles of trail wind through a lodgepole pine forest, allowing no distant prospects. It's early in the season but the trail is already dusty with lots of foot and hoofprints. In places, the path has actually become a two-foot trench in which rocks and branches and other debris have fallen, making for some rough footing. Because the lakes are a relatively easy hike in with reputedly good fishing and fine views, the area is showing clear signs of being loved to death. But most of the River of No Return Wilderness is inaccessible, far from any roads. A place like this thus becomes a kind of sacrifice area, which is regrettable but perhaps necessary. Folks in these parts would never stand for closing trails or rationing access to a popular lake basin.

I'm a bit early arriving at the trailhead — it's taken me only two hours to walk the six miles — so I pass the time waiting for Becky to arrive by sitting in the sun and scribbling in my journal. At seven thousand feet the air seems heavy and thick; I guess I have become a native of the mountains, accustomed to living on thin air.

Before long I hear the grinding engine of a rig in low gear as it descends the curves from Vanity Summit. It's Becky in the standard light-green Forest Service pickup. As I climb in she hands me an ice-cold dark Lowenbrau from a cooler in the front seat. Bless her sweet soul! Then we fly down the road at what seems to me a rocket-like thirty miles per hour, and before I know it we're out of the thick forest and through the spacious meadows paralleling Beaver Creek and gliding along on the smooth blacktop of Highway 21, heading south to the raucous town of Stanley. At least I hope it'll be raucous. If not, then I intend to help make it so.

We stop for another beer in a deserted park at the edge of town near the base of the Sawtooths. Having eaten little up to this point and guzzled my first beer, being in town for the first time in a month and still an Easterner at heart awestruck at the sight of towering mountains seemingly within arm's reach, I'm feeling more than a little heady. Jagged peaks soar four thousand feet into the air while I bask in the high, dry, clear air and make small talk and drink beer with an interesting woman. It all seems unreal, dreamy, fantastic. Becky catches me up on the latest Forest Service gossip, tells me about the photographic work she's done along the Middle Fork (she hopes to publish a coffee-table book about the river someday) and her plans of doing some horseback riding for the next couple days while she's off. The riding will do her some good. She's still recovering from two separate tragedies: a terrible accident over two years ago in which she broke her back and was laid up for months, then a house fire in which she lost most of her possessions. Suffering excruciating pain followed by depression, she finally turned to Prozac and now feels much better. I listen and nod now and then; it seems that after all the weeks of talking hardly at all to anyone, the physical act of forming words with the tongue and lips is a challenging exercise. Besides, what can one say as an adequate response to the revelation of such hardships? Better to simply be quiet; sometimes all someone wants is a good listener.

Becky finally runs out of things to say and takes off in the truck. I stroll down Stanley's main street, which is still unpaved and fronted with wooden structures right out of a John Wayne Western. They house the standard business establishments: laundry, post office, general store, hardware store, a couple of restaurants, hotels, and, of course, saloons. Plus the offices of a couple of river-rafting companies, bait and tackle shops, curio and gift stores. Although Stanley was settled in the 1890s, today there are still officially only a hundred or so residents. But ominous signs of progress are starting to appear — T-shirt shops, spanking new and obscenely large A-frame log homes sprouting on the sagebrush slopes, and the incongruous espresso stands mentioned earlier. Harrah's of Nevada became the major landowner in the basin in the 1970s, which doesn't bode well for Stanley. It is on the verge of becoming one more mountain town threatened by the spoils of development in the late twentieth century.

At the southeast end of town a state historical sign explains that "long before miners and ranchers settled Stanley Basin, bear dominated this area." Alexander Ross of the Hudson Bay Company in 1824 wrote in his journal of observing four acres of mountain meadow "dug up and turned over." Upon closer inspection he and his party encountered "no less than nine black and grizzly bears at work, rooting away" for wild onions and celery. It's been a long time since the last grizzly disappeared from these mountains. But they will return, from northern Montana via the Selway-Bitterroot and the Frank Church wilderness areas, if the bears themselves have anything to say about it. They already are in the Frank Church, if some random furtive sightings can be believed.

I've got a few bucks (plus a credit card), so after weeks of thinking how to spend my first paycheck I'm eager to visit the local bookstore and outdoor shop. First, though, some lunch (and another beer) to calm my nerves and put me in the right frame of mind for some serious shopping. I push through the swinging doors of the Sawtooth Saloon and order a local microbrewed beer, a burger, and fries. Marvelous. Followed by blackberry cobbler à la mode. Can life get much better than this?

The conversation certainly can. I'm the only person in the bar at the moment aside from the bartender and (apparently) a local chum. They both appear to be in their early thirties and are commiserating over their recent divorces and child-support payments. Women are bitches, they conclude. They swear they'll never get married again. Both their ex-wives left them — imagine this — for other guys. Listening to these two Neanderthals rant on in their misogynistic vein, I can't help but conclude that the women made a smart move.

It's my observation that in small Western towns there are very few single people. Why? Because the towns are so isolated and cities are usually so distant; because winter can get mighty long and lonely out West; because if you're going to live off the land in some fashion it takes more than one person to survive; and because the pressure to conform to the norms of society in small towns is great. But the West is changing. More and more people are in service work as small companies relocate to the region and the population continues to grow. As the West gets more populous, as it becomes more modern, the accompanying social evils — crime, unemployment, divorce — increase. And so the vicious cycle continues, more people relocating to an area because it's more livable than where they came from, which ultimately makes it less livable. Paradise found, then lost. Ask the natives (if any still exist) of Aspen, Telluride, or Santa Fe.

It's no fun thinking of the decline of the American West. Time for some bookstore browsing. The Sawtooth Cafe has a good selection of local and regional titles. I buy a couple of regional histories to complement my collection of natural history field guides, then saunter back out into what seems to me to be the oppressive heat of afternoon in the lowlands of the six thousand-foot basin. I make one more stop, in the outdoor store, but am quickly put off by the over-eager and officious young clerks who are obviously bored by the lack of business on a slow afternoon. Don't really need any of the expensive, gawdy clothes or gewgaws on sale anyway. It appears that everybody is out recreating, hiking in the mountains or rafting the local rivers. Who can blame them?

It's not long before I'm feeling the same way myself — realizing how lucky I had it in my cabin atop the mountain. I sit on the steps of the general store licking a homemade huckleberry ice cream cone. What's next on the agenda? I decide to have a few more beers to drown (or at least soak) my sorrows in the other tavern in town, the Rod 'n Gun Club, before hitching a ride back on Highway 21 to the turnoff to Langer Lakes. It's late afternoon, and some more people have appeared — loggers, a few seasonal Forest Service employees, some day hikers and river rafters. The conversation is now more animated, more positive, a natural result of having spent much of a beautiful day outdoors. I sit at the bar and take in the exhilarating social scene of Stanley. The trip to town suddenly seems worthwhile.

After a pizza smothered with pepperoni, mushrooms, and black olives, I decide I've had my fill of civilization and its food and drink for another couple of weeks. It's early evening and Stanley now lies in the shadows of the Sawtooths. I stick out my thumb and in no time (I've always been a damn lucky hitchhiker) a pickup pulls over. A guy wearing a Potlatch baseball cap and a long drooping mustache offers a ride back in the open bed of his truck. No room in the front with his three kids, he explains, as three innocent girls with lots of blonde curls smile shyly at me. I gladly accept the offer and hop in the back. In a few seconds we're doing 70 MPH and the wind is whipping through my hair and T-shirt and the Sawtooths in all their craggy splendor are receding in the distance. Marvelous: it's a drive and view I'll remember forever. Before I know it the truck is slowing down at the Cape Horn turnoff and I'm leaping off, thanking the driver. As the truck speeds away I head up the gravel road. It's two miles to the Halstead Creek trailhead, then eight miles to the lookout. I have about three hours till dark.

No problem. I tank up on some water once I reach the trail, then put my head down and shift into low gear for the climb through the thick forest ahead. It's four miles before I'm out of the trees and by that time I'll need whatever light remains.

Ten P.M. I reach the steps of the lookout and take a deep blow. Incredibly, there's still light in the sky at this hour. After checking the cabin to make sure everything is in order, I call Bernie on Little Soldier to find out what I've missed. Not much, he says, it's been a quiet sunny day without storms. I sign off on the radio then collapse on the bed, exhausted and exhilarated.

11. friends

It's the second week of August, and I get a call from the FMO. Jack says Ron is planning to resupply me later this week. What do I need in the way of food for the month or so I have left up on Ruffneck?

My stores are running low, it's true, but more on my mind these days are things like whiskey and cigars. I like a shot of JD in my tea now and then late at night, and there's nothing finer than an occasional meditative smoke after a hard day at the office, even if the office is in the midst of the wilderness. I'm plumb out of booze and down to my last cigar. I suppose I could have bought a bottle when I was down in Stanley on my day off, but I was traveling light then and didn't want to weigh myself down with a fifth of whiskey in my pack. The trick is to get Ron the good Mormon to haul these sinful vices up to me along with other staples like bread, cheese, fruit, etc.

So when I order my necessaries over the radio later that night, I tell Jack (who enjoys a drink and a smoke now and then himself) to smuggle the contraband in some specially wrapped package to avoid arousing Mormon Ron's ire. He readily agrees, though knowing his penchant for ribbing I'm sure he'll let Ron know after the fact that he was implicated in the devil's work.

Ron and his assistant, Abe, arrive a couple of days later around noon with the pack string. As is customary, Ron unravels the mannies holding my goodies and proudly checks the two dozen eggs I've requested. Not a one is cracked or broken. "My perfect streak is intact," he says proudly. After we unstrap the cardboard boxes and set them in the shade of the cabin, I invite them both in for lunch. They gladly accept but politely decline all my offers of food; it's part of Forest Service decorum not to take anything from a lookout, knowing that he or she might well be needing it sometime down the line. So we each eat our own lunches and talk about goings-on down below.

Becky and her boyfriend, Ron tells me, "have split their blankets" (meaning they've broken up).

This comes as no surprise, as Becky had hinted at such a development when we last talked. I feign indifference to keep the conversation going and see where it will lead. "So what else is new? If I had a dollar for every time she threw a hissy fit over her cowboy lover, I'd be a rich man," I say.

That observation sets Ron and Abe to laughing out loud. Then they want to know if I've been visited by any good-looking women.

I mention, with a straight face, that a member of the fire crew, Ms. So-and-So, a real looker, came up and decided to spend the night, and since she didn't bring a sleeping bag that meant we had to share mine.

They guffaw and utter the famous Idaho declaration of disbelief: "Sheeiit."

Suit yourselves, I say, in mock seriousness.

The flag hangs in the calm air. Flies buzz around the horses and they swish at them now and then with their tails. There isn't a cloud between here and Oregon.

Before I know it Ron (who's never been known to take the regulation forty-five-minute lunch break) gets up and says, "Time to head down the hill, huh Abe?"

Abe, barely out of his teens and not quite through with his lunch, rolls his eyes but says nothing. Does nothing. He wants to stay longer and pump me about lookout life, find out if I'm coming back next year. I think he's after my job.

"It's not a job, it's a vocation," I tell him. "It's a calling. Are you sure you're ready to take on the weighty responsibilities of this position?"

By this time, Ron has had more than enough of my B.s. and yells to Abe, "Are you coming or should I tell the FMO you've become a lookout's assistant?"

I wave to them as they disappear below the summit and think about our visit later that night as I sip my whiskey and chuff on a cigar. It was good to see them, and it was even better to see them go. Restocked with supplies, I have come to realize that solitude is usually preferable to society.

The Transcendentalists, my favorite coterie of American writers, are famous for their views of nature, but they also had some important insights to offer about friendship, through both their words and their relationships. Emerson and Thoreau of course were good friends, mentor and disciple, for many years, until their gradual falling out. Hawthorne and Melville mingled, to good literary effect, in the Berkshires. Whitman, true to his democratic character, made friends with all of America. Thoreau wrote often and eloquently of friendship in his journal, often complaining (in typical Transcendentalist fashion) that his friends (like William Ellery Channing) nearly always failed to match his ideal of friendship. Thoreau's first book, *A Week on the Concord and Merrimack Rivers*, written as an elegy to his brother, John, and to commemorate their boat trip in New England, contains some eloquent passages on the virtues of friendship. Here is one of my favorites, relating to the bonds that form when friends share meaningful time together in the out-of-doors: "Is it of no significance that we have so long partaken of the same loaf, drank at the same fountain, breathed the same air summer and winter, felt the same heat and cold; that the same fruits have been pleased to refresh us both, and we have never had a thought of different fibre the one from the other?"

I dwell on friends a lot when I'm up in the lookout, in part, as the cliché goes, because absence makes the heart grow fonder. Thoreau once wrote in his journal, "Nothing makes the earth seem so spacious as to have friends at a distance; they make the latitudes and the longitudes." But when I sent that quote to a friend in a letter she got insulted, claiming that I was insinuating we got along better when far apart. It wasn't what I meant at all, I wrote back, trying to explain; rather, it was only after I left Portland to work in the woods for the Forest Service in Idaho that I realized how valuable a friend she was. That was many years ago, and we still keep in touch to this day. Her letters are among my most cherished pieces of mail.

Other friends have fallen out of touch. As Thoreau observed in *A Week*, "Friendship is evanescent in every man's experience, and remembered like heat lightning in past summers." I have found this to be true in most cases. One friend in particular comes to mind in this regard, the guy I met when I first began working with the Forest Service and who introduced me to Western mountains. George, a native Oregonian, and I began climbing and backpacking at around the same time and ascended many of the old volcanoes of the Cascades together. After I moved to Idaho we still wrote and visited each other regularly. Then he got married (to a friend of one of my friends, whom he met on a backpacking trip). His wife, a lawyer and a very demanding, contentious, and humorless person, slowly began to suck the joy of life from my former hiking partner. Then she insisted that they have kids, requiring a major change in their life-style. Gradually we drifted apart. The last time we talked was on the phone in March 1989, when word got out of Edward Abbey's death. We commiserated over Abbey's passing, recalling the profound way his words had changed our lives. We didn't know it then, but a friendship had died too. I later sent George this passage from Emerson's *Nature* as a final act of correspondence:

> We are associated in adolescent and adult life with some friends, who, like skies and water, are coextensive with our idea; who, answering each to a certain affection of the soul, satisfy our desire on that side; whom we lack power to put at such focal distance from us, that we can mend or even analyze them. We cannot choose but love them. When much intercourse with a friend has supplied us with a standard of perfection and has increased our respect for the resources of God who thus sends a real person to outgo our ideal; when he has, moreover, become an object of thought, and whilst his character retains all its unconscious effect, is converted in the mind into solid and sweet wisdom — it is a sign to us that his office is closing, and he is commonly withdrawn from our sight in a short time.

Another friend visits the lookout for a couple of days. I've known him since graduate school in Idaho. I was returning to school after dropping out of law school and spending a few seasons with the Forest Service; Mike was entering grad school right out of college and was experiencing the same kind of academic burnout I'd felt the first year of law school. We partied hard that first year, a release from teaching freshman composition and spending much of our time grading papers as office mates. Then we started hiking together, visiting some marvelous country in Idaho that I hadn't even heard of and that Mike had dreamt about visiting ever since he was a kid growing up near the Lochsa River. Late at night he'd come over to my apartment after we'd done our class prep for the next day (or maybe not having done it) and drink Rolling Rock and eat homemade chocolate chip cookies and complain about having to take courses in Spenser and Milton when good writers of the American West like Abbey and Richard Hugo and Wallace Stegner were saying profound things about the world immediately around us. Then we'd break out the cigars and the books and read passages aloud well into the night, arguing about their significance and meaning. Opposition is true friendship, as someone once said.

We drifted apart physically over the years. Mike dropped out of grad school and then opted for medical school, eventually becoming a physician and general practitioner. But we continued to stay in touch. When the opportunity arose we visited each other in various parts of the country, often getting in a wilderness trip. Winter camping in Johnson's Shut-In in the Missouri Ozarks. The Marble Mountains Wilderness in northern California. The Buffalo River in Arkansas. The canyonlands of Utah. Quetico Provincial Park in Ontario. And each time the ritual was the same: drink lots of beer and whiskey, smoke some fine cigars, cook sumptuous meals, and talk — about words, women, and the wild. Often I have asked myself, why did we become and remain such good friends? I think it has to do with basic demographic and geographic similarities. We're both small-town, working-class kids, both bookish and athletic, and having grown up in the mountains, we both will always hearken to the call of the wilderness. Like Jake and Bill in a famous scene in the Spanish countryside of *The Sun Also Rises*, we know and love country when we see it, and we love to explore it as often as we can.

Mike arrives early in the evening, hardly puffing at all despite the long hard pull up the switchbacks from the lakes. We shake hands, embrace, and crack open the first of many beers — a fine microbrewery ale from eastern Washington. He empties a humongous pack in the cabin and reveals some clothes, a couple of books, and delicacies like venison steaks and homemade chocolate chip cookies (for old-times' sake).

Sometimes it's hard for friends to visit me in the lookout. They don't know the routine or don't realize that I'm pretty much stuck in the cabin for most of the day and have to keep my eyes always peeled for smokes and an ear cocked to the radio in case someone is trying to reach me. It can tax a friendship, and there have been several friends over the years who've visited once and never again (though we have been on fine terms when seeing each other elsewhere, away from the confines of the cabin). But Mike has a lookout's personality and sensibilities. He's very independent, quiet much of the time, alert, a fine reader of the landscape. He even threatens to scoop me on spotting a fire. There is always a healthy sense of competition between men, especially former athletes, though fortunately for my sake he's not yet been able to make good on that particular promise.

For the occasion Mike has purchased some gentlemen's cigars from a good smoke shop in Boise, and we pour ourselves some stiff drinks and chuff away. At this altitude the whiskey and tobacco soon achieve their desired effects, and we're waxing eloquent (or at least voluble) about the best-looking women we knew in graduate school: Cindy, who in both dress and mannerisms reminded us exactly of Annie Hall; Ellen, a dark-haired Finnish beauty from a small farming town near Moscow; as well as others whose names we can no longer recall. We re-analyze the many great films we saw at the cubicle of a theater in Moscow known as the Micro: *Manhattan, The Raging Bull, Aguirre: The Wrath of God, Room with a View, Platoon.* We talk of former wilderness experiences together — remember how cold it got that first night of winter camping in the Missouri Ozarks? How about the five straight days of freezing rain in the Marbles? And how could we forget the time we hitched a ride with the mail boat back down the Snake River in Hells Canyon after an excruciatingly long day hike? And we piss and moan about our current workaday lives and all the shit we have to put up with. Before we know it there's a hint of false dawn in the eastern sky and we say, oh what the hell, let's eat some breakfast. So I cook up home fries, eggs over easy, homemade elk sausage (another gift from Mike), and lots of coffee. And we continue to talk as the new day dawns.

Not much happens while we are together on the mountain. We spend the days alternately chatting, reading, and walking. The skies are spectacularly blue and cloudless, which means little fire activity. Just as well for me, since I have to worry less about looking for smokes. Mike recognizes the sly grin on my face for what it is and promises to visit me again, only during stormy weather, so as to have another chance to beat me at spotting a fire.

The next day after breakfast he departs, having to catch a plane out of Boise. This is one of the toughest times on the lookout for me, dealing with the spell of aloneness after a good friend leaves. I walk Mike out to the summit drop-off and bid him farewell.

Back in the cabin, I read Gary Snyder's poem, "August on Sourdough, A Visit from Dick Brewer":

> You hitched a thousand miles
>   north from San Francisco
> Hiked up the mountainside   a mile in the air
> The little cabin — one room —
>   walled in glass
> Meadows and snowfields,   hundreds of peaks.

We lay in our sleeping bags

        talking half the night;

Wind in the guy-cables   this summer mountain rain.

Next morning I went with you

        as far as the cliffs,

Loaned you my poncho — the rain across the shale —

You down the snowfield

        flapping in the wind

Waving a last goodbye   half hidden in the clouds

To go on hitchhiking

        clear to New York

Me back to my mountain   and far, far, west.

12. pleasing prospects

There's a smoke pall in the air, reducing visibility. It's the result, I'm told, of a large sagebrush fire in northern Nevada. I can no longer see the Wallowas in Oregon to the northwest, or the Bighorn Crags to the east. The smoky skies add to the somnolence of midsummer.

Scattered journal entries:

Like the ocean, this River of No Return Wilderness inspires and awes not through any particular vertical feature but by its general immensity. A sea of wilderness. Sometimes I want to drown in it, immerse myself in it, and never come back. Take the plunge.

Walk down to Langer Lakes and spot a college-aged woman in tank top and headband, tall and athletic, with the sweetest of smiles.

Make chapatis this afternoon and use them instead of tortillas in enchiladas. Excellent.

Find a single piece of scat near the cabin this morning, four to five inches long, black, with berries in it. Bear?

The wilderness exists whether we establish it or not, whether we recognize it or not, whether we visit it or not. Avoid the anthropocentric fallacy at all costs. But can we? How can we escape the confines of our own species? Should we?

No radio, no TV, no computer up here. I get all the news I need from the weather report.

After several days of unsuccessful attempts — splat! bam! — a chickadee succeeds in finding the open door to visit me in the lookout cabin, this time knocking itself silly on the *inside* of the windows. I find it prostrate on my desk, beak open, and pick it up with leather gloves, placing it outside on the catwalk. Eventually it recovers and hops, then flies to a nearby whitebark pine a couple of feet away. I think of it all day, lying in my palm,

> the trembling heart
> of a captive bird.

Some visitors, noting the four-by-six-foot map of the River of No Return Wilderness on the ceiling (the only place to hang it since I can't block the view out the windows) remark that they'd heard of people with mirrors on their ceilings, but never maps! What can I say? — I'm a geography geek, a map freak.

Buildup, a thunderstorm, lots of hail, but no lightning. Like the line in the Bruce Springsteen song, you can't start a fire without a spark. Walking back from a water run after the hailstorm, I pick up the cold white marbles and taste them —

> They are delicious
> so hard
> and so cold.

Pearly everlasting, yarrow, and fireweed now in full bloom.

Roughneck (rúf nek). Noun. A pugnacious fellow; a rowdy (*American Heritage Dictionary*).

A Hammond's flycatcher is my companion for the day, flitting from one subalpine and whitebark to another, feasting on ant flies. Good show, mate!

Like a lizard I spend all morning in the sun on the steps of the catwalk. Recent storms have scoured the air clean once again. Fair-weather cumulus blossom like wildflowers across the sky. It's a day of pleasing prospects.

That's a phrase I recall from Raymond Williams's *The Country and the City*, a study of the British pastoral tradition. For how long have humans been enamored of a view? This is a theme much examined by scholars (see, in addition to Williams, Paul Shepard, *Man in the Landscape*; Roderick

Nash, *Wilderness and the American Mind*; Marjorie Hope Nicolson, *Mountain Gloom and Mountain Glory*; Albert Boime, *The Magisterial Gaze*). The theme has been on my mind for much of my life, ever since I left the Appalachians to attend college. It was then I first began to miss the mountains of memory, the wooded hills of my boyhood. I remember doing an independent study with a professor in political science during my senior year and insisting that the nature writing of Supreme Court Justice William O. Douglas — books like *East to Katahdin* and *My Wilderness* — be on the reading list (as well as works of political theory). On weekends during my college years in Philadelphia, I went back home to hike the Appalachian Trail near Hawk Mountain. There I was restored by the liberating views from the open, boulder-strewn ridgetops.

Then came the long litany of peaks and mountains ascended in the Pacific Northwest, Idaho, and California.

Only in graduate school did I become self-conscious about my love of mountain scenery and critical of my ignorance of other kinds of environments. Having read a great deal of the scholarly literature about landscape art, literature, and history, I still ask myself, "But why do you want to continue to defy gravity and climb to the highest prominence in an area for the view?"

It's exactly the question on my mind this marvelously clear afternoon in late August, when the densely visible Sawtooths seem within arm's reach. I can think of a few answers. Because I love the language of mountains and mountaineering: couloir, arête, bergschrund, crevasse, glacial erratic — lots of hard-sounding, masculine words signifying something real, something you can hold onto and clutch in your hands. Because I love the camaraderie that can develop with fellow mountaineers in a common quest for the summit. Because I love the physical challenge that comes with thigh-burning and lung-searing ascents and knee-crunching descents. Because I love the solitude of high, lonely, rocky places. Because I love the sense of liberation and freedom that comes from being on a summit with all-expansive views. And of course, as Malory said, because it's there.

From climbing mountains it seemed a natural progression for me to want to live on mountains. Not in the mountains but on top of them.

Fire lookout: one who inhabits mountain summits.

Jack Turner writes in *The Abstract Wild* that true wilderness literature and art can only come after long inhabitation of a place. He goes on to say that "Many of our best writers on wilderness — Abbey, Snyder, Peacock, — worked as fire lookouts for the U.S. Forest Service." He also observes that when we talk about any form of literature, we commonly write that "it takes place in. . . ." Setting, an old-fashioned term in literary studies long out of vogue, is again being recognized in some critical circles as an important element in storytelling. Ecocriticism — the study of the role of the nonhuman environment in literature — is gaining prominence for its insistence on the fundamental role that nature plays in shaping our thoughts and actions. Stories about places have long captivated readers who have their own intimate experiences with some cherished spot on earth.

The history of how humans have become enamored of views is a long, intricate, and ultimately mysterious one. Raymond Williams traces mountain appreciation back to the times of classic Greece and the eclogues of Vergil. A later influential figure in the tradition was Petrarch, the fourteenth century Italian poet who, says Williams, "climbed Mont Ventoux in Provence to see the panorama but when he had got to the top remembered a conflicting model, in a passage from Augustine: 'Men go forth and admire lofty mountains and broad seas and roaring torrents and the ocean and the course of the stars, and forget their own selves while doing so.'" Petrarch and Augustine reveal a very important effect of experiencing the alpine wilderness: coming to the realization that there is a universe wider and more powerful than we had thought.

To his credit, Williams recognizes that we have only the vaguest and most inaccurate sense of the history of the aesthetics of mountaineering (all the more remarkable an insight when one considers that he is a literary scholar, a student of written sources): "Yet we have to remember that we do not know, from the times of disturbance, what was seen, what appreciated, in the long hours of watching, by generations of men. Most of the men who did the watching have left no records."

Who was the very first human being to ascend this mountain now called Ruffneck Peak? Was it some member of the Big Game culture on a hunting quest, after the glaciers receded, unsuccessfully stalking a giant elk, who then decided to rest on top of this promontory and take in the view, read the country below, and try to ascertain where camp was located? We will never know, for most of prehistory is lost to us.

The rocks on which the lookout cabin rests represent one kind of solid reality. The rocks, however, do not write history in a language that is legible to most people. The view still prevails, especially among academics, that reality is only that which gets recorded. Meaning written down. We need to learn — or better put, relearn — another kind of language, the language of nature, and its tawny grammar. We need to reacquaint ourselves with the "words" — and the wildness — of the nonhuman environment. We need to reattain a natural literacy.

I think of "Witness" by W. S. Merwin:

> I want to tell what the forests
> were like
>
> I will have to speak
> in a forgotten language

13. getting to the source of things

Another day, another dolor. One early evening late in August I decide to head down the hill once again to clear my head, stretch my legs, snap out of the funk that inevitably comes from being cooped up for too long in the cabin. Even living on a mountaintop, despite the all-encompassing views, can become inhibiting if it remains one's only perspective. Open spaces can confine as well as liberate the spirit.

As I start the hike I have in mind the usual plan of walking down to the Langer Lakes. But when I reach the first junction, I stop and realize that I'm falling into yet another rut of routine. Why not head in a different direction? Why not take the path less traveled? Why not create your own path to the unnamed lake southwest of the lookout, the headwaters of Fall Creek? For a change, take the pathless way.

This spontaneous plan immediately strikes me as a grand idea, a fitting confirmation of my goal to celebrate the surrounding area of Ruffneck Peak. *Celebrate* in Latin means to visit frequently. And as that pontificating Anglophile, T. S. Eliot, once wrote:

> We shall not cease from exploration
> And the end of all our exploring
> Will be to arrive where we started
> And know the place for the first time.

Right. Part of becoming native to a place, is, paradoxically, to visit other places, expand one's home range, see what else is out there, compare and contrast territories, then choose one's optimal landscape. Explore the world around you till you become an expert, as Thoreau said, in "home cosmography."

I walk also because I feel the need to dispel ideas from my mind, to flee the world of books, to be free of the intellectual life for a brief time. No ideas but in things. But of course I recognize that as a statement of another intellectual, William Carlos Williams. Whether I like it or not, I can't escape the textual universe, even as I enter a world of things — namely trees, what books are made of. If some books have been (wrongly) accused of having too many trees in them (meaning that they're too much about nature), I wonder if it's possible for a book to have too many ideas in it. Come to think about it, I know of many such books.

As I trudge down the trail I try hard to become aware only of my immediate physical surroundings, which in this case is nothing but trees. I've entered a shaggy forest of lichen-draped Engelmann spruce and subalpine fir. The understory is an obstacle course of a hundred years' worth of accumulating blowdown — unless a wildfire has cleaned it out in that time. Given the remoteness and inaccessibility of these trees, and the fact that this tract of the Salmon River Mountains has been preserved as wilderness in one form or another since the 1930s, I'm convinced that I'm now walking in a virgin forest — that is, one unsubjected to widespread commercial logging. It's too remote and inaccessible for loggers earlier in the century to have exploited it. But it's not the classic ancient forest that people envision when they hear the term "old growth" either: the ten-foot-wide trunks of the cedar and Douglas fir found in Olympic National Park on the Washington coast, for example. No, at this high elevation where the growing season is shorter, the climate drier, and the conditions much harsher, many of the trees have a stunted, gnarly look, and few of the fir and spruce I see around me have a girth more than two feet. It's a thick forest, not a tall one, the antithesis of the classic open gallery look of a mature stand of pines in the lower elevations. It's hardly a place conducive to a stroll in the woods.

To make matters worse, the slope is much steeper now that I'm actually on the ground than it appeared from afar or on the topo map, and it's hard to shake the growing, sickening feeling in my stomach that it's gonna be a real *mutha* of a climb back up to the lookout, once I've finally reached the lake. If I finally reach the lake. Where the hell is the lake anyhow? I can hardly see the forest for the trees, much less any sign of water. It occurs to me that I'm somewhat lost, at least not exactly sure where I am in relation to the unnamed lake I want to visit. Of course I could retrace my steps (vaguely) and head uphill, knowing that I'd eventually intersect with the trail that runs along the ridgetop to the lookout. But that's not the direction I want to go, at least for the moment. I'll continue to take the easier course and head downward, obeying gravity's call.

Besides (ever the intellectual) I can't help but think of something Thoreau said in similar circumstances: "It is surprising and memorable, as well as a valuable experience, to be lost in the woods any time."

There are actually several lakes (plus a spring) that form one of the head-waters of Fall Creek. I have in mind the lake marked as 8,069 feet in eleva-tion on the Cape Horn Lakes quadrangle, the easternmost of the three lakes that together mark the western source of Fall Creek. On the map it looks like a mere eighth of a mile descent if I drop directly west from the trail on top of the ridge. But as I'm making the actual drop, the walk seems farther than that — more like a half-mile at least. As is always the case, the map seems not quite to correspond to the actual terrain. The woods look just as shaggy and dark and formidable as they did when I first left the trail. Sun-set is only an hour away.

Once again I retrieve a file stored in my brain, a scene from the film *Black Robe*, based on Brian Moore's novel. It's about a Jesuit priest in seventeenth century Canada whose mission is to convert Eastern woodlands tribes to Christianity. The main character, Father LaForgue, leaves an Indian camp for a walk in the woods and before he knows it, becomes hopelessly lost. When some hunters by chance encounter him on their way back to camp, his sense of relief at being found is poignant. The natives cannot understand the overwhelming joy he expresses upon seeing them, and they poke fun: "If you were lost, why didn't you look at the trees, Black Robe?" No doubt the James Fenimore Cooper myth of the noble savage who's never without his bearings is being perpetuated here. But the scene still resonates within me, in part because when I was a boy a friend and I got lost in the woods be-hind our homes during a raging blizzard. For what seemed like hours (but probably wasn't half that long) we wandered in the woods as the snow con-tinued to fall. Then, in an incongruous miracle we were saved not by an an-gel but by the town bum, Snuffy Smith, who inexplicably came upon us as we huddled under some trees, saying the rosary (like the good Catholic kids we were then). I have rarely been lost since. But as Thoreau said, it is a mem-orable experience to be disoriented, whether because of getting turned around in unfamiliar country, or (as is sometimes the case) when the maps are wrong.

Is the fear of forests atavistic, cultural, or both? I think of yet another treatment of forest fear, Robert Pogue Harrison's *Forests: The Shadow of Civ-*

ilization. He argues that Euroamerican culture has long been a society of sky worshippers. "Where divinity has been identified with the sky, or with the eternal geometry of the stars, or with cosmic infinity, or with heaven, the forests have become monstrous, for they hide the prospect of god." So is that what explains Black Robe's, and my own, sense of panic amidst the trees? Perhaps E. O. Wilson's theory of biophilia is correct; perhaps humans do have an innate preference for open landscapes, attributable to our emergence from Africa's dark, threatening woods onto its open, sunny savannas.

My search for open spaces continues. Finally I arrive at what seems like the floor, or at least a small platform, at the head of the drainage, where it is likely that a lake exists. Sure enough, after fighting my way through the final tangle of primeval woods, there it is: a relatively small body of water, maybe a hundred feet wide at most, an island of openness and light in this otherwise dark, desolate wilderness. Judging from the original perimeter of the basin, the water level appears to be down at least five feet from its highest mark, expanding the shoreline and thus making circumambulation of the lake rather easy. That's a nice recompense given the arduous hike to get here. Fifteen-inch trout dimple the surface, snapping at anything that floats. Otherwise, a dead calm prevails in this sheltered, mysterious basin.

I have reached the headwaters of Fall Creek. Like Lewis and Clark, like Henry Rowe Schoolcraft, I realize the explorer's sense of delight in discovering a river's origins. Fall Creek could be considered one of the sources of the fabled Middle Fork of the Salmon River, since it lies very near the headwaters. Of course, others have no doubt been here before me, but that knowledge does not diminish my feelings of having encountered terra incognita. As far as I'm concerned, this territory was undiscovered until I came along.

Poking around the shoreline in the dusky light of this forest clearing, I see in the mud near the water's edge tracks of deer, elk, and . . . a palm-sized print with four toes showing. Mountain lion.

The incontrovertible evidence of a lion's presence in this lake basin makes the place feel all the wilder. Suddenly I realize that I am indeed all alone in this spot, with no trail access, with no one aware of my location. (I hadn't told anyone about my intended destination, largely because when I set out I hadn't known it myself.) So if something were to happen I'd be in a challenging situation, to say the least. The solitude takes on a newer, graver meaning.

Immediately, I once more relate my experience to something I read. Edward Abbey's account in "Freedom and Wilderness" of his first encounter with a lion in a dark desert canyon comes to mind. Hiking some forlorn canyon in the Southwest one late afternoon, Abbey happened to notice tracks in the sand and recognized instantly what had made them. He followed the prints for as long as he could but had to turn around for lack of light. Heading back, he heard noises and then realized the lion was following him back along the trail. The hunter had become the hunted. Abbey turned around to check out his stalker and saw the silhouette of a lion in the twilight canyon. He felt fear, of course, but also, as he says, "a kind of affection and the crazy desire to communicate, to make some kind of emotional, even physical contact with the animal." So he raised his hand and beckoned the cat by saying something ridiculous, like "Here, kitty, kitty." The lion did not respond. Abbey decided after all that he was not quite ready to shake hands with a mountain lion.

I don't have any desire to do so either. I know that, statistically, mountain lion attacks on humans are rare; I also know that when they attack people they seem to prefer smaller members of our species, like children. I know too that I'd put up one helluva fight — there are too many more places to visit and books to read and write for me to die this young. But the sight of the lion print, along with what appears to be the all too rapid onset of nightfall, is sufficient impetus to hurry back out of the basin and up through the trees.

Where it's even darker, of course. But now, fueled by an energy surge I didn't think I could have mustered earlier, I'm up out of the lake basin in no time and back on the ridgetop, where I intersect the trail once again. It's an awful ascent, in the Burkean sense of the term. This time the trail appears as a veritable highway in the wilderness, and I profusely thank those hardworking CCC crews of the Depression era for their heroic, civilizing efforts. Hikers take for granted the existence of things like trails, bridges, and even signposts in official wilderness areas, forgetting that without them the woods would be a real wilderness where in all likelihood a lot more people would get lost, get hurt, and die. So we need even wilder wilderness to remind us of the importance of places that we have allowed to exist beyond our control — where no trail exists, where no bridge spans a raging stream, where no sign tells how far it is to the next junction. We need the tonic of the wildest wilderness possible.

Trudging back up the final hump over the summit, where the lookout cabin is silhouetted against a blue-black sky, yet one more author comes to mind. David Brower once wrote that "sometimes luck is with you, and sometimes not, but the important thing is to take the dare. Those who climb mountains or raft rivers understand this."

I have not escaped the intellectual world after all. Rather, the world of ideas has enhanced my wilderness experience. The ideas and words I remember from books have made more precious my wanderings in the woods. I cherish wild places and wild thoughts.

14. The bighorn crags

One of the few drawbacks of working a lookout is the fundamental fact of being stuck in one place for an entire summer, in the center of so much wild country that begs to be investigated. As I have said, among the human species' basic instincts is the desire to see new country, the urge to explore. As much as we are possessed by the homing instinct, the desire to go native, we are also urged on by our genes, by our past as hunter-gatherers, to wander. Although I loved and lived for my daily saunters from the lookout, I also hungered for longer sojourns into the great expanses of alpine wilderness that lay on the horizons: the White Clouds, the Sawtooths, the Wallowas. For some reason, of all the rugged horizons that I could discern from Ruffneck, the one I found most intriguing lay fifty miles to the northeast, where the ragged peaks of the Bighorn Crags slice the sky. Topping out at just over ten thousand feet, the Crags are among the highest and certainly the most well-known of the Salmon River Mountains within the Frank Church Wilderness. However, sixty-five miles from the nearest town and accessible only by unpaved, twisty, Forest Service roads, they are certainly not easily reached by vehicle. A few years after working Ruffneck I finally fulfilled my dream of backpacking and climbing in the Crags. To see mountains from afar is one thing, to walk and climb in them is quite another. I felt it was important to get both perspectives.

The Crags campground in the Salmon National Forest consists of a dozen or so drive-in sites with picnic tables, fire rings, two outhouses, and a few water pumps scattered about a loop drive. One August aternoon in 1998 when I arrive, it happens to be deserted, which is just the way I prefer it.

There is not a breath of air stirring the thick forest of lodgepole pines. A few clouds obscure an otherwise flawless blue sky. The only sound comes from a stream trickling next to the site where I choose to camp.

I crack open a bottle of Full Sail amber ale, take a deep gurgling swallow, sit back on the picnic table and let the tension of the long, slow drive over steep, twisty, rutted mountain roads rinse off me like a passing summer shower.

Around noon I departed the river town of Salmon, Idaho, after chowing down a huge Mexican breakfast at the El Rancho Cafe (chorizo, eggs, potatoes, lots of salsa), and after stocking up on supplies for a weeklong backpack. I also stopped at a recently opened brewpub in town. The yuppification of Western towns certainly has its drawbacks — like the driving up of real-estate prices and the construction of ranchettes on former premium wildlife habitat — but among the advantages that accrue is the production of good, unique, local products like raspberry ale. To ensure that I got my daily requisite of Vitamin C, I sampled several of these tasty beverages before heading out.

Saying farewell to the obvious outsiders sauntering down Main Street in their new Tevas, long-brimmed sunhats, and Goretex raingear — all prepared for a run with a local outfitter down the Main Salmon River — I head south along Highway 93 before stopping briefly at the ranger station to make some inquiries about the road to the Crags trailhead and trail conditions in the wilderness. As usual the information officers at the main desk are friendly and informative. Some trails in the Frank Church — in the southwestern corner, near Ruffneck lookout — have been closed because of lightning-caused fires which have been declared PNFs and allowed to burn. I wince upon hearing this news, thinking of what it would have been like to observe the storm from Ruffneck, see the lightning strikes that caused the fires, report the smokes to dispatch, and monitor the fire and fire management activity. Then I'm told that Ruffneck isn't manned this year, hasn't been manned for several years in fact, a casualty of budget cutbacks.

Maybe I'll be able to see the fires from the summit of some peak in the Crags, maybe even make out the profile of Ruffneck Peak through the smoky haze.

The last seven miles of the road to the trailhead, say the Forest Service officials, are not recommended for regular passenger vehicles. Too steep, too many ruts and rocks. Since I'm driving a high-clearance, all-wheel drive vehicle, I should be OK (damn those environmentalists who drive gas-guzzling SUVs).

I cross the Williams Creek Summit (elevation 7,057 feet) and drop down into Panther Creek, in which the isolated outpost of the Pine Creek Inn is niched. WE SUPPORT THE TIMBER INDUSTRY reads a sign prominently displayed above the entrance. So do I, I think — as long as it doesn't pose a threat to wilderness. Then I pass through the town of Cobalt ("Population one," says the Forest Service sign), before beginning the serious final ascent up Porphyry Ridge to the Crags campground and trailhead. The warnings about the road prove to be well-grounded: this is one of the "better" approach routes to a backpacking destination. In addition to the ruts and rocks there is the typically narrow width of the Forest Service road to consider; I wouldn't want to meet a vehicle coming down the road in the opposite direction around one of the many blind curves — not with the steep thousand-foot drop-offs on the outside of the turns. It's a real *mutha* of a road, hacked out of the wilderness in the late nineteenth century by optimistic prospectors hoping to make the proverbial big strike. The map indicates that just south of the Crags the Yellowjacket Mine is located, one of several in the area in which gold and cobalt were found in significant quantities.

I have in mind prospects of another kind, however. Soon the road tops out along a heavily forested ridge and the reassuring Forest Service campground sign appears. I do a quick circuit of the campground to check out all the sites and decide on the most remote one tucked away at the opposite end from the entrance. It doesn't really matter, since the place is deserted, but you never know who your neighbor is going to be, and, as previously noted, I believe strongly in the maxim that good distances make for the best neighbors.

Then comes the familiar ritual of setting up camp. I quickly put up the two-person Eureka dome tent (the ample room a real bonus when soloing), set out the two-burner Coleman stove, haul out the cooler full of beer and other essentials, along with the grocery bags full of food. Wood has already been provided and stacked by some hard-working, conscientious recreation guard. I open the first beer and toast the great out-of-doors. Here's to government preservation of our forests and mountains. If the government doesn't do it, who will?

At eighty-five hundred feet the air bears the fresh scent of pine and fir and is much cooler than down in the canyons. It's late afternoon, too early for dinner, and I need to stretch my legs after the long, tortuous drive. After consulting the map I decide on an easy half-mile hike down to Golden Trout Lake at the edge of the wilderness. I head toward the trailhead near the campground entrance. To my dismay I soon come across an over-sized pickup with extended cab parked partway down the trail, which at this point is really a jeep track. There are other people here after all. As I make my way down the plummeting trail I can hear laughter from the lake basin. Damn. The grand illusion of mountain solitude is over; I have to share the wilderness with another party. All my worst, most selfish, and misanthropic feelings surface.

Nothing to do but accept that they were here first. I'm invading their space, I realize. Even though this is a national forest and government-owned land and thus open to everyone, I feel like I'm an intruder. So I try to be as quiet as possible. Upon reaching the shore I see that it's a family of four, a group of Idahoans out on a picnic. Dad and son are decked out in military-style fatigues, mom and daughter in cutoffs. They've brought gallon jugs of Kool-aid and heavy canvas packs no doubt stuffed with potato salad, hot dogs, and all the fixings. The males are holding fishing poles, dipping their lines in the water, in the age-old posture and hope of the angler.

I rim around the lake on the opposite shore. It's really a lovely setting in spite of the presence of others. Solid granite spires shine in the sun, their images reflected across the glimmering waters. Fish occasionally dimple the lake surface. Thrushes flute from the treetops. It's a classic scene from one of America's great national forests — made better, not worse, I have to admit, for the people who recreate in it.

Leaving the family to the solitude of the basin, I climb back out cross-country over exfoliated granite domes, hoping for a glimpse of the Crags. The rock, in its texture and forms, reminds me of Yosemite — but without the maddening crowds moving at a glacially slow pace all over the valley, wearing down my spirit. Soon I'm rewarded with views of the high peaks, including the rounded-off summit of Mount McGuire, at 10,082 feet the highest peak in the range. I recognize it from the photo in Tom Lopez's *Exploring Idaho's Mountains*, a guide I'd consulted and have along in the rig. According to Lopez it's an easy Class 2 climb from the west side, the route I plan to take, using Airplane Lake as my base camp. I glass the mountain's boulder-covered slopes with binoculars, searching for good routes. To see this mountain from close up, after gazing at it from a distance atop Ruffneck, is immensely satisfying — and tantalizing. I'm not there yet.

I intersect the main trail from the campground to the Crags and stop along the ridgetop, noting an acre-size fire scar of fairly recent origin. The blackened whitebark pines, many sawed and bucked in chunks now lying on the ground, tell an intriguing story. It appears there was a lightning strike on this ridge within the last year, and smokejumpers were dropped on the fire where they engaged in minimum impact suppression tactics (MIST). Because this fire occurred just within the border of the wilderness area, the firefighters were required to avoid heavy-impact practices like digging a footwide trench around the fire's perimeter. No doubt they had to use bow saws rather than chainsaws to buck up the wood. Perhaps they were aided by a helicopter making water drops from the nearby lake. This fire could have taken off, torching thousands of acres of forest, perhaps burning down one of the tributary streams into the canyon of the Middle Fork or into the Crags, threatening rafters on the river or hikers and parties on horseback. One of the key criteria in deciding whether to allow a natural fire to burn in a wilderness like the Frank Church is the threat it poses to human life and recreation in a heavily used area. Obviously this particular fire met the criteria, and the decision was made to suppress it. All around, then, there is evidence of both the visible and invisible hand of humans on the land.

Back at camp, early evening, I make my own fire and begin preparations for dinner. Hungry from the walk, I throw a thick steak on the grill after the fire burns down and some good coals form, pour a can of beans in one pot and put some ears of fresh sweet corn in another pot of boiling water on the Coleman stove. I crack open another beer and take in the solitude. There's no sign of the family I saw earlier, so I can enjoy an imagined if not real state of aloneness. Solitude is a construct of the imagination, I think. Yeah, right. I turn my attention to truer propositions, things more real: like the hike ahead. I pore over the maps, read the guidebooks one more time. I've got several ridges to traverse, lots of elevation to gain, lose, and regain. That's reality. So is the sumptuous meal I devour, followed by equally real pleasures like a cigar and jigger of whiskey for dessert. The night air is sweet with the scent of lodgepole pines, and I lapse into a profound sense of sedentary satisfaction.

The next day dawns brilliant and clear. By midmorning, better acclimatized to the higher elevation, I'm tromping along the ridgetop trail that leads from the campground to Cathedral Rock, a ninety-four hundred-foot granite monolith dominating the immediate horizon to the north. The trail is high and dry, and I'm glad I hydrated well before hoisting my fifty-pound pack. At the rock I pause for a water break. I run my hand down the face of a rough-hewn granite dome that forms a wall to my right, admiring the reassurance of solid rock, the certainty of stone.

Farther along, on a knife-edged ridge just east of Fishfin Pass, I pause to take in the breathtaking, U-shaped gorge of Clear Creek. Ralph and Jackie Johnson Maughan in *Hiking Idaho* report that "Clear Creek is a large, pristine drainage, heavily fought over by the timber industry before it was included in the River of No Return Wilderness." Now there's not a clear-cut in sight, thanks to the efforts of wilderness preservationists. I imagine walking down, down, down the drainage, from the headwaters near this ridgetop to Panther Creek, and from there to the Main Salmon River. I suspect that I'd see no people but lots of wildlife. It's a tempting alternative.

I choose to stay on the ridgetop, however, for the prospects — as well as the solitude. I've met no one else today in spite of the dozen or so vehicles parked at the trailhead. Where could they all be?

I soon discover that most of them are at Wilson and Harbor lakes, exactly my destination for today. For the wilderness solitaire, could there possibly be a more dreaded announcement than "There's a troop of scouts camped at the lake ahead"? This is what I'm told by two guys I meet at Fishfin Pass, a narrow gap between the towering granite fins that separate Clear and Wilson creeks. Sure enough, as I approach the spectacular glacial cirque that contains Harbor Lake, the upper of the twin lakes in the basin, I can already hear the shouts and screams of prepubescent, hyperactive boys scurrying like rodents around their campsites. Coming closer I also hear the chopping of an ax, smell wood smoke in the air, and then see a crowd of kids cavorting on a narrow peninsula of the lake.

I've come seven hard miles along a roller coaster of a ridgetop trail and I'm not about to turn around and try to make another two or three miles towards the next lake — at least not today. I resign myself to the company of crowds and find a good if heavily trampled campsite just across from the outlet of Harbor Lake with fine views both up and down the basin. After setting up the tent and throwing in the Thermarest and sleeping bag, I heat up some water for soup on my backpacking stove and change into a warm dry polypropylene top. It's late afternoon, the clouds are building, and long shadows fill the basin. A thunderstorm is brewing.

Before the thunder begins, however, there's a disturbance of another kind. The scouts are setting off cherry bombs, and the explosions that echo throughout the cirque are a far greater disturbance than any thunderstorm. The little fuckers, I think. Where the hell are the so-called scoutmasters who are supposed to be in charge?

The answer to this question comes a few minutes later as a couple of older guys troop up the trail with fishing lines. They smile and wave when passing my camp. I respond by yelling at them to stop their scouts from ruining the wilderness experience for others in the area. They fail to reply.

The human fireworks end and nature's begin, infinitely more powerful and terrifying. I barely have time to make myself a mug of soup before the first flash of lightning flares behind the ridge, followed three seconds later by the CRACK! of thunder. I sit on my insulated pad and scribble in my journal in the tent as the storm passes overhead, moving down the basin. As always, the effect of being caught in a thunderstorm is a fearful, alienating experience. The flimsy shelter of a nylon tent is all the more obvious at times like these, and try as I might I can't help but think of the campers I've read about who were struck and killed by lightning while in the wilderness. Nothing like a lightning bolt in close proximity to make one a believer in existentialism.

I read and write while the storm lights up and pounds the basin. One of the few published accounts about the Crags that I'm aware of is a chapter in Harvey Brome's *Faces of the Wilderness*, which I've brought along. Unfortunately the narrative is dominated by the inexplicable disappearance of a member of the party, a botanist who somehow managed to stray off the trail on a day hike in the Puddin Lake basin (which lies just to the southwest of where I'm camped). Three days and a helicopter search by the Forest Service later, she was found, in good condition, not too far from base camp. Apparently, erroneous assumptions were made by various members of the party about the cross-country route back to camp and who was traveling with whom.

Much of Brome's prose is understandably devoted to search and rescue.

But just prior to the point at which the woman got lost, the author, a leading activist for the Wilderness Society in the 1950s and 60s, focuses on the surrounding wilderness. Here is his description of the Puddin Lake basin:

> There was a fringe of trees around the entire lake from which protruded rocky bluffs and above which were the stark chalky-gray angles of high above-timber line ridges. It was untrailed, remote. The lake lay open to the sky in a vast maze of intersecting ridges. It was a wild and beautiful lake.
>
> Above the forest on the north and west were gray-fractured, angular faces of cliffs. Again I had reached a spot completely given over to wild game and seldom visited. The ruff of trees and beach, the rays of grass and flowering draws stretching up from the shore did not dilute my feeling. All around were gaunt pyramids of broken rock pushing above the forest into the domain of the thunderbolts. And back of us was the wide basin laced only with game ways. This was indeed wilderness — perhaps the wildest place I have ever been — and a part of the great Idaho wilderness.

I envy Brome his feelings of ecstasy and solitude. With the passing of the storm, the annoying sounds of the scouts resume, and I can only console myself with the hope that the next camp will be more isolated.

When my candle lantern burns down, I close my book and journal to catch some sleep. Only to be awakened in the middle of the night by light showers. I get out to piss and am struck by the awful stillness of the basin. Finally, quietude. The hulking silhouettes of the surrounding peaks loom in the night.

From Fishfin Pass the trail to Gentian Lake takes a dramatic plunge in a series of switchbacks before leveling off, then dropping again to the next set of lakes. The only snow I encountered during the entire trip lay in a north-facing bowl where the trail crosses from one side of the slope to the other. Since I'm crossing the snow in the cool of early morning, I have to kick steps in the snowbank for about a fifty-foot stretch. The slope is so steep that a slip would result in a one-hundred-foot skid down into a boulder field. As I gingerly walk across with my full pack, I try hard not to think about a mishap. Suddenly I recall a description in one of the guidebooks about an author encountering the carcass of a dead horse which had fallen in this same spot. Memory, I have come to learn, is like the wilderness: both are wild and uncontrollable.

There is a party of horse campers at Gentian Lake just breaking camp.

We nod at each other but say nothing, choosing not to disturb the silence of morning in the mountains. Then it's one more ascent to the final divide at eighty-eight hundred feet separating Clear Creek from the Ship Island basin. Through the scattered whitebark pines I have a good view, finally, of Mount McGuire, Ship Island Lake (Idaho's largest alpine lake), and the massive granite cliffs at the end of the lake forming Ship Island Canyon. These are scenes about which I have read and dreamed for years. I am at last near the end of my quest.

Airplane Lake lies at the head of Ship Island basin, and it is there, where the trail bottoms out after a long, gradual, switchbacking descent over numerous talus slopes, that I plan to establish my base camp for the next three days. And as I arrive at the bottom of the upper basin, it looks like I have the lake to myself, at least for the moment. I drop my pack at water's edge and circumambulate the shore, searching for the best campsite. Leaving the fifty-pound pack behind is liberating, and I can now see much more, unburdened by the heavy load which made it an effort to look anywhere but down towards my feet. I'm looking forward to several days of hiking without the beast on my back.

After all my searching the best site proves to be right where I'd dropped my pack. No matter. There is virtue in exploration of any sort. While walking around the lake I had a chance to check out the many different species of wildflowers in high bloom: paintbrush, valerian, penstemon, elephant-head, lupine, columbine, lousewort, purple aster, shootingstar. I also stopped to listen to the lyrical plashing of the stream feeding into the basin from the lakes above, Shoban and Sheepeater. Lured by the sound of mountain water, I consider a cross-country trek to these upper lakes, where I'd guess few parties have ventured to explore.

I set up camp once again, then decide to go for a dip. At eighty-four hundred feet, the water, of course, is quite cold and I'm in and out in seconds. But with an unimpeded sun blazing down on me I'm soon warm again and basking on a makeshift dock of rocks and branches that some alpine fisherman once fashioned. There is not a human sound to be heard in the basin. I seem to have succeeded in my search for wilderness solitude.

For the rest of the day I alternately bathe, bask, and putz around camp. The time passes slowly, deliciously, meditatively, measured by the angle and length of the ridgetop shadows across the basin. I am back on lookout time, and loving every precious moment of the experience.

Before sunrise the next morning I'm out of my bag, headlamp on, groping for layers of clothing and some food to shove into a belt pack for the ascent of Mount McGuire. Breakfast is a quart of water and a PowerBar; I've no time to heat up water for coffee. I want to be on the summit before noon and off the mountain by midafternoon in the event of developing storms. A new moon shimmering in the light of dawn seems like a good omen.

As I begin the uphill climb from the lake, I remind myself to walk slow and steady. My mind is plagued with doubts: at age forty-five, climbing alone, can I, should I, still be doing this kind of thing? It's sixteen hundred feet higher to the summit, with no trail, and likely no people around in the event I hurt myself and am unable to walk out. In all likelihood it would be days, even a week, before I'd be discovered as missing. These kinds of thoughts haunt me much more now than when I was younger. But still I persist. Why? Perhaps it has something to do with making further self-discoveries. And with wanting one more solo physical challenge in the wild, where there is nothing to compete against — except nature. But I'm not competing against nature, I think; I simply want to try meeting it on its own terms, to understand it better, to learn from it. To engage in outward as well as inward exploration.

Soon the fight against gravity, the heavy tug on the legs, forces me to focus solely on the task at hand. I'm grateful for that. I pause for breath several times before reaching the mountain tarn that, at 9,150 feet, lies maybe a quarter-mile from and less than a thousand feet below the summit. This would be a good place to camp, I think, seven hundred feet above the main trail, with a guaranteed water supply. True alpine solitude. With juncos and mountain bluebirds for company. Another time, perhaps.

From the lake to the tarn, the climbing had been on solid ground, through the trees. Now the ascent above timberline begins, across and up boulder fields, once I rehydrate and fill my water bottles and munch on another PowerBar. The sun is just arcing over the east ridge as I resume the climb from the tarn. I soon reach the southeast ridge and pick my way among the rocks, always conscious of good footholds and handholds.

Just below the summit I stop at a lone whitebark pine that has somehow managed to grow between some rocks. Stunted, gnarly, no more than ten feet tall, it gives me pause, embodying the phrase "the will to live." I then notice other signs of life around me: lichen splashed on the many faces of the granite boulders; some faded pink moss campion niched between some rocks but still apparently vital; and scattered plots of krummholz — dwarf pines — greening occasional spots on the mountainside. I take heart at these tenacious examples of life at altitude, then climb on.

Once atop the summit, the first thing I do is bow in all four directions

Ship Island Lake.

and thank the mountain for allowing me to climb it. Then and only then do I take in the stupendous views. Below, to the south and southwest lies the Ship Island basin, the lake a long lovely blue ribbon hemmed in by thick un-broken forests and massive mountains and cliffs. Farther south tower the rest of the crags, many of the peaks without names, their namelessness thus making them all the more mysterious and alluring. Due west is the fire-scarred Middle Fork of the Salmon River canyon, much of it torched by the Ship Island fire of 1979, which eventually burned almost eleven thousand acres. North and northwest undulates ridge after ridge of the Frank Church Wilderness. On the southwest horizon I can barely make out the Sawtooths through the smoky haze. Somewhere in the pall stands Ruffneck Peak, but try as I might I cannot quite make it out, not even with the binoculars. No matter: it is clear enough still in memory.

I feel good, having found the climb up surprisingly quick and easy. I'm not a big-time mountaineer, have never climbed anything higher than Mount Whitney (which is really just a long hike), and have done only a little glacier climbing with ice ax, crampons, and rope. I've never climbed with ropes and all the other hardware up sheer rock walls and am really more a scrambler than a climber in the technical sense. But there is challenge enough in solitary scrambling up boulder fields in remote wilderness areas. I have met one more challenge, feel good about it, and already begin to anticipate the next mountain climb.

I remain on the summit for a spell, checking the map against the actual terrain, glancing occasionally at the sky, trying to read it too, wondering what it will do later in the day. There's a thick, wide band of high cirrus clouds developing to the west, the direction of the weather in these parts, and I know I should get down off the mountain soon.

A lone mountain swift boomerangs around the summit. The winds accelerate, which I read as a sign to depart. But not before bowing once again to the mountain spirits and asking for safe passage back down (knowing that the descent is often as dangerous if not more so than the climb up). Then and only then do I repack my things and slowly, reluctantly, obey gravity's call.

Back down in the trees I catch glimpses of the biggest buck I've ever seen, a mule deer with seven tines on each side of its rack. The deer slowly, nonchalantly picks its way across the slope below me, only occasionally pausing to glance my way. Come winter it will probably head down Ship Island Canyon to a warmer domain where (I hope) it will remain safe from hunters for another year. That animal is a trophy the wilderness alone should claim.

Back at camp, early in the afternoon, storms develop, though with little lightning in the immediate vicinity. I lie in the tent atop my bag listening to the soporific hissing of rain on the lake. In the evening after dinner I treat myself to a jigger of whiskey and a cigar. The smoke wafts across the water's surface in the still aftermath of the storm. I hear only the steady background plashing of the creek and in the foreground the chirruping of crickets and the "peenting" of sandpipers along the shore. I relish this natural poetry, the onomatopoeia of the wild.

Back in the tent, well past dark, I compose this haiku:

> Wherever there is
> granite water pines solitude
> is a good place.

The next morning I awaken to the "eh eh eh" of red-breasted nuthatches in the massive spruce that shelters my tent. Today there's no need to rise before dawn and when I emerge from the tent, the sun, already above the eastern ridge, bathes the lake basin in a soft light.

I fix a hot breakfast of coffee and oatmeal, contemplating my activities for today. I consider moseying on down to Ship Island Lake, all the way to its outlet and the beginning of legendary Ship Island Canyon. Here's what the Maughans have to say about the canyon in their guidebook: "At the outlet of the lake, immense granite spires line the canyon walls, and here Ship Island Creek begins to tumble down a steep, trailless canyon. It drops forty-five hundred feet in five miles to the Middle Fork of the Salmon River. Few have ever descended this canyon."

Just the suggestion of a little-explored canyon is enough to lure me to its brink.

I stand on the dock at lake's edge and sip my coffee and drink in the stillness. I am immersed in the present of this place, with no plans for tomorrow, totally at home in the wild, at my own personal listening point.

Around noon, after having descended the mile and a half of trail connecting Airplane and Ship Island lakes, I emerge from the thick forest onto the eastern shore of immense Ship Island Lake. It seems a long way to the opposite end, where the towering granite cliffs mark the beginning of the canyon. In no hurry, I pause to drink some water and eat some gorp, listening to the waves wash up on the gravelly beach. Once again I have an entire lake basin to myself.

Making my way down the milelong lakeshore on the north side, along a faint foot trail, I take note of some excellent campsites niched between long granite fingers that reach out into the water to form tiny peninsulas. The prominence of the rocky shelves reminds me of the Boundary Waters Canoe Area Wilderness in northern Minnesota and the infinite number of stunning campsites in the north woods where thick forests, exposed Precambrian granite, and countless lakes predominate. This basin has a north woods feel, a dominating presence of water and woods. What it also has are towering ten thousand-foot peaks to define the basin in a way so much more dramatic than anything I've seen in the Quetico-Superior region.

It's at the lake outlet where I am truly awestruck. I cross the creek where it begins its downward tumble just after the grassy lake narrows. Then I scramble up the side of a gigantic granite dome that must have risen millions of years ago to dam the creek and form the lake. On top I'm surrounded by a titanic display of geology: thousand-foot walls, topped by impregnable spires and fins that I would guess, because of their remoteness and difficulty, have never been scaled by climbers, and a sinuous, mysterious canyon that I doubt has seen more than a dozen human visitors. I am in a spot that the indigenous peoples, the Tukudeka, must have felt was a power place, a sacred site that induced awe and reverence. And a place that nineteenth century explorers would have called sublime had they ventured here. It's a fantastic campsite, isolated, hard to get to, with great prospects, one I know I must revisit.

Walking across the dome I discover a single lodgepole pine twenty feet tall and looking quite healthy, growing out of a crack in the granite dome and hanging over the canyon. More evidence of the will to live. I eat lunch and scribble in my journal, taking in the surroundings. Several truck-sized boulders lie precariously balanced on the slope of the dome, inch by inch coming closer to tumbling down into the rocky defile below. Two ravens soar and honk above, breaking the silence. Are they speaking to me? What are they saying? Should I take this to be an omen, interpret it as part of a vision? Perhaps their appearance means nothing at all. Perhaps they would have appeared whether I was here or not. More than anything else, this place seems to say to me, you are insignificant, you are nothing in the face of these million-year-old rocks, this enduring granite.

Before leaving I bow, in worship and supplication, to this place.

That night back in camp, quite late I am awakened by a rockslide on the ridge above. Bighorn sheep? Mountain lion? Or maybe it's the ghosts of the Tukedeka, still roaming the ridgetops, trying to reclaim their lost lands.

Hiking out all the way the next day, I encounter several horse parties, one over a dozen in size, making me all the more grateful for my solitude the last few days. Then follows the long, hot, dry drive to town. Luckily I'd saved a few beers in the cooler for the ride out. On the final descent into the Salmon River valley, late afternoon, I take in the stunning views of the knife-edged Beaverhead Range along the Idaho-Montana border to the east, foregrounded by tawny meadow grasses waving with the desiccating canyon winds.

At the brewpub back in Salmon, a waitress serves me raspberry ale. To a man who has just emerged from the wilderness after a long journey, she seems a beautiful and exotic apparition. Laetitia is her name. She's from northern California and goes to school at the University of Idaho, working down here for the summer to help get through college. I ask her what's she's studying; she says she's an English major. That's good to hear. Out of curiosity I ask her, what does she think of Ernest Hemingway? She loves the way he writes but hates the way he portrays women. Typical response from young women nowadays. And justified. I tell her about my trip in the Crags. Wish I could get off enough days to do that, she says wistfully. Why ask

The Dome and the Crags.

about Hemingway? Because he used to live in Sun Valley and hunt in these parts for many years. Yeah, she had heard about that. In fact, he did a pack trip to the Salmon River Mountains in the late 1930s and later wrote a short story called "The Shot" in which he mentioned them. I quote from memory: "We rode to the top of the range where we could look over all the way into the Middle Fork of the Salmon," the main character observes, "across the loveliest mountains that I know."

Laetitia serves me another beer. I tell her, "That's the way I feel about the Crags."

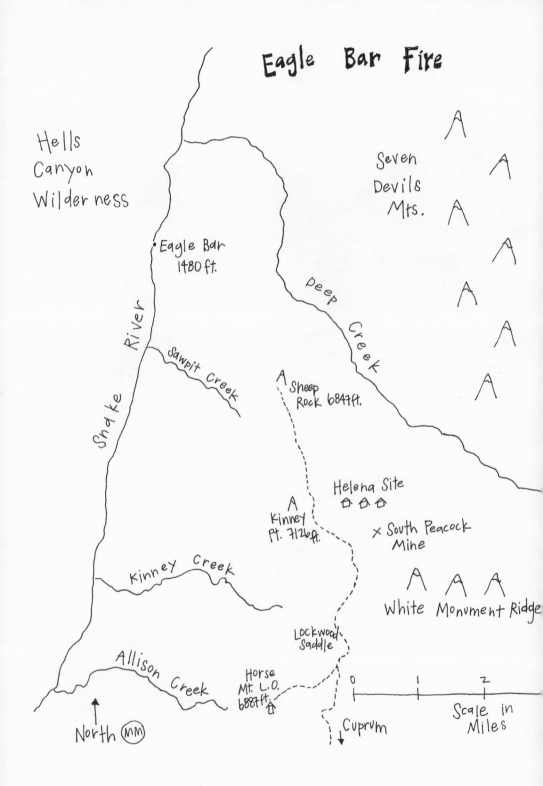

Eagle Bar Fire

Hells
Canyon
Wilderness

Seven
Devils
Mts.

• Eagle Bar
1480 ft.

Deep Creek

Snake River

Sawpit Creek

△ Sheep Rock 6847ft.

Helena Site
⌂ ⌂ ⌂

△ Kinney Pt. 7126ft.

× South Peacock Mine

Kinney Creek

△ △ △ White Monument Ridge

Lockwood Saddle

Allison Creek

Horse Mt. L.O. 6887ft.

Cuprum

North ⓂⓂ

0   1   2
Scale in Miles

15. The eagle bar fire

Although there is plenty of time on the lookout for leisurely activities like hiking, reading, and doing nothing at all, work is real and important. Fires occur. Sometimes small fires become big fires. Sometimes a few of these big fires become big news, headlined in major newspapers, eventually mentioned by national news anchors on television, finally having attained enough notoriety to draw reporters in their just-off-the-rack outdoor clothing to the hinterlands to talk with firefighters on the line. This account of a lookout's life would not be complete without reference to a big fire. A few years back, on another lookout, I was intimately involved in such a spectacle. What follows are journal entries subsequently polished after being initially jotted down hastily during a frenzied three-week period in which my lookout became the locus, the epicenter, of fire and firefighting activity. It was a sobering reminder of the life-and-death gravity of fire management. I preserve the journal format here to convey the immediacy of the events.

SATURDAY, AUGUST 20. For a lookout, Saturday night is like any other evening. I sign off on the two-way radio at 6 P.M. ("eighteen hundred hours" in firefighter parlance), eat dinner, take a hike, return to the tower and read until darkness descends, then fall asleep.

But sometime later in the evening the unmistakable smell of wood smoke awakens me. I look north, the direction from which the wind is blowing, and in spite of the light of a waxing moon I can make out an orange glow behind the silhouette of Grassy Ridge in Hells Canyon.

Fire! I note the time — 10:15 P.M. —then take a bearing of the blaze to determine its location. Next I radio Dispatch in McCall, headquarters of the Payette National Forest, and give my report: "This is Horse Mountain lookout reporting a fire burning in Hells Canyon in the vicinity of Sawpit Creek, about five miles north of the lookout. My azimuth is 342 degrees. The legal location is township 21 north, range 3 west, section 4. I can't see the base of the fire but my guess is that it's about fifty acres in size."

Both Dispatch and I know, though we don't say, that it's the worst possible scenario. Because it's night, firefighters can't be flown to the fire. Because they'll have to be transported by trucks and it's a long way around by switchbacking canyon roads from the nearest ranger station, it'll take three to four hours to drive to the scene. And because of the steep, rugged terrain with explosive cheatgrass fuels along the bottom of Hells Canyon, the fire is sure to take off quickly. Combine these factors with the current high winds and there is a very good chance that a small fire will explode into a big one.

SUNDAY, AUGUST 21. Events blur and become surreal. All night and into the morning I relay calls from fire crews in the depths of the canyon to Dispatch and provide updates on the fire based on the firefighters' reports and my own view of the growing mushroom cloud of smoke. In the darkness there is little for the crews to do except evacuate fishermen, campers, and river runners. Fanned by northwest wind gusts, the fire races up the grassy slopes of the canyon into higher-elevation stands of Douglas fir and ponderosa pine. Burning debris occasionally tumbles downhill onto the Idaho Power road that dead-ends at Hells Canyon Dam where rafters put in, and fire crews extinguish these spot fires while looking warily uphill for more logs and rocks to fall.

By morning the fire rages across 750 acres. Most fires that a lookout reports remain small — no larger than one-tenth of an acre — and usually require three to four helitackers or smokejumpers to extinguish them. But this blaze, the Eagle Bar fire (so named because it apparently started near Eagle Bar on the Snake River) has become a Class I fire. This means that top fire management personnel from across the country are being assembled to form a team to contain and suppress the fire. Four hundred firefighters in twenty-person crews have been called for, and a fire camp is to be established at Kinney Point, three miles north of the lookout.

War has been declared on the Eagle Bar fire.

Throughout the next day, DC-3 retardant planes lumber overhead, making drop after drop of pink-red ammonia phosphate (or "mud," as the pilots call it), in an attempt to halt the advancing flames. The pilots' reports to Dispatch — "Heading back to McCall for reload and return" — dominate the airwaves.

But things begin to go wrong in the afternoon. The air attack plane in charge of the overall aerial operations reports that the lead plane (used to guide in the ponderous retardant planes) has just crashed in the backwaters of Hells Canyon Dam. Air operations are then shut down until another lead plane can be found. In the meantime the fire grows, whipped by winds and heated by afternoon temperatures soaring into the nineties.

By early evening Horse Mountain becomes a helibase for the numerous helicopters shuttling crews to various locations on the fire. Word finally gets out that the pilot of the downed lead plane swam away from the scene of the crash to a nearby island. The good news is passed on to Dispatch.

TUESDAY, AUGUST 23. An August dog-day dawns, sultry and still. Smoke hangs heavily in the air. At 7:30 A.M. I hear the thwock-thwock-thwock of the first helicopter feeling its way through the pall. The smoke is too thick for the retardant planes to make their drops safely in the canyon narrows, so we wait for the winds to pick up and warming temperatures to lift the inversion.

I meet firefighters from all over the country. We all complain about the hornets, which are as thick as the smoke and, chased from their nests by the fire, even more bad-tempered than usual. Everyone gets stung and some people, unknowingly allergic, are taken by helicopter to the hospital in McCall.

WEDNESDAY, AUGUST 24. Choppers again appear through the smoky haze of sunrise. I find out from others the cause of the fire: a motorcyclist in the canyon who tried to burn his toilet paper in very dry grasses on a hot, windy afternoon. Unbelievable! We all have a good laugh over that explanation, which helps to relieve the stress of the situation. I soon learn that, among firefighters, black humor helps to keep everyone loose in otherwise dirty and very dangerous conditions.

More laughter follows when we learn that a local crew member is stranded overnight on an island of the Snake River. Apparently he'd been assigned the cushy duty of watching over the plane that had crashed in the river to make sure that the evidence of the accident wasn't tampered with before federal investigators arrived on the scene. But in the pell-mell of the firefighting operations he was lost track of after being dropped off by helicopter and had to spend the night without food after his radio batteries went dead. The next morning he was spotted and rescued by a passing fire truck, appearing to be in good condition. His new nickname is Robinson Crusoe.

Later in the day another lead plane is initially dispatched to the Eagle Bar fire but is then diverted to a new start on the Salmon National Forest. The Forest Service adheres to this strategy because it's better to divert personnel and equipment to a small fire so it can be contained quickly and prevented from becoming yet another large fire, rather than to devote every resource to a large fire that may burn uncontrolled anyway. This strategy will prove prophetic in the case of the Eagle Bar fire.

Meanwhile, down on the fire line, the situation grows increasingly serious when a firefighter collapses from heat exhaustion. The column of smoke towers to twelve thousand feet, creating its own cumulus. With binoculars I can see trees torching off like matchsticks on the slopes of Sheep Rock and Kinney Point only five air miles away.

Then at 5:20 P.M. we learn that the fire camp on Kinney Point is being evacuated and relocated to Horse Mountain. The fire brass calls it a "strategic retreat." The rest of the day helicopters shuttle crews from the fire to the ridgetop where I work and live. The FMO of the district on which I work radios me to say, "It looks like you're gonna have some company for awhile."

The road to the lookout becomes as congested as a freeway during rush-hour traffic. National Guard trucks ferry equipment and crews, and tractor-trailers haul food and shower units. Steam-cleaned Idaho Fish & Game tank trucks transport potable water while sprinkler trucks spray water to keep down the dust. Caravans of green Forest Service rigs appear. And at dusk an F-4 fighter jet screams high in the sky over the fire, doing infra-red aerial reconnaissance. Photo-maps of the fire will appear in camp the same evening, transferred electronically via computer, informing fire management of the fire's behavior and perimeter.

The invasion has begun. So much for my summer of wilderness solitude.

THURSDAY, AUGUST 25. The latest estimate of the size of the fire is twenty-one hundred acres. I hear this report during my tour of Horse City, as the fire-camp on the ridge is now dubbed. Declaring myself benevolent mayor-dictator of the new metropolis (population seven hundred), I stroll down Main Street past rows of porta-potties, a food trailer and kitchen, mess tents, and shelters housing the various facets of a large fire organization: planning, communications, finance, logistics, supply, ground support, and

Fire camp below Horse Mountain lookout.

first-aid. On the outskirts of Horse City, slightly removed from the drone of generators and glare of lights, are the tent camps of the twenty crews assigned to the fire. On the southeast point are the helibase, the landing spots for the helicopters working the fire, and the camps of the helitack crews. Overnight, Horse City has become a sizable Idaho town with a restaurant, bank, and airport.

FRIDAY, AUGUST 26. *Firestorm*. One of the Overhead Team members tells me just after midnight that the fire suddenly shifted direction, trapping twenty to thirty firefighters. As a result they are forced to deploy their fire shelters, one-person A-frame tents made of an aluminum foil-like insulation.

Although firefighters routinely joke about the procedure of employing a fire shelter as a "shake and bake" move when they practice it, in reality it is absolutely the ultimate nightmare for a firefighter. To deploy a shelter implies that a firefighter believes there is no escape route. Fortunately only one injury is reported during the fiery siege, a dollar-size burn on someone's calf. Once the fire sweeps by after an hour or so, the firefighters emerge from their shelters.

By 3:30 A.M. the firestorm advances to within two miles of the lookout. Smoke obscures the view, colder temperatures dampen the blaze somewhat, and the fire seems to come to a halt, at least temporarily. Nothing to do but try to get some rest. But sleep is fitful and short.

After breakfast I learn that the crews who were forced to deploy their shelters are being shipped to McCall for trauma therapy. This is standard operating procedure for any firefighter who has gone through such an ordeal.

The decision then comes down that no crews are to be sent out on the fire lines today. Conditions are too smoky, too uncertain, hence too dangerous. So firefighters do laundry, play hacky-sack, read newspapers, magazines, and junk literature from the library, and stock up on candy bars and pop at the commissary. I take my first real shower in two months and feel almost human again. The camp laborers fashion a large sign that reads MAYOR OF HORSE CITY and hang it at the base of the lookout tower. I spend much of the day mingling with my constituents.

At a fire camp one of the ways to pass the time is to check out people's T-shirts. On a large fire it's customary for commemorative shirts to be designed and sold. My favorite is from one of the Yellowstone fires currently raging in Wyoming. With a firestorm for a backdrop, Boo-Boo says to Yogi the Bear, "Yogi, Mr. Ranger isn't gonna like this."

SATURDAY, AUGUST 27. The fire is now estimated to be thirty-one hundred acres. It begins to make runs to the east, up toward White Monument Ridge, where it torches the archaeological remains of the old mining town of Helena and the site of the Peacock Mine near the head of Copper Creek. The big concern now is that the fire will make a run into Deep Creek, a sinuous, steep, heavily timbered tributary of the Snake River in the Hells Canyon Wilderness where there are no roads and where it's too dangerous to place firefighters. The word from the top is that once the fire becomes established there, forget it; there will be no choice but to let it burn into the wilderness area until winter snows put it out.

SUNDAY, AUGUST 28. Another windy day. The fire blows up once again, this time in Copper Creek. Retardant planes are ineffective because it's too smoky for them to fly low enough to drop their loads effectively, and the wind scatters their mud before it reaches the hot spots. Three helicopters operating with water buckets are somewhat more effective.

Early in the evening I fly over the fire in a helicopter with the district ranger. First we inspect Grassy Ridge, where backburning has begun. The entire ridge is now charcoal. Next we fly through Hells Canyon. Though at first glance it appears that there is nothing to burn — the canyon consisting mainly of sheer cliffs — closer inspection reveals that something is indeed burning: lichen draping the rock walls. In the drainages of Deep and Copper creeks there is no question about what is burning. Thousands of trees are aflame, and I trace the fascinating mosaic patterns of the fire in green and black outlines of burning and untouched Douglas fir, ponderosa pine, Engelmann spruce, and subalpine fir. The helicopter labors up the steep gorge of Deep Creek through billowy smoke clouds and over conifers crowning out in flames. On the return we get a spectacular view of Horse Mountain, now a tent-city atop a hill.

MONDAY, AUGUST 29. The media discovers the Eagle Bar fire. Cameramen and reporters from a Boise TV station appear in camp and seek out interviews, and an information officer from the Payette National Forest arrives to take photographs and talk with firefighting personnel.

TUESDAY, AUGUST 30. The fire slops over White Monument Ridge into Camp Creek, adding an entirely new dimension to the containment strategy. Camp Creek is a tributary of Indian Creek, which runs through the tiny, still extant mining town of Cuprum, only two miles south of the lookout. The threat to human lives and private property from the fire grows, so resources are refocused on halting the fire's progress on White Monument Ridge. And on another front, in the Deep Creek drainage, the fire has entered the Hells Canyon Wilderness, which means that the Wallowa National Forest will now be involved. This is a jurisdictional nicety about which the woods — and the fire — know nothing.

Following breakfast I make the rounds, scanning the bulletin board (which lists reports of fires across the country) and visiting with fire management officers in Plans and Communications, hoping to glean some new information. More than thirty injuries have now occurred, mostly bee stings. The latest estimate of the fire's size is seventy-four hundred acres. The Eagle Bar fire has now become the number one priority fire in Region Four of the Forest Service (covering the Intermountain states). Ten more crews have been requested, but with the fires still raging in Yellowstone it's unlikely we'll get them anytime soon.

WEDNESDAY, AUGUST 31. After I turn in my morning weather observations to Dispatch, I'm told that I was featured on the Boise news programs last night, identified as the mayor of Horse City.

The fire has acquired a ho-hum quality in spite of the fact that it has yet to be contained. As in war, destruction and life-threatening situations become routine, even mundane. Firefighters are even talking about demobilization, but don't mention a projected containment date. After chatting with various crew members, I get the feeling that everyone wants to leave to go to a new fire — where things won't really be any easier or less dangerous, just different.

THURSDAY, SEPTEMBER 1. The rumormongers are hard at work: camp to bug out in a few days; camp to remain for weeks; some crews to be demobed; more crews coming in. It's hard to get a straight answer out of the top brass. Much depends on whether or not the fire can be confined to the wilderness, which in turn depends largely on weather conditions. If the fire does enter the wilderness, it will be allowed to burn within certain prescribed parameters and a skeleton crew will remain to monitor its progress.

Allow a human-caused fire to burn unchecked into a wilderness area? What kind of fire management strategy is that? The hard truth is, there's not much that we can do about stopping the Eagle Bar fire given these dry, windy conditions and steep terrain. A few years ago, John McPhee wrote a book with an ironic title that now comes to mind: *The Control of Nature*. It's about natural disasters like floods, volcanic eruptions, and avalanches that defy human attempts to prevent their recurrence. This fire is one more example of nature's dominance.

Following the morning weather forecasts, Dispatch announces the fire situation report. The acreage of the fires burning in Yellowstone draws particular attention: North Fork fire 109,000 acres; Wolf Lake 40,000; Fan 23,000; Clover Mist 213,000; and Snake River 186,000. In comparison, the Eagle Bar fire of 8,000 acres is but a flicker.

Another dog day proceeds. Smoke lies like a lid on valleys and mountains. Visibility is down to two miles. If there were other fires out there they would be undetected until they raged out of control. Fortunately we've had no lightning for weeks, so there is little chance of sleeper (smoldering) fires developing. All we need be concerned about then are human-caused fires.

Say, how did the Eagle Bar fire start?

FRIDAY, SEPTEMBER 2. Another eerie red sunrise to begin the day. After breakfast I chat with John Russell, the incident commander (I.C.) in charge of all fire operations. He is a pipe-chuffing, bearded barrel of a man, a veteran of many, many forest fires in the West. He predicts that the fire will eventually burn about twenty-five thousand acres, most of that in the wilderness. The cost of the fire is now $4.8 million. Of that amount, $2 million is in suppression costs, billed (as required by law) to the unlucky, stupid motorcyclist who started the fire (who, I'm later told, fled the country to escape paying the bill). The remainder is the amount lost in property and timber.

SUNDAY, SEPTEMBER 4. You can see fatigue and despair on the face of the firefighters today. They want out of here. Pounding line, inhaling large quantities of smoke and dust without making progress towards containment of the fire, has long since become mere drudgery.

I, too, want the fire to be over, all the people gone. The appeal of plentiful food cooked by someone else and showers and interesting folks from all over the country to talk with has dissipated. I long for some solitude, a night of sleep without being awakened by generators. While eating we're entertained by the ZAP! of electric bug-killers stationed strategically near the salad bar. Very appetizing.

I study the latest infrared photos. The fire is now at 14,900 acres. "Hey we're just about respectable," jokes a member of the Overhead Team. That's total acreage within the perimeter of the fire, not actual burned acres. One can clearly see the mosaic of burn patterns along the ridges, how at its whim the fire has torched some swaths of timber but left others untouched. And much of the burned acreage is the result of backburning. Still, fifteen thousand acres is nothing to sneeze at.

TUESDAY, SEPTEMBER 6. Two-thirds of camp is to be taken down today; at the same time, a cold front with high winds is forecast to move into the region. Most of the crews and the entire Overhead Team break camp, load up in school buses, and head down the hill. Good riddance. I remain in the tower most of the day, avoiding good-byes, watching the queues of vehicles crawl away, savoring the relative silence that returns to the mountain.

As the cold front advances, for the first time in weeks I can see distances of five, ten, then twenty miles, the wind scouring the air clean and bringing with it row after row of fair-weather cumulus.

Smoke from the Eagle Bar fire roils out of Deep Creek.

The fire seems unaware of the containment strategy planned for it. During dinner we're provided with one more awesome display of its power, as the biggest smoke column yet roils out behind a ridgetop near the head of Deep Creek, topping out at fifteen thousand feet. It arcs all the way across the head of the basin to Smith Mountain, whipped by northwest winds.

THURSDAY, SEPTEMBER 8. A sunny, cold, clear day. There's an unmistakable feel of fall in the air. The aspen leaves are gilded, the brush is turning russet on the mountain slopes. The latest estimate of the fire is 15,275 acres. The fire is doing exactly what the Overhead Team predicted: blow up in Deep Creek but eventually peter out as it moves higher up into the patchy timber and rocky outcroppings of the wilderness. We seem to be better at predicting the fire's behavior than at controlling it.

The latest rumor: what's left of camp will bug out in a few days. Another cold front is expected to pass over by then, bringing snow to the higher elevations.

FRIDAY, SEPTEMBER 9. I talk with Carol Ciliberti, a member of the Wasatch National Forest crew from Utah, a firefighter in the summer and a ski patrol guide in the winter. Asked why she has chosen firefighting as a seasonal pastime, Carol says that it has something to do with the brute simplicity of the work, the basic, physically demanding task of pounding line for twelve to fourteen hours a day, sleeping out in the elements, and seeing clear evidence of your accomplishments as an individual and a team. Not to mention the camaraderie that develops among the crew members, the bonds that are formed between people who face the same brutal, dirty, and dangerous conditions day after day. "This must be what war is like," she says.

SATURDAY, SEPTEMBER 10. It's been three weeks since I reported the fire. The blaze that started in the heat of summer is now continuing into the cold of winter. The air temperature has dropped to twenty-seven degrees, and the winds are howling at more than 20 MPH, reducing the windchill to minus four. For the first time in months I fire up the wood stove and invite Carol up to the cabin for hot chocolate. Together we listen to the morning weather forecast, which mentions snow levels dropping to seven thousand feet. Dispatch warns that "Lookouts should beware of winterlike conditions." Mercifully, the crews are not sent out on the fire line this morning, for fear of hypothermia.

In fact, they're not being sent out at all. They're being sent home! Or at least to another, hopefully warmer fire. There is dancing in the streets of Horse Village today as eighty happy firefighters break camp. Within hours the tent-city disappears, leaving in its wake a dust bowl of trampled grasses.

What about the fire? It still burns within Deep Creek, lying low because of the cold temperatures. With the advent of this wintry weather there's little chance for it to escape from the wilderness area. Millions of dollars have been spent on suppression, but the fire has done its own thing and will be extinguished, ultimately, only by snow and cold. Whoever said fire management was an exact science?

The population of Horse Mountain returns to one. As snowflakes flutter through the air I go on one last long hike. Down to the meadows where I can wade once again through the chest-high tawny grass. Under the aspen niched in the draw of a creek, their yellow leaves rustling in the wind. Past the silent dark groves and the spires of subalpine fir and spruce. I return home at dusk, to enjoy once more the delicious solitude of working a fire lookout.

fall

16. hunting, the fundamental diversion

For lookouts, September is the coolest month.

The brush along the trails has turned russet after the desiccatingly hot summer and below-freezing temperatures of late. In fact, autumn hues have appeared everywhere over the last few days — the golds of aspen, tawny browns of meadow grasses, reds of mountain ash berries, and darker browns of the shrubs and brush. Now that the fire season is coming to an end, there is little if any smoke around, and the low humidity and cooler temperatures have combined to lend a crystalline quality to the air. As in spring I can once again see for long distances, westward all the way to Oregon where the Wallowa range retains only the barest traces of snow, and eastward to the wall of the Bighorn Crags. I glass all the countryside with delight, luxuriating in the lay of the land.

The decrease in wildfires means a corresponding decline in radio traffic. In front of ranger stations across Idaho and Montana, that wonderful cultural icon Smokey the Bear is pointing to the fire danger indicator at LOW. Many of the seasonal employees on the fire, timber, river, and recreation crews have gone back to college, leaving relatively few personnel still in the field. The little conversation that does occur on the radio is relaxed, low-key, the tension gone from everyone's voices now that the chance for wildfires has diminished. It's a bittersweet time for firefighters, who've racked up lots of OT pay for hazard duty while battling blazes but who now know that they too are short-timers, soon to be laid off for lack of work.

I sit on the steps of the catwalk overseeing my domain, neither lord nor monarch of all I survey, just one more member of the biotic community. Basking in the sun out of the wind, wearing a wool sweater and shorts, I become aware of another fall delight: no bugs. Well, hardly any. Sure there are still a few flies droning about, the only noise noticeable at the moment. But the mosquitoes, ant flies, and wasps have all disappeared for the year, and it is an absolute pleasure to sit and not have to flail at various pests while trying to enjoy my morning coffee. Yes, fall is truly the most colorful, comfortable, and solitary time of the year on the lookout. Hemingway captured the enchanting qualities of an Idaho autumn in this stanza of a poem he once wrote (now inscribed on a bronze plaque at a memorial to him in Sun Valley):

> Best of all he loved the fall
> The leaves yellow on the cottonwoods
> Leaves littering the trout streams
> And above the hills
> The high blue windless skies.

I don't look forward to the rush of visitors over Labor Day, the last holiday weekend of the year. Like the fourth of July, it's one of the few times that I'm required to be on the lookout for most of the day (including before and after official 9 to 5 hours) in order to perform my responsibilities of greeting the public and serving as a representative of the Forest Service. It's not part of my temperament to be gregarious and social, but I grin and bear this weighty responsibility as best I can. And as I continue to discover, there are actually a lot of good folks out there hiking and camping in the woods.

The first visitors of the weekend are a party of five women, all of whom must be at least sixty years old. They offer me fruit and candy bars, which I gratefully accept. We chat while on the catwalk about where they're from and what they're doing up here. Rosemary, the leader of the group, has hiked up to Ruffneck's summit seven times, and the journey for her has now become a pilgrimage. Apparently, the organizing principle of the group is divorce; all formerly married, the women are now dating eligible men in Nampa — such as they exist, I suggest, and Rosemary readily replies, "You got *that* straight, cowboy." We talk about the advantages of living in southern Idaho: proximity to both Boise and its many recreational possibilities in the surrounding mountains, canyons, and rivers; the temperate climate of the high desert; the uncrowded freeways and easy commutes. Ah, she sighs, but Californians have discovered Idaho and are gobbling up land and jacking up home prices. "They've ruined their state and now they want to come up here and ruin ours too." Although I'm an ex-Californian myself (though not born and raised there) I can see her point. But what, I ask, would they have the government do — lock out all immigrants? Invasion has become the perpetual problem in the American West, once dotted by former Shangri-las. Strict growth limits and land-use controls do not generally sit well with natives of the West, known for the inhabitants' love of frontier freedoms and resistance to government control.

The women are absolutely my favorite visitors of the season — funny, friendly, and feisty — and I'm genuinely sorry to see them go after an hour or so of real conversation. They head back down the Langer Lakes trail, intending to spend the weekend camping in Stanley, where they can attend church on Sunday. Rosemary urges me to visit a chapel on the outskirts of town with a picture window of the Sawtooths. Sounds good, I tell her. When they depart I can't help but marvel that the feminist revolution has come to Idaho, where people seem so proud of the T-shirt that proclaims: NOW ENTERING IDAHO — SET YOUR WATCHES BACK FIFTY YEARS. I'll be damned!

Among the dozen or so people who visit over the three-day holiday, the most troubling party is a father (probably in his forties) and preteen son. The boy is as shy as a doe, very well behaved, tow-headed and cute as a button. The father, soft-spoken but dictatorial, immediately got on my nerves by constantly bossing the son around, ordering him to pose here, then there, for pictures. Occasionally I noticed the boy rolling his eyes, very quickly, so as to go undetected by the father. I sensed that something was amiss.

Fortunately, they don't stay long. But I think long afterwards of the boy, of the father, of fatherhood. As someone who's deliberately chosen not to have kids (mainly for environmental reasons), I occasionally wonder if that's the right decision to make, especially when I see poor parenting in action. I was the third child of parents, both in their forties when I was born, and grew up pretty much as an only child, thus acquiring independent habits of mind. Although my parents argued often over my dad's drinking, which in retrospect seems like a way miners cope with hard and dangerous working conditions, I look back on my upbringing not as an idyllic experience but as a generally healthy period of my life. Somehow, perhaps accidentally, they fostered a strong spirit of independence in me, for which I'll be forever grateful. So I suppose that is a quality I'd pass on to my kids, if I were ever to have them (possibly through adoption). Independence, fostered by lots of experience in the outdoors. There are far worse ways to raise children.

The remainder of the Labor Day weekend is unusually quiet and fire-free. Typically at this time there are a few fires started as campfires which get out of control or by a cigarette carelessly tossed along some road. But this year the crews on duty for the weekend (getting double OT pay) have little to do other than to patrol and check campgrounds. As summer comes to a close in the valleys (where the temperature still reaches the eighties), we relax and gear up for the last big influx of people for the year in a week or two, come the start of hunting season.

In fact, the grouse season has already begun in these parts, and though there have been few hunters who have actually hoofed it all the way to the top of this mountain, I've been hearing the reports of their guns down below periodically. A pity (for their sake, not the grouse's) that they haven't ventured higher, for each morning of late I've seen an enormous spruce grouse waddling around the summit, pecking for crickets. Earlier in the season I'd heard its drumming call, caused by beating its wings to attract a mate. Now it's all I can do not to throw rocks at it to drive it away (so hunters wouldn't shoot it if they did come up) or klunk it myself for a delicious supper some night. The bird allows me to get remarkably close when I walk by it, as if it were tempting its own fate; or perhaps it's trying to protect the rest of its family by distracting me, though I've yet to see any other grouse in the vicinity. At any rate, watching the bird's antics has become part of my morning ritual and a source of entertainment.

The real hunting starts with the opening of elk season. Like the fishing opener in Minnesota, the start of elk season in the American West marks the beginning of an annual rite of passage for many people (mostly men). Because there are relatively few roads still legally open in the River of No Return Wilderness, the kind of elk hunting that occurs in this neck of the woods is of the more traditional type, featuring pack trains and hunters on horseback. A hunting party of a half-dozen or so men and boys will typically set up a base camp around some lake, then spray out in various directions to track down and shoot an elk, preferably a large bull with a sizable rack — a trophy animal, in other words. The party will then gut the animal and pack out the meat — and horns, if any — leaving the remains for scavengers like wolves, coyote, ravens, jays, etc.

Hunting of any sort has traditionally raised the hackles of environmentalists, and not without reason. They have in mind the worst sort of hunter, the booze-swilling brutes who tool around the logging roads of the national forests in their oversized pickups (always with gun rack featured in the back window), shooting at anything that moves and who generally are more a menace to their own species than the animals they hunt. While these subspecies of humans do exist (I've seen a few myself), the kind of hunting I've been witness to in the wilderness area is a laudable practice which honors the time-tested tradition of the chase. These hunters recall what José Ortega y Gasset wrote about the sport in *Meditations on Hunting*:

> For all the grace and delight of hunting are rooted in this fact: that man, projected by his inevitable progress away from his ancestral proximity to animals, vegetables, and minerals — in sum, to Nature — takes pleasure in the artificial return to it, the only occupation that permits him something like a vacation from his human condition. . . . when man hunts he succeeds in di-verting himself and in distracting himself from being a man. And this is the superlative diversion: it is the fundamental di-version.

Ortega goes on to write, "This is the reason men hunt. When you are fed up with the troublesome present, with being 'very twentieth century,' you take your gun, whistle for your dog, go out to the mountains, and, without further ado, give yourself the pleasure during a few hours or a few days of being 'Paleolithic.' And men of all eras have been able to do the same, without any difference except in the weapon employed." I would take exception to a couple of points claimed here — as someone not raised as a hunter or ever having taken it up myself, and fancying myself a hiker instead, I disagree when he argues that hunting is the "only occupation that permits [humans] something like a vacation from [the] human condition." There are certainly other vacations which can have a similar effect — and *vacation* is a poor choice of words, to my way of thinking, one which diminishes rather than elevates the spiritual significance of various forms of outdoor recreation. A better word is *re-creation*: a process whereby one rejuvenates the self through elemental activities like backpacking, mountain climbing, and river-running. But generally I find a compelling truth in the claim that there is an atavistic appeal to hunting which can't be ignored or devalued.

The issue of class is involved in the debate over hunting as well. In Pennsylvania where I grew up (the state with the largest deer population) one reason to hunt is to put food on the table. The subsistence value of hunting is far greater still in the West where an elk (or moose) can provide a family with several hundred pounds of lean, chemical-free, delicious meat for a winter. Hunters turn elk into steaks, sausage, pepperoni, hamburger — all of which I've tried and liked very much. For working-class families it means saving hundreds of dollars, a sum more easily dismissed by environmentalists from the city and suburbs with swanky, A-frame, log cabin summer homes than by people who log, ranch, or otherwise work with their hands for a living.

There is also the long view, the evolutionary justification for hunting. This argument is advanced by Richard Nelson, an anthropologist and nature writer whose work I much respect. He points out that "For ninety-nine percent of our history . . . human beings lived exclusively as hunter-gatherers. On a relative time scale, agriculture has existed only for a moment and urban societies scarcely more than a blink." Of course one could argue, as Thoreau does in "Higher Laws" in *Walden*, that vegetarianism represents a "higher" state of being and that with the continued "progression" of our species we all will "advance" beyond carnivorism. "[The young man] goes thither at first as a hunter and fisher, until at last, if he has the seeds of a better life in him, he distinguishes his proper objects, as a poet or naturalist it may be, and leaves the gun and fish-pole behind." But Thoreau himself never fully gave up eating meat or fish, nor am I aware of any vegetarian cultures that have flourished for a significant duration in human history. There *are* good reasons not to eat meat in the modern industrial era — to protest the ways that animals are treated and raised or because one is repelled by the poisons present in processed meat. But a truly sad thing about meat-eating is how far we as a species have distanced ourselves from the procurement of meat through the hunt itself, which was once and still can be a noble act. As Paul Shepard observes in *Coming Home to the Pleistocene*, we have lost touch with the predator in ourselves, our ancient ancestor, and in a larger sense we are losing touch with our basic wildness as well as with the wilderness around us.

A party of horse hunters visits the lookout, and one of their first questions (asked with an ironic grin to be sure) is, "Seen any elk?" Since I'm paid to look, they assume that I will have devoted some time to spotting game as well as fires. Why else would a grown man imprison himself like this in a glass house for most of the summer? Since I'm not much inclined to do their hunting for them, though, I smile and shake my head. Of course they don't believe me when I tell them that I haven't seen a single elk all summer (though I have encountered plenty of deer). These hunters have been coming to the Langer Lakes each hunting season for more than a dozen years. Since they've gotten at least one elk every season, they don't intend for their streak to be broken. They're good men, really, with red leathery faces and lean, hard bodies and clear blue eyes undimmed by too much print — the countenances of folks who have spent their entire lives working outdoors. I wish them well and hope their streak remains intact.

Chances are I won't be around for the opening of elk season anyway. I have other lives to live and the long-range forecast I heard the other day predicted wet, cold weather for the weeks to come, so it's likely that the few remaining lookouts will soon be brought down for the season. The hunters are grateful to hear of the prospect of snow in the mountains — it makes tracking animals a lot easier and serves to muffle the sounds of people in the woods. The snow will also, of course, dramatically lower the fire danger — no small consideration, as many forest fires in the fall are started by careless hunters who don't properly extinguish their campfires or who build warming fires in places where they ought not to be built (a fact I don't bring up). As they depart they invite me down to their camp for a nip and a smoke. It's an offer I'll certainly consider.

But for now the weather remains clear, crisp, and cold. In the evening I'm witness to a magnificent harvest moon which seems to rise just behind the Tango Mountains to the east. With the binoculars I observe its full appearance for ten minutes, watching the surface slowly change in color from bright orange to yellow to white. The lunar craters look like they're the result of silent explosions on the moon's surface. It's a preternatural event, dramatized all the more by an owl in the treetops of the whitebark pines near the cabin. I discover it not by sound (it makes no call) but by its spooky silhouette against the darkening blue-black sky. What kind is it? I immediately have to know. It looks large, though in the dark and without a real good standard of comparison I can't say exactly how big it is. I don't see any tufts on its head, which suggests it's not a great horned owl, and it seems larger than a barred owl, which I've seen on a number of occasions. A great gray owl, then? I want it to be this species, since I've never seen one before, and my bird book (which I read by headlamp) informs me that this is the right habitat (though at the very southern limit of its range). Before I can get another decent look at it, though, it flies off, disappearing into the dense cover of conifers below. I agonize the rest of the night over whether it's ethical for me to claim it as a great gray owl on my bird list.

Not until I review the following passage from *Walden* do I calm down sufficiently to go to sleep: "I rejoice that there are owls. Let them do the idiotic and maniacal hooting for men. It is a sound admirably suited to swamps and twilight woods which no day illustrates, suggesting a vast and undeveloped nature which men have not recognized. They represent the stark twilight and unsatisfied thoughts which all have."

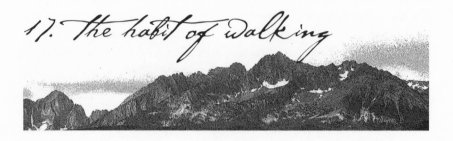

17. the habit of walking

I'm running low on water again (not to mention food) with only a few cubies left, and since my exact termination date is still unknown I figure I'd better make one last water run. I could get caught up here for a few days in a sudden blizzard and have to wait out the storm before the packer arrives. It's happened to other lookouts, though never to me. So one more time I hoist an empty cubie and packframe on my back and head down the hill.

As usual, I need to get out of the cabin anyway to once more dispel the ennui that has accumulated over the course of the day. I find that walking is the best way to rejuvenate my spirits and awaken my senses to the world around me. I've always been a walker, perhaps due to the fact that I come from a family of walkers. My mother and father loved to walk around our small town niched in the Pennsylvania hills, talking with townsfolk, checking out others' homes and gardens, and to take walks along the coal and slate-ridden roads through the woods behind our house, before the strip mines obliterated them. So I followed their example. When I reached sixteen I was in no hurry to get my driver's license — I preferred to walk (though my high school sweetheart eventually convinced me that a car was a good thing to have). Once I moved to Philadelphia to attend college, I lived off-campus in the center of the city, happy to have left my car behind, taking the subway or trolley to school, and every night after dinner returning to my apartment I would walk back and forth along Pine and Chestnut and Spruce streets, from Independence Mall to Rittenhouse Square, pondering the books I was reading in classes, life in the city, the beautiful girls in classes I was too shy to talk to — all the while politely declining the offers of the many men who asked me to visit their apartments. Philadelphia, City of Brotherly Love! And of course hiking in the woods and mountains of the Appalachians in places like Glen Onoko Falls, near Jim Thorpe, where I once saw three rattlesnakes on a single hike during an unbelievably hot, sticky, summer day, as I was making my way up the trail past the three separate terraces over which waterfalls tumble in increasingly dramatic fashion, smelling the snakes' split-cucumber scent before spotting them slither away. Then on to the Pacific Northwest and all those epic hikes in the Cascades — the Three Sisters, Goat Rocks, Indian Heaven, the Olympics, North Cascades. As well as regular city saunters in Portland, city of Roses: enduring the constant rain, walking the gauntlet of bums along Burnside Avenue, sampling the treats of Chinatown, Frankenstein's, Produce Row, Elephant & Castle, The Streudel House, Forest Park. That interminably gray, cloud-shrouded, drizzly, conifer-darkened landscape! Followed by the northern Rockies of Idaho and many epic climbs and hikes, from the Selkirks to the Seven Devils to the Sawtooths. On to northern California: walks along College and Telegraph avenues in Berkeley, Market and Montgomery streets in San Francisco, hikes on the trails of the East Bay Hills, Point Reyes, climbs in the mighty Sierra skying out at nearly fifteen thousand feet! Finally, Midwestern exile, Iowa and Minnesota, the sweeping skies, the expansive prairies and lakes, the claustrophobic North Woods. In my life I have walked many landscapes. And hope to walk many more.

I think of my favorite section of Whitman's "Song of Myself":

I tramp a perpetual journey, (come listen all!)
My signs are a rain-proof coat, good shoes, and a staff cut from the
     woods,
No friend of mine takes his ease in my chair,
I have no chair, no church, no philosophy,
I lead no man to a dinner-table, library, exchange,
But each man and each woman of you I lead upon a knoll,
My left hand hooking you round the waist,
My right hand pointing to landscapes of continents and the public
     road.

Not I, not any one else can travel that road for you,
You must travel it for yourself.
It is not far, it is within reach,
Perhaps you have been on it since you were born and did not know,
Perhaps it is everywhere on water and on land.

Shoulder your duds dear son, and I will mine, and let us hasten
    forth,
Wonderful cities and free nations we shall fetch as we go.

I once read an estimate, based on a reading of Wordsworth's journals, that the great Romantic poet walked something like over one hundred thousand miles in his lifetime, all over the hills and dales of the Lake District. I want to out-hike Wordsworth.

In one of his most famous essays, "Walking," Thoreau wrote that "I think that I cannot preserve my health and spirits, unless I spend four hours a day at least — and it is commonly more than that — sauntering through the woods and over the hills and fields, absolutely free from all worldly engagements." The ultimate provincial, he boasted that "an absolutely new prospect is a great happiness, and I can still get this any afternoon. Two or three hours walking will carry me to as strange a country as I expect ever to see." For Thoreau, the wild — which he believed was inextricably connected to walking — always lay nearby, if only one was attentive and ambitious enough: "I can easily walk ten, fifteen, twenty, any number of miles, commencing at my own door, without going by any house, without crossing a road except where the fox and the mink do: first along by the river, and then the brook, and then the meadow and the woodside. There are square miles in my vicinity which have no inhabitant."

Imagine what Thoreau would have written had he been unleashed in the 2.4 million acre Frank Church–River of No Return Wilderness.

The pleasures of walking. They are suggested by our various words for the act, each with its own history and nuances: stroll, saunter, amble, perambulate, sojourn, promenade, march, tramp, traipse, trek, trudge, hike, mosey. Whatever the connotation, to walk requires that you move with your senses alive and alert to the surroundings.

I head down the trail, focusing on the now, the immediate, the world around me, the real world, the only world that matters. Arriving on the shore of the first lake, I take a deep breath, smell the rich, sweet scent of decaying vegetation in the air, feel the cool damp air of the lake basin on my arms, listen to the ever-present sound of water tinkling downhill.

The show begins. While filling up the cubie I spook a spotted sandpiper, and it "peet-weets peet-weets" in panic and flies to the opposite shore, bobbing up and down, teetering precariously on its ridiculously thin legs. I walk around the shore and flush some strange birds out of a dwarf subalpine fir. Once I focus in on them with the binocs, I realize they're a new species for me — pine grosbeaks! (orange-headed, buffy-breasted, with white wing-bars and exaggerated, overlapping, dark beaks). *Yes.* Rounding the lake I hear a WHOOSH! and cry, and spot a prairie falcon dive-bombing the sandpiper. Moments later I glimpse a Cooper's hawk plunging into the brush after a songbird of some kind. It apparently fails, then perches in a nearby snag, seemingly unperturbed.

I trudge up the switchbacks once more with forty pounds of water sloshing on my back. Just as I ascend the final summit plateau I see the glow of what appears to be a fire burning behind a ridge. I stop dead in my tracks. Then I realize that it's the light of a gibbous moon rising through some clouds, having just breached the horizon. I laugh, recalling the story of the lookout who once reported a moonrise as a forest fire. The blaze was promptly dubbed "the lunar complex," and the lookout was never allowed to live it down.

Back in the cabin I write and read till I can read and write no more.

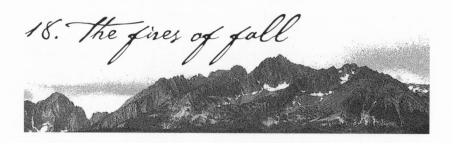

18. The fires of fall

The next day, a brilliantly warm Indian summer afternoon, I'm standing on the catwalk, completely in the buff, cleaning the windows for what I truly hope is the last time of the season. There is no chore more tedious than cleaning all 144 window panes, inside and out, of a fire lookout cabin.

Suddenly I hear Bernie on Little Soldier lookout report on the radio: "Low-flying military jet flying over Little Soldier heading toward Ruffneck."

Too late.

For even as I turn my head northeast, in the direction of Little Soldier Mountain, I see then hear the dot of an aircraft approaching at subsonic speed (400 MPH?), and before I know it the jet roars by not more than fifty feet from the cabin. I can almost see the pilot's face in the cockpit of the F-15, a fiery metal projectile that represents for scientists, engineers, and military men the very best combination of technology and physical skill: Top Gun. Since this kind of incident has happened a number of times before — it's common for the military to schedule training runs for their pilots and planes across the empty spaces of the American West, wilderness areas though they may be — I try hard not to flinch and, in the most demonstrative gesture I can muster, flip the pilot the bird. But the noise alone just about knocks me off my feet. Truth is, I'm terrified by the encounter. Imagine then if this were war and the pilot had launched a thousand pound smart bomb at the lookout.

The military has long used the West as its playground, and every summer I've been on a lookout, I and my fellow firewatchers report numerous buzzings by fighter jets on training runs. The pilots, I'm told, are particularly interested in flying close by lookouts to see if there are women sun-bathing in the nude on the roofs of the cabins (which they have been known to do). I'm terribly sorry to have disappointed this particular sky cowboy, but maybe the sight of me naked on the catwalk will be enough to dissuade him from undertaking future practice bombing runs near fire lookouts. Though I doubt it.

The next day I awaken to ragged, fleecy clouds and howling winds from the southwest. We haven't had a storm in these parts for what seems like weeks, and my lookout instincts tell me that we're due for one today. The morning weather forecast bears out my feeling: LAL today is four to five. Ollie the dis-patcher reports that a late-season thunderstorm is heading our way. North-ern California got caught by surprise and was hit hard yesterday; today may well be our turn. Good thing I cleaned the windows.

By early afternoon the clouds have been whipped to a frothy fury by the ever-increasing winds. Lightning, accompanied by little rain, begins to strike to the northwest about six miles away, on the flanks of Big Soldier Mountain just east of the Middle Fork of the Salmon River. Once again I'm pumped full of fear and adrenaline.

It's a quickly developing and fast-moving front, and within half an hour the storm is tracking east along the canyon of the Middle Fork towards Little Soldier Mountain. Now is the time for maximum watchfulness, as the spots struck by lightning heat up in the afternoon warmth and decreasing humidity. Perhaps, fanned by winds, some of the spots will begin to burn and smoke — in a stump, a snag, a still-living tree. I have seen lightning scars spiraling up and around a hundred-foot Doug fir like a staircase, the tree still intact, alive, even thriving.

The waiting continues. Then, at 3:05 P.M. I spot a clearly defined column of smoke rising on the south slopes of Big Soldier Mountain. I rush to the firefinder and take a bearing: 305 degrees. I look at the fire with binoculars again, then study the map, check the actual terrain once more, and decide that the fire is located near the head of Patrol Creek, just south of Cut Throat Lake. This time I don't even write the info down but radio it immediately to Challis Dispatch. I'm worried that Thunderbolt Mountain lookout to the northwest of the fire on the Boise National Forest probably has a good look at this same smoke, too, and I don't want him to scoop me in reporting it. Dispatch records the info, then, in an unusual display of emotion, tells me, "Good job!" They too are excited about some action after weeks of drought and inactivity.

Within half an hour, smokejumper plane 4-0 Zulu from McCall is over the fire dropping colorful plastic streamers — to ascertain wind direction and speed — then unloading the jumpers, four in all. Once on the ground they gather their gear and assess the fire. It's less than an eighth of an acre in size, burning in a couple of subalpine firs. There's water from a creek nearby to help them extinguish it. I make contact with jumper Hudson, the incident commander, and we chat for a bit, knowing each other from previous forests and fires. "Have a good fire," I tell him, then sign off.

The next morning they have the fire extinguished and are flown out by helicopter back to McCall.

19. Worship

A wet cold front moves in by mid-September. I walk along the lookout trail and sniff the rich sweet scent of decaying vegetation — the leaves of the brush are fading, falling, dying. It reminds me of what a friend who lived in the backcountry of northern Idaho once said about the onset of sadness that she always felt in autumn. The mass disappearance of life depressed her, and she took to baking and quilting and other indoor projects as a way of coping with the inevitable melancholy of fall.

I have always loved autumn for its rich hues and textures and scents, so her remark struck me as poignant. I remember that near the end of *Pilgrim at Tinker Creek*, Annie Dillard comes to cope with the general dominance of death over life and the resulting melancholy of autumn by interpreting simple and seemingly insignificant events — a maple key falling from a tree, or a goldfinch sowing a field with thistledown — as evidence of the cycle of life renewed. It was her way of reconciling the existence of mass death and suffering of many different creatures with the Christian belief in an omnipotent, omniscient, and loving God.

Rosemary, my visitor from southern Idaho the other day, told me to visit the church in Stanley sometime. Maybe I will. But I think I have been in church all summer. As Emily Dickinson once wrote,

> Some worship God by going to church
> I worship him staying at home
> with a bobolink for a chorister
> and an orchard for a throne.

Sunday morning. As I write, clouds swirl and fill up the valley below, enveloping the peaks and ridges. I am temporarily whited out, and a sense of disorientation sweeps over me — I have lost my bearings. For balance and comfort I look inward. On this fog-filled day, it's a time for introspection. I think about church, about worship, about religion.

Sunday morning. This phrase denotes not only the time and day but also the title of my favorite poem in all of literature. Written by Wallace Stevens in the 1920s, it describes the inner conflict a woman experiences as she wakes up on Easter morning and feels guilty over indulging herself in the sensuous delights of home rather than going to church.

> Complacencies of the peignoir, and late
> Coffee and oranges in a sunny chair,
> And the green freedom of a cockatoo
> Upon a rug mingle to dissipate
> The holy hush of ancient sacrifice.
> She dreams a little, and she feels the dark
> Encroachment of that old catastrophe,
> As a calm darkens among water-lights.

I was introduced to this poem in college when I first began to question the relevance of Catholicism, the religion I had been raised on. As I grew older and read more and more critiques of Catholicism in particular and Christianity in general — most notable among them Lynn White's "The Historical Roots of the Ecologic Crisis" — I came to reject the Church because I found it remote, overly institutionalized, and hypocritical. The priests who had never known a woman admonishing me not to fantasize about girls. The insistence on giving more money as the collection basket went around. The high style of the fathers who drove around in Cadillacs. To say nothing of the Church's role in colonialist enterprises across the globe.

But what would take its place? I realized that I felt a deep, resonant spirituality when out in the woods, particularly after I moved to the West and spent much of my free time hiking and backpacking. Gradually I came to experience this same reverence in all places out-of-doors; I discovered, as theologian Belden Lane has put it, "*sacred place is ordinary place, ritually made extraordinary.*" I realized that there is more to the wilderness than sublime, monumental landscapes; that the wild — like God, Spirit, call it what you will — is present everywhere. So I identified with the woman in "Sunday Morning" who was inspired by everyday sensual delights:

Why should she give her bounty to the dead?
What is divinity if it can come
Only in silent shadows and in dreams?
Shall she not find in comforts of the sun,
In pungent fruit and bright, green wings, or else
In any balm or beauty of the earth,
Things to be cherished like the thought of heaven?

Yet the woman is not convinced, not quite ready to sign on with a religion of the tangible. She vacillates between feeling that there is nothing, no system of religious beliefs "that has endured / As April's green endures," and comes to recognize that "in contentment I still feel / The need of some imperishable bliss." Then come my favorite, most paradoxical words of the entire poem: "Death is the mother of beauty." This is one way to explain the necessity of death and suffering: it makes way for those yet to come, for the beauty of birth, the beginnings of new life. Death gives birth to beauty. Those falling, dying leaves on the brush below the lookout will form the detritus, the organic material necessary for future plants and animals to grow and flourish.

In the penultimate stanza, the woman envisions a pagan ritual in which men "chant in orgy on a summer morn / Their boisterous devotion to the sun." In this newly imagined version of religion it is god, not God, who dances with the worshipers, "Naked among them, like a savage source" — an accessible, democratic deity much more in keeping with the tangible presence of the speaker's religious passion. But the last stanza ends on an ambiguous note, as if to suggest that she has not — and perhaps never will — decide with finality her religious beliefs.

We live in an old chaos of the sun,
Or old dependency of day and night,
Or island solitude, unsponsored, free,
Of that wide water, inescapable.
Deer walk upon our mountains, and the quail
Whistle about us their spontaneous cries;
Sweet berries ripen in the wilderness;
And, in the isolation of the sky,
At evening, casual flocks of pigeons make
Ambiguous undulations as they sink,
Downward to darkness, on extended wings.

This is what I have taken from this poem: One can be intensely religious and spiritual without being Christian, without being a member of any religious institution or group. I prefer to worship (if that is the term that must be used) alone, in nature, at any time, uttering no chant or hymn or prayer, making no predetermined set of gesticulations, paying homage to no one or thing in particular. The term I invoke for myself (through reading Annie Dillard) is *anchorite*: one who seeks seclusion for religious reasons. I have a few close friends, whom I prefer to keep at a distance; but the older I get the more it seems that I prefer to spend most of my time alone in nature. Loren Eiseley writes in *The Immense Journey* that "it is a commonplace of all religious thought, even the most primitive, that the man seeking visions and insight must go apart from his fellows and live for a time in the wilderness." That statement, along with Stevens's poem, has functioned as a kind of touchstone for most of my adult life. Another guiding light on this subject for me has been Kathleen Norris, a contemporary essayist and poet from the Midwest who has spent a significant amount of time in monasteries. She observes in *The Cloister Walk* that "the monastic life has this in common with the artistic one: both are attempts to pay close attention to objects, events, and natural phenomena that otherwise get chewed up in the daily grind. One of the things I like most about monastic people is the respect they show for the holy hours of sunrise and sunset." Norris would make a good fire lookout, I think.

To live up here, in this monastery in the clouds, is to live a life mostly unobtruded on by all the indulgences and distractions of syphilization, closer to the fundamental realities and spiritual essence of life. When Jack Kerouac, a former fire lookout himself, wrote *The Dharma Bums*, based in part on his and Gary Snyder's lookout life in the North Cascades, he created a character named Japhy Ryder (modeled after Snyder) who avowed:

> The closer you get to real matter,
> rock air fire wood,
> the more spiritual the world is.

I came to lookout life twenty years ago troubled and confused and angry about religion and my religious beliefs; now I am no longer troubled and angry, just confused. Comfortably confused. Or maybe not so much confused as still searching for answers to questions about the way the world appears to work. I am far less judgmental of Christianity, recognize that much good has been and continues to be done in its name, have no desire to appropriate religions from other cultures that do not appear to suit my own

Season-ending snowstorm on Ruffneck.

Americanized tastes and preferences, and am happy to combine in eclectic fashion whatever religious beliefs I see as offering something appealing and worthwhile.

I am an alpine anchorite.

By late afternoon the temperatures drop and the rain turns to snow. I have been enveloped in clouds all day. I make tea, write in my journal, and stare into the clouds. I have not seen one other living thing for days — not a bug, bird, or mammal. I am completely alone and quite happy in this mountain solitude.

The next day I awaken to a world of white: swirling clouds and a snow-glazed summit. On the cabin, the trees, the ground is an inch of ice-encrusted snow. The wind is howling and with the air temperature at twenty-five degrees and the winds (I'd estimate) at 30 MPH, the windchill is well below zero. I hurriedly put on all the clothes I can — polypropylene long underwear, sweater, parka — hustle outside and back in with fire-wood, and stoke up the little wood stove. I fire up the Coleman stove and heat water for coffee and begin to fix an enormous panful of *huevos rancheros*. I'll have to consume a lot of calories today to stay warm.

The cloud ceiling has risen above me but just barely, revealing a snow line around nine thousand feet. I call Bernie on Little Soldier and he tells me that he got hailed and rained on last night, but no snow fell. At eighty-eight hundred feet he's a bit lower than Ruffneck, confirming my estimate of the snow line's elevation. We chat and joke for a bit. This storm has the feel of a terminator, signaling the end of another fire season. And with it the end of our employment as fire lookouts.

Dispatch confirms this hunch later in the morning. "We'll get the packer up to you guys in the next couple days," Ollie tells us after the weather forecast. "In the meantime looks like you'll have an easy one today." Yes indeed — it's a good day to

> wrap up in a blanket
> and just read.

But first I want to walk out into this wintry world and feel the sting of cold air on my face. That's one of the many advantages of working a fire lookout; if I were backpacking in the mountains and caught in a storm like this, I'd most likely hike out or certainly down below to warmer, hopefully drier weather. Living up here in the cabin, on the other hand, I've got a cozy and comfortable base camp on the mountaintop from which to explore. So after breakfast I saunter around the summit, exploring this *terra blanca*, a landscape blanketed by the snow. I have the satisfaction of breaking trail, of knowing for certain that where I go no person has gone before — at least since the storm.

Amazingly, I see a pair of finches flitting from tree to tree. Cassin's finch: a bird of the high mountains, its rosy red head adds a cheery hue to the otherwise monochromatic landscape. The whitebark pines on which these two perch now remind me of Christmas trees, their strong sinewy boughs laden with snow and ice. I break out into song, belt out a carol or two, and I find that singing improves my mood measurably. I'm soon going down, heading home, returning to civilization, and for that I am grateful.

All good things must come to an end.

winter

20. last visitors

> Get ready for the snow
> get ready
> to go down.

And then there was one.

I got the word today from Dispatch. I'm to be "terminated" (without prejudice) in two days. Since Bobette on Pinyon Peak went down weeks ago and Bernie on Little Soldier is being packed out today, that leaves Ruffneck as the last remaining lookout on the Challis National Forest for the 1990 fire season.

The quiet radio suggests that there is no civilization to return to. That can't be, I insist; there's too much I've been longing for, too much I've been anticipating, these last few days, now that I know for sure the season is coming to an end. I want to walk the chaotic, funky, bohemian streets of the Uptown neighborhood of Minneapolis, chug a frosty cold mug of Summit pale ale, eat a five-star dinner at Lucia's, chomp on a brick of a raspberry-chocolate brownie from Roberto Gelati's, browse the bookshelves of Border's and Maguin's, perhaps finish the night with a café latté at Starbucks. I've had it with Langer Lakes, the Sawtooths, the Middle Fork, the River of No Return Wilderness; now I want to circumambulate the shore of Lake Calhoun, check out all the beautiful people, hear the white noise of nearby freeway traffic, inhale the diesel exhaust of a Metro Transit bus, run a gauntlet of panhandlers on Hennepin Avenue, and gawk at the downtown skyscrapers from my car on I-35. I look forward to coming home after a hard day at the office and collapsing in my La-Z-Boy with remote in hand, turning on ITN's "World News" and swooning over Daljit Dhaliwal, my favorite news anchor, then laughing out loud while watching *Seinfeld* reruns. Most of all, I yearn to again be with my wife, my best friend and lover, and put an end to this self-mythologizing narrative of one (more) white male wandering in the wilderness. Good-bye Idaho, home to neo-Nazis, troglodyte politics, potato heads and grousebrains; hello again to the upper Midwest, Minnesota nice, Scandinavian social liberalism, land of Youbetcha. It's not, it's never been, the city *versus* the wilderness; it should always be the city *and* the wilderness. People, to retain their humanity and their wildness, desperately need them both. My definition of an ideal home is a place in or close to a major metropolitan area within a half day's drive of a large wilderness area. Where one can reap the benefits of both culture and nature.

But first there are still more sensory delights to experience in the River of No Return Wilderness.

Puttering about the cabin in the morning, trying to stay warm by drinking lots of coffee, keeping the stove well-stoked, I happen to look out the west windows and detect some movement. About ten feet away, there's an animal hopping and prancing about in the inch or so of snow that remains on the summit since the last storm. It's maybe a foot long, has a three-inch tail, with a lovely red back and tawny belly, sleek and slim, a muscled ribbon. It seems to have turned snow-white to match its surroundings in the winter. I consult the mammal guide. Yes: an ermine! A member of the weasel family, the ermine like its other cousins has a valuable fur prized by trappers; according to the guidebook, its black-tipped tails are the traditional trim on the robes of royalty. I value the ermine solely for the pleasure I derive in watching its antics. It pauses, then leaps up into the air and pounces into the snow, apparently searching for mice. I implore it to rid me of the pests that have all summer raided my supplies of rice, pasta, cereal, etc. The ermine prates about for half an hour before it finally relents, then departs, prey-less. Near the end of my mostly solitary stay, it has proved a welcome companion on the summit.

The silence is broken by a call from dispatch. I'm to have one last uninvited visitor of the season, a lake surveyor from the Forest Service in the area who will be using the lookout as a base camp from which to operate the next day or two. She should be arriving later in the afternoon.

As with other uninvited guests I've had this season, I feel ambivalent about the surprise visit. On the one hand, company — especially female company — would be nice, since it's been a couple of weeks since my last visitors. On the other hand I was hoping and expecting to spend my last days on the lookout alone, savoring the solitude and privacy of the cabin. Now I'm faced with sharing my home with another person, a stranger at that, and the thought kind of rankles.

I watch for my visitor in the morning from the lookout. I soon spot a hiker and a dog making their way over the divide that separates the Finger Lakes from the Langer Lakes basin, each carrying a bright red pack; they must be my pending guests. My guess is confirmed a couple hours later when a petite woman comes striding up the summit with a huge German shepherd and introduces herself as Seeta and her dog as Blacky. She breaks open her pack and pulls out a bag of Pepperidge Farm cookies — my favorite, double chocolate Milanos! Let's celebrate my arrival, she says, and I'm glad to oblige.

Seeta is from the Bitterroot Valley in Montana, where she has been homesteading with a number of other alternative life-stylers for the last ten years. As a small but cohesive community, they've collectively built their own passive solar houses and farm as much of their food as they can during the short growing season of the northern Rockies. Many of them work seasonally for the Forest Service, and in the winter take to the road and market various artisans' products. Seeta herself makes and sells daypacks at college fairs across the West. I examine one of her products: tough triple stitching, padded shoulder straps, heavy metal zippers, rugged and colorful fabric. It's durable art.

Curious to know more about the work she's doing on the lakes, I ask her for details. The Forest Service, concerned over the potential effects of acid rain resulting from pollution blown into the Salmon River Mountains from the more populated West Coast, has hired technicians to sample water from the lakes in the River of No Return Wilderness. Her job on this trip is to return to Challis with one-pint bottles of water taken from Finger, Mable, and Langer lakes, where they'll be shipped to a university lab in Missoula and analyzed for their acidity. It's unclear exactly how the Forest Service will help determine government policy regarding the amount of emissions on the West Coast when the effects are being felt in the Rocky Mountains, but at least the agency appears to be doing something about the problem. Which may be exactly its strategy: pacify through some form of action, even if the action is superficial or ineffectual.

As longtime seasonal employees of the Forest Service, Seeta and I are rightfully skeptical of the agency's motives and practices. She has been working for the agency since the 1970s: as part of a helitack crew in Alaska, as a lookout in California and Montana, and as a member of a river patrol on the Middle Fork. She loves the outdoor work in the American West, has loved it ever since she left home in Rhode Island when she was seventeen to work for the Curry Company in Yosemite National Park. From there Seeta managed to work her way all over the West, spending significant time in the most spectacular scenery in the country. Now employed regularly on the Middle Fork District of the Challis National Forest and owner of land in the Edenic Bitterroot Valley, she has achieved stability and beauty in her life.

Seeta warms up by the wood stove, shedding layers of clothing. She passes on a good lookout story. A few summers ago she was working Hells Half Acre lookout on the Bitterroot National Forest. Her boyfriend of the time managed to get a few days off from his job as a river guide on the Middle Fork and hiked up to her cabin to see her for the first time in weeks. Understandably they didn't get much sleep during his visit, and not only because a thunderstorm raged one night. A party of visitors arrived the next morning. One of them cast a wary look at a nearby ridge and said, "Isn't that what a forest fire looks like?" Seeta rubbed the sleepiness from her eyes and said nonchalantly, "Oh, that's just another control burn being done by the Forest Service." This statement may have struck the visitor as rather odd, given that the fire was burning during the height of summer in a wilderness area. As soon as the party left, Seeta called in the smoke, and no one was the wiser for it.

For dinner I make spaghetti. To the sauce Seeta adds broccoli fresh from her garden, and we drink the red wine she's brought up for the visit. As a former lookout she is mindful of lookout protocol: when visiting a lookout, especially towards the end of the fire season, always be sure to bring goodies from civilization like fresh produce, chocolate, and alcohol. I thank her profusely for these treasures and tell her she can visit anytime.

We talk about life in the Bitterroot Valley. Since it's only fifty miles south of Missoula, which is home to the University of Montana, residents can enjoy the benefits of both the rustic life and the more cultured metropolis, without having to endure congestion, crime, and pollution (though Missoula does suffer many inversions and bad air, especially during the winter months, because it lies in a valley surrounded by mountains). There is a sizable contingent of Earth First!, the radical environmentalist group, living in the area. Howie Wolke, a founding member, is a neighbor of Seeta's. We get into a discussion about the group's tactics and strategy. As a longtime admirer of Ed Abbey, the spiritual founder of Earth First!, I'm sympathetic to the group's goals but am troubled by its disregard for the consequences of radical environmentalism, particularly for working class people. For instance, by spiking trees — driving large metal stakes into timber slated for logging — and then warning logging companies and the Forest Service that they have done so, Earth First!ers have successfully blocked some of the cutting of old growth forests in the West. But what happens to the loggers and mill workers who were to earn a living wage from harvesting those trees? Of course, as environmentalists have pointed out, many of the trees are shipped raw to Japan anyway, rather than processed by American mill workers, so few people besides corporate executives actually benefit monetarily from the logging. But with no trees to be cut, workers in the timber industry must inevitably suffer, and I worry about what happens to them and their families.

Seeta seems unconcerned with their fate. Let them retrain, she says, like I have; they can find other, more earth-friendly, marketable skills if they try. But what is a guy who's worked all his life as a logger supposed to do instead? Work as a chambermaid in some tacky tourist resort? It's not that easy to find alternative careers that are meaningful and pay a living wage, especially in the rural West. Adapt or die, Seeta says. It's time for a new wave of inhabitants of the West — smart savvy youths who've lived elsewhere and can satisfy the demands of the global economy — to repopulate the region. As for the older residents with their traditional extractive skills in logging, ranching, and mining — well, they don't seem to have much of a future in the increasingly high-tech, ecologically conscious marketplace.

I'm impressed with her determination but appalled by her arrogance. Doesn't the tale of native inhabitants removed against their will by arrogant outsiders have a familiar ring to it? If the history of the West, if the history of the Americas, if the history of the world for that matter, teaches us anything, it is that colonization and narrow-mindedness have far-reaching, unforeseen, disastrous consequences for both oppressor and oppressed. Shouldn't we try to avoid repeating the tragedies of the past?

To Seeta I must seem like a cautious academic, one paralyzed by inaction because I'm forever worrying about the various consequences of each alternative — the What-if syndrome. She has never been to college, she tells me, which is surprising; I find her bright, articulate, confident, and assertive. She goes on to say she has little respect for Christianne and Lisa, the two college volunteers from Harvard and Brown who'd worked on the Middle Fork district earlier in the season. Snickering, she says there's no place for "Ivy leaguers" in the West because "ivy doesn't grow well out here." Moreover, she had no patience for their "classroom feminism." "They haven't even been out in the real world yet. What do they know about working for or with men? I live feminism, rather than only study it from some book," she says.

All this gets very heavy for what should be a festive visit between two strangers. Suddenly the cabin gets very quiet. We both feel awkward, and Seeta apologizes for being rude in my home. I tell her that I respect the honesty of her opinions.

The awkwardness ends abruptly with a radio call from Jack the FMO, who wants to thank me for another good season and wish me well for the winter. I tell him to have a good off season too — "Don't get too bored stuck in the office all winter, you hear?" — then sign off.

The next morning after breakfast — Seeta has brewed some wonderfully exotic coffee she bought in Missoula — we exchange shy, embarrassed good-byes. She and Blacky head down the trail to take more water samples, first from the Mable Lakes chain, then Langer Lakes, on their way out. I spend the rest of the morning scribbling furiously in my journal. Around noon the sun finally emerges from a thick cloud bank.

I get yet another unexpected visitor later in the day. A friend from nearby Lowman comes stomping up the trail, backpack heavily laden with beer and other goodies for the night. I'd been expecting him earlier in the season, but when he didn't show up, figured he had made other plans. "Better late than never," he says, pausing for breath on the steps of the cabin. "We better drink this case of beer tonight, because I'm sure as hell not gonna pack it back down." It's a proposal with which I readily agree.

The Vickster and I go way back. We grew up together in the coal country of northeastern Pennsylvania. We played against each other in Little League baseball, and competed for the same girlfriends in high school. Not anywhere near as athletic or intelligent as I, the Vickster chose the one sport which requires neither athleticism nor intelligence: wrestling. I, meanwhile, went on to play basketball, a sport that demands both. After college we headed west, he as a schoolteacher in Montana and me to law school. We soon started backpacking and climbing in the mountains of the West. Gradually it became a custom for us to rendezvous at least once a year for some trekking in the wilderness. We hiked the Muir Trail together and have also backpacked in the Wind River and Bighorn ranges of Wyoming, as well as the Sawtooths. Vick worked his way up from teacher to principal, then got burned out after a stint as an administrator, and decided to demote himself, becoming a janitor at a one-room schoolhouse in Lowman, where his wife teaches. He's much happier now, making far less money but having far more free time to climb mountains. He's redefined the concept of upward mobility.

As well as bag peaks, he likes to harass friends who work on nearby lookouts; visiting me atop Ruffneck, he can do both. He guffaws when I tell him what a busy fire season I've had, claiming that someone must have set all the fires with my knowledge so I could then speedily and accurately report them, just to make myself look good. He chides me for taking a sedentary job like this when I could be climbing with him every weekend in the Sawtooths. He tells me how easy I have it as a college professor, teaching only a couple classes a semester and getting paid a huge salary to boot, when teachers like his wife are slaving in the trenches for peanuts. Finally he wants to know how my book on lookout life is coming and how many chapters are devoted to him. After all, he reminds me, "I'm the only person to have visited you on every lookout you worked. I deserve recognition!"

The Vickster is a born skeptic. He doesn't believe in freeze-dried food; instead, he cracks open a huge Tupperware container to reveal a deep-dish pizza he's made himself for our dinner tonight. No complaints from me on that score. Nor does he believe in purifying his water in the wilderness; when I offer him some iodine tablets or a pump-filter to use for the water I've hauled up from the lake, he waves me off and chugs a quart's worth, claiming, "The day I have to filter my water from the wilderness is the day I stop going to the wilderness." Maybe that's why you have to take an emergency dump after every meal you eat, I suggest. Finally, he apparently doesn't believe in banks either. He tosses his wallet wadded with cash on the table and I ask him what he needs all the money for. "You never know when you might need to bargain for — a ride, a beer, or something else," he says with a sinister smile. And I respond: that's the only way you're gonna get any.

The mutual ribbing goes on all night. After many beers and slices of pizza, we are rolling on the floor, hysterical with laughter. We tell for the umpteenth time the same stories about our basketball and wrestling coaches from high school days. We also give each other massive shit about mishaps and bailouts on The Trail. Like when Victor had to pull out of our Muir Trail hike back in 1991 with only three days left (after backpacking most of the 220-mile route for nearly three weeks) because of aching feet. Or like when I nearly collapsed from exhaustion on a backpack in the Sawtooths a few years later after he badly miscalculated the miles we needed to go one day. I mimic him hobbling on swollen feet, arm extended, thumb out, hitchhiking a ride home; he imitates me bent over my walking stick on a steep switchback, unable to go a step further. We reprise endless scenes from *Seinfeld* episodes, a show to which we both have become addicted. Master of Your Domain, the Ass Man, the Soup Nazi. In fact, I call V the K-Man, after Kramer, the sitcom's most zany character, because his surname begins with a K and because, like Kramer, he is one of a kind.

Shit-faced and bleary-eyed, we both wake up late the next morning. After a light breakfast (a snort of JD, one more for the road), the K-Man heads down the hill, promising to give me a ride to the airport when I come down. Adios, compadre.

I decide to go for one last walk before the packer arrives tomorrow.

21. Disappearances

The temperatures have remained surprisingly cold since the last storm blew in — thirties during the day and twenties at night, with strong winds — so the little snow that fell, an inch or two, remains as it lay a couple of days ago, piled up in cornices in the cabin's windward sides, forming balls in the turned-up boughs of the conifers, dusting the ground with powder. I recite Emerson's "The Snowstorm" as I walk down the trail:

> Announced by all the trumpets of the sky,
> Arrives the snow, and driving o'er the fields,
> Seems nowhere to alight: the whited air
> Hides hills and woods, the river, and the heaven,
> And veils the farm-house at the garden's end.
> The sled and traveller stopped, the courier's feet
> Delayed, all friends shut out, the housemates sit
> Around the radiant fireplace, enclosed
> In a tumultuous privacy of storm.
>
> Come see the north wind's masonry
> Out of an unseen quarry evermore
> Furnished with tile, the fierce artificer
> Curves his white bastions with projected roof
> Round every windward stake, or tree, or door.
> Speeding, the myriad-handed, his wild work
> So fanciful, so savage, nought cares he
> For number or proportion. Mockingly,
> On coop or kennel he hangs Parian wreaths;

A swan-like form invests the hidden thorn;
Fills up the farmer's lane from wall to wall,
Maugre the farmer's sighs, and at the gate,
A tapering turret overtops the work.
And when his hours are numbered, and the world
Is all his own; retiring, as he were not,
Leaves, when the sun appears, astonished Art
To mimic in slow structures, stone by stone,
The frolic architecture of the snow.

I love that last line in particular.

No sun appears today in these parts though. The clouds, hovering at around ten thousand feet, seem stalled over the Salmon River Mountains. The morning weather forecast confirms as much; Ollie at Dispatch, reading the report, spoke of this cold front as a season-ending "terminator," chasing all seasonal employees back to their winter homes.

Far down in the basin, I see dark birds flap through the mist, hear them croaking for blood. Ravens. Closer, I see a couple of Canada jays flitting about the trees, searching for food in these cold hard times. A lone Clark's nutcracker is also on the prowl, its black and white wings on showy display. Otherwise, aside from the occasional gust of wind, it's eerily quiet around the mountain. The cold and the silence enhance rather than stifle my senses, however, and I'm feeling ecstatic about being out-of-doors again, sniffing the fresh snow-scented air, kicking my toes against the solid rocks on the trail, feeling the bite of cold air on my cheeks. Despite the hangover, I'm quite alive and well on this late-September day in the River of No Return Wilderness.

The River of No Return. The name is associated with, conjures up, all kinds of historical memories. Of Lewis and Clark, of course, their turning back, daunted by the geography of the Main Salmon River. Of Impassable Canyon, the lower stretch of the Middle Fork which defied the trail builders of the CCC era. And, sadly, of the number of river runners who have drowned trying to take on the Salmon and Middle Fork.

I also think of another Western figure, nowhere near as well known as Lewis and Clark, someone who chose — so the legend goes, anyhow — not to return from the wilderness. Everett Ruess was a dreamy romantic raised in southern California in the early 1900s primarily by his mother, Stella, a devotee of the arts and an artist of sorts herself who wrote poetry and painted. In his late teens Ruess decided to shuck off the shackles of civilization and spend as much time as he could in the deserts of the Southwest: where better to minimize one's needs than in the land of endless sun? With a burro to carry his meager subsistence rations and artist's materials (he loved to sketch and once traded prints with Ansel Adams), he wandered from one desert to the next, in pursuit of his dream to achieve oneness with nature. Then in 1934 he vanished without a trace (as the saying goes) in the canyon country of southern Utah. Actually, traces did turn up years later, though whether they were of Ruess are still disputed. The word NEMO was found etched in a rock wall near where he is said to have disappeared. Followers of Ruess have theorized that perhaps this was an allusion to Captain Nemo of Jules Verne's *Twenty Thousand Leagues Under the Sea*, a figure who desired to escape all ties with humanity. NEMO is Latin for no one, and if scrawled by Ruess it suggests that indeed he did succeed in losing himself and his identity in the wild. Old camping equipment discovered in 1957 by an archaeologist along a tributary of the Colorado River may also constitute evidence of Ruess's whereabouts on his last outing. But the most intriguing memento he left behind is in the form of many letters he wrote to his parents and friends, collected and published in 1983 as a book entitled *Everett Ruess: A Vagabond for Beauty*. He wrote to his brother Waldo in 1932 that "I have been thinking more and more that I shall always be a lone wanderer of the wilderness. God, how the trail lures me. You cannot comprehend its resistless fascination for me. After all the lone trail is the best. . . . I'll never stop wandering. And when the time comes to die, I'll find the wildest, loneliest, most desolate spot there is." As a lone wanderer in the wilderness myself, I have long been fascinated with this dreamy, romantic hermit.

Did Everett Ruess deliberately set out to disappear and die in the desert at the young age of twenty? For someone who apparently loved life and the wilderness as much as any other, his death seems the epitome of living out one's philosophy to a contradictory extreme. At times I would prefer to think that Ruess's luck simply ran out — that he met with some unfortunate accident, got too close to the edge of a canyon rim and fell to his death, or drowned in the Colorado River. Or that he got swallowed up in the abyss of the desert, where his body was eventually scavenged and savored by vultures. But at other times, when I am in my most romantic, melancholy mood, I like to consider that Ruess simply chose not to return to syphilization, to remain and live — then die — in the wilderness.

Like his modern counterpart, Chris McCandless. Many are no doubt familiar with the details of his case. He was a graduate of Emory University in Atlanta who gave up several thousand dollars of savings to charity and wandered all over the West, from Mexico to Alaska. McCandless' heroes were John Muir and Jack London, and he renamed himself Alexander Supertramp, choosing to live in the wild with as little as possible. Finally in 1992 he hitchhiked to Alaska, near Denali National Park, and with a small-caliber rifle and ten-pound bag of rice sought to live off the land. His emaciated body was found several months later by a moose hunter in an abandoned school bus. The journals McCandless left behind reveal that he tried to return to civilization when he found he could not subsist in the wild. But, inexplicably, he did not reckon with the rise of the Alaskan rivers in spring when the snow melts, and so was stranded (or thought he was) and starved to death. Many people (especially Alaskans) dismissed him as a kooky novice ill-prepared to deal with the harsh rigors of the bush. But Jon Krakauer, who wrote *Into the Wild*, a riveting and sympathetic best-selling account of McCandless's travails, saw him as a symbol for many American males who are irresistibly drawn into the wilderness, who feel possessed by its spell as part of our nation's frontier heritage, and who seek to test and prove their manhood other than in combat and war.

One summer, on another mountain, my lookout routine was interrupted on an otherwise uneventful day by two frantic visitors. A man and his daughter from Illinois wanted to know if I'd seen any sign of his teenage son, who'd gotten separated from the rest of their hiking party on a trail in the wilderness area and whom they hadn't been able to relocate. No, I told him; I hadn't seen anyone until they arrived for weeks. This was in the Gospel Hump Wilderness, an isolated and seldom visited area just north of the Main Salmon, a region of steep rugged drainages. The boy had been missing for half the day, and if he'd wandered down into one of the creek bottoms full of boulders and blowdown his situation could get ugly fast. I called in to dispatch a description of him, and a search and rescue team was sent out. I then accompanied the father and daughter back to their camp at the trailhead, shouting the boy's name periodically as we walked the trail back along the ridgetop. Our shouts forlornly echoed back to us, making the wilderness suddenly seem dreary and desolate. A thunderstorm brewed in the late afternoon.

When we got to camp we discovered that the boy had been found by other members of the party. He'd fallen behind the group and taken a wrong turn at a junction in the trail. Hours later, after failing to catch up, he realized his error and backtracked. After seeing the joyous look in the father's eyes, I was grateful that this was one disappearance that was only temporary in nature.

As I walked back along the trail to the lookout, with the dark, dense, pathless maze of conifers on either side of me, I thought for a moment of how easy it would be to simply disappear in the woods, walk until I could walk no more, walk until some accident befell me, walk until I encountered a mountain lion or grizzly bear, which are rumored to be lingering in these mountains. Why not? How much better could life be than this, exploring and enjoying the last remnants of wilderness near the end of the twentieth century, before we're all done in by some toxic cloud, some incurable disease, some natural disaster actually of our own making?

But the fatalism of these thoughts appalled me, stopped me abruptly in my tracks. I reawakened to the reality that there is more day to dawn. No, I decided, I'm not quite ready to submit, to be vanquished by the doom-and-gloom predictions of overpopulation, pollution, exhaustion of natural resources, etc. If I'm going to disappear and die in the wilderness I want the decision and action to be an affirmative gesture, a sign of strength not weakness, a victory not a defeat. As I bounded up the last leg of the trail over the summit and the cabin came back into view, I thought *here* is where I'll make my last stand, write my last will and testament and ode of triumph to the world. And no smarmy, sentimental, costly funeral for me, with people gawking at my cold corpse in some fancy casket. Absolutely not. I want my remains cremated and my ashes scattered over these Salmon River Mountains, over this wilderness, where I've lived a full and richly textured life.

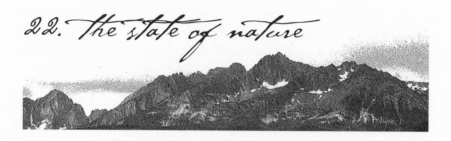

22. The state of nature

Ron the packer has just arrived on his horse, leading a string of a half-dozen mules. In addition to my books are a bunch of empty cubies and some trash to be hauled off the mountain after we button up the lookout for the season. So our load will be lighter but just as bulky going down as when we came up. I leave the little leftover canned food for the next resident of Ruffneck. Ron, very active as always, no sooner arrives than he is unwrapping the mannies and hoisting boxes onto the mules, grunting with the effort and muttering (in a good-natured way) about "the heaviness of the professor's books." I haul the boxes down from the cabin to help him out and tell him at least none of them is filled with bottles of alcohol, for which, good Mormon that he is, he's grateful.

The cabin, glass-walled for months, is turned into a cave again as we lower the shutters to protect the windows from the rigors of winter over the next nine months. I've mopped the floors, cleaned out the cupboards with antiseptic, and dusted the furniture. Finally, I cover the Osborne firefinder. I hate housework generally but take real pleasure from leaving the lookout in just as good shape as I found it a season ago.

I help load up the mules as Ron works his magic with the mannies and knots. He's ready to go after a quick sandwich. I tell him that as usual he can't stand to sit in one place for more than five minutes. He merely shakes his head in mock grief and drawls, "I know one thing — I'd never make it as a lookout."

He shakes his head again when I tell him that I'd prefer to walk down rather than ride a mule. But I insist that that's the way I want to leave: as slowly as possible, savoring the departure, making the descent under my own power. The temperature has warmed up into the fifties and snow lingers only in shady spots above the nine thousand-foot line. It's a good day for a last saunter down the mountain.

Once Ron and the pack train disappear below the summit plateau I take one final look at the surrounding countryside, all 360 degrees of mountains and ridges and valleys. The air is clear, having been scoured clean by the last couple storms, and I can't recall seeing the mountains in such brilliant relief. The Sawtooths, softened only a little by a recent dusting of snow, look rugged as ever. The castle-like ramparts of the White Clouds to the south are also snow-draped, as are the Bighorn Crags to the northeast. The Wallowas to the northwest in Oregon present the snowiest summits of all, thirty miles' worth of ten-thousand foot peaks.

I can see official, capital W wilderness in all directions. I have worked lookouts, and written this book, partly in order to meditate on the significance and importance of wilderness in my life and in American society generally; and to distinguish it from culture, its supposed antithesis, but also to emphasize its cultural roots. As I have mentioned, a number of environmental historians today are rightfully questioning and rethinking the meaning of wilderness. I agree with some of their concerns. On the one hand I recognize the possibility of the wild anywhere, from the River of No Return Wilderness in Idaho to Central Park in New York City, where wildness sometimes manifests itself in terrifying human behavior aptly named "wilding," to one's own backyard, where it can take the simple form of an invasive species of plant or animal. But, on the other hand, I also know that there exist few places on the globe that are truly free of some form of human activity or influence, past or present. We cannot neatly separate humans from wilderness because for more than twelve thousand years (in the Americas) we have been modifying our environments and because wilderness is in a sense an invention of human culture anyhow — at least in the sense of it as wild land, "where man is but a visitor." In the twentieth century, Americans like to think they can still escape to pristine lands, vast tracts of forests and mountains and desert where there is virtually no trace of human presence. But if we look closely, if we inquire into the local history of any landscape, we find that the notion of a pristine wilderness is a myth: there is or has been a human presence just about everywhere. The belief in a pristine wilderness is a very powerful one, to be sure, one that continues to exert all kinds of psychic and cultural influence. But it is a myth nonetheless. This has been a very important personal insight from my going native in the Frank Church.

Yet I also feel the need to defend the concept and existence of wilderness. We need a philosophy and practice of wilderness management that encompasses the Big Outside as well as the wilderness of everyone's backyard. Of course we ought to treat all land as sacred, live with every landscape in a sustainable way. But in at least one important respect my backyard wilderness will never equal the Frank Church: I will never be inspired or awed by it as I have been by the mountains and rivers of central Idaho. I will never be able to roam in my backyard as I have roamed in the 2.4-million-acre River of No Return Wilderness. I need a physical space commensurate with my capacity for wonder, a place big enough to wander on foot as well as in thought.

Thoreau is often celebrated as the exemplary inhabitor of the backyard wilderness, someone who discovered and praised the tonic of local wildness at the edge of Concord. Far fewer readers know about or remember the tales of his trips to the Big Outside, which in mid-nineteenth century New England meant the Maine woods. In 1851 Thoreau made the second of three wilderness excursions to Maine, all of them chronicled in the posthumously published *The Maine Woods*. He journeyed into the interior with an Indian guide and subsequently wrote an essay entitled "Chesuncook." So inspired was he by the existence of a large remnant tract of wildlands in the Northeast that in the conclusion of the essay he made one of the earliest calls for wilderness preservation:

> The kings of England formerly had their forests "to hold the king's game," for sport or food, sometimes destroying villages to create or extend them; and I think that they were impelled by a true instinct. Why should not we, who have renounced the king's authority, have our national preserves, where no villages need be destroyed, in which the bear and panther, and some even of the hunter race, may still exist, and not be "civilized off the face of the earth," — our forests, not to hold the king's game merely, but to hold and preserve the king himself also, the lord of creation, — not for idle sport or food, but for inspiration and our own true recreation?

Among environmental historians there is a controversial essay written by William Cronon entitled "The Trouble with Wilderness." I maintain that the main trouble with wilderness is that there's nowhere near enough of it.

Perhaps the biggest revelation resulting from my life in the wilderness is that in this culture of overconsumption, of rampant commercialism and ubiquitous commodification, we have come to assume that our wide-open expanses of wilderness exist as a matter of course. We forget too easily, or are unaware, that in other countries, in other cultures, the idea and existence of wilderness recreation is at best a luxury and at worst a laughable form of leisure activity carried on by affluent Americans who don't know what to do with all their money or free time. I mean, are people in Chiapas, in Bosnia, in Rwanda wondering where they'll go and what they'll do for the weekend in the local wilderness area? I think not. They are too preoccupied with survival: worrying about the source of their next meal, worrying about the state of their subsistence crops, worrying about escaping the horrors of ethnic cleansing. We take freedom for granted in this country, especially freedom of movement. The next time I canoe in the Boundary Waters Canoe Area Wilderness along the U.S.-Canadian border I'll be grateful that because we have long been at peace with our neighbors to the north I don't have to be concerned with avoiding land mines, snipers, or Stealth bombers. I will glide silently over the water and cross the portage trails comfortable in the knowledge that the only physical threats to my existence are perhaps getting caught between a mother bear and her cubs or getting trampled by a moose or being a victim of my own stupidity. That is exactly as it should be in the wilderness.

I have made it my life's work to experience and reflect on the possible connections between culture and wilderness, between freedom and nature. A few years ago I read *Landscape and Memory*, a wonderful work by historian Simon Schama tracing the evolution of Euroamerican attitudes towards nature. Schama's basic thesis is that buried in the collective memory of all cultures are myths and images of landscape that are important to them, that resonate throughout their history. In discussing forestry in Germany, for example, Schama points out that the Nazi state exercised strong control over the forests and even transformed forestry into a branch of state security. Order, over both the human and nonhuman world, was of paramount importance to the Hitler regime. Subsequently, in East Germany and in other countries behind the Iron Curtain, the Communists exerted similar degrees of authority over the woods.

One of the things that appeals to me about Schama's work is his emphasis on the power of place and the value of fieldwork. Schama followed the advice of his graduate school mentor: when doing research, always experi-

The author on Ruffneck Peak lookout.

ence the physical environment by using the "archives of the feet." So he paid a visit to Eastern Europe after the toppling of the Berlin Wall, where he toured a formerly state-run forest with a guide. Here is what he reports:

> The day before, our forester-guide, Wlodek, whose startling blue eyes smiled from a face the color of tree bark, had given us his landscape memories: of the woodlands east of Minsk where he grew up; of the borderlands of Hungary where he was caught by Soviet troops fleeing from the debacle of 1939; of the Arctic *gulag* where he watched friends die of hunger and exposure, a prisoner with a fever of 103 degrees forced to sit with his feet in a bucket of ice water for six hours as a penalty for "malingering"; the arid landscape of northern Iran through which he trudged with the rest of the "Anders" army of Poles, released once Hitler attacked Stalin, on its way to British-held Iraq; the tropical landscape of the African coast where he caught malaria en route to Durban and the troop ships; the rolling meadows of Essex where he trained as a pilot in the exiled Polish Air Force; the burned-out shells of German cities where he threw bars of chocolate to small children;

the desperate women whom he and his mates called "Dutch" when they wanted a night of illegal fraternization.

And all the time he had hung on to his memories of the Lithuanian woods as if they were the parachute cords of his identity. He had remembered the dark smell of the bison and the almond-sweet fragrance of the bison-grass vodka. "I don't care about the state," he said when I asked him about the Great Alteration from communism to democracy. "This is my state" — he smiled, waving airily at the trees — "nature; you understand: the state of nature."

I am of Eastern European stock. A Bohemian. I ponder the various connotations of the phrase "the state of nature" as I switchback down the trail. The lookout, no longer visible, becomes part of a marvelous and indelible past, the mountains of memory.

And the life of a lookout already lies like a dream behind me.

coda

> There is great good in returning to a landscape that has had extraordinary
> meaning in one's life. It happens that we return to such places in our minds
> irresistibly. There are certain villages and towns, mountains and plains that,
> having seen them, walked in them, lived in them, even for a day, we keep
> forever in the mind's eye. They become indispensable to our well-being; they
> define us, and we say: I am who I am because I have been there, or there.
> — N. Scott Momaday, "Sacred and Ancestral Ground"

Although I officially retired as a firewatcher a number of years
ago, I have, through the writing of this book, relived lookout life and revis-
ited Ruffneck Peak and its surroundings continuously. So intensely have I
lived on the mountain, in both the literal and figurative senses of the term,
that I like to think I have become its genius loci, the guardian spirit of the
mountain. In retrospect, I view the writing of this book as a way of finding
a place in the world, even if I no longer physically inhabit the place that I
write about. Having found this place, having gone native on Ruffneck, I will
be better able to find and go native in other places, too.

I can't say that I have had much of an influence on the mountain on
which I worked and lived (aside from walking upon it and chopping some
of its dead trees for firewood). But I do know that the mountain has affected
me in a number of significant ways. It has made me realize the necessity of
leisure in one's life. Not a day goes by now when I don't take at least a moment to daydream, think freely, and focus on nothing at all. Working a
lookout has further enhanced my love of solitude, to the extent that I now
largely prefer to travel in the wilderness alone, whether it be in the North

Woods of Minnesota and Canada, the Sonoran Desert of Arizona and Mexico, or the wooded canyon behind our house. It's when by myself that I can best realize my goal of contemplative recreation, the opportunity for exploring both outer and inner landscapes. Even when confined indoors at home I find that some of my happiest moments occur when alone in my study, poring over maps, anticipating the next journey to some wild place, visiting the wilderness in mind if not yet in body. There are more mountains to climb, there is much more wilderness to explore.

I still visit lookouts whenever I can. A few towers remain in northern Minnesota, and some are still in use during periods of high fire danger. A couple of summers ago I was driving through the Chippewa National Forest in north-central Minnesota when I glimpsed a tiny house atop tall steel legs barely protruding above the white pine forest. My curiosity and sense of nostalgia were piqued, so I pulled into the nearest turnoff and proceeded down the gravel road. After a short distance, a track to the tower appeared. I parked at the base of the structure and craned my neck to look up at the little house in the sky. One hundred and fifteen steps later, I was at the base of the cabin, gasping for air. The cabin entrance through a trapdoor was locked up and boarded off, so I could go no further. Still, I had commanding views in all directions from where I sat. There were no mountains to be seen, but the expanses of trees and water were impressive, even sublime.

I sat there for I don't know how long glassing the countryside, scanning the forest for smokes. Flocks of fair-weather cumulus formed and floated through the afternoon sky. I saw a few hawks and even an eagle soaring by at eye level. I sat there and relaxed and saw nothing at all, lost in the distant horizons that are the gift of every fire lookout.

select bibliography

Abbey, Edward. *Abbey's Road*. New York: Dutton, 1979.

——. *Black Sun*. New York: Harold Matson, 1971.

——. *Desert Solitaire*. New York: McGraw-Hill, 1968.

——. *The Journey Home*. New York: Dutton, 1977.

——. *One Life at a Time, Please*. New York: Dutton, 1988.

Abram, David. *The Spell of the Sensuous: Perception and Language in a More-Than-Human World*. New York: Pantheon, 1996.

"The Adventures of Alexander Ross in the Snake Country." *Idaho Yesteryears* 14.1 (Spring 1970): 8–15.

Albanese, Catherine L. *Nature Religion in America: From the Algonkian Indians to the New Age*. Chicago: University of Chicago Press, 1990.

Alt, David, and Donald W. Hyndman. *Roadside Geology of Idaho*. Missoula, Montana: Mountain Press, 1989.

Arnold, R. Ross. *Indian Wars of Idaho*. Caldwell, Idaho: Caxton Printers, 1932.

Arnold, Tillie. *The Idaho Hemingway*. Buhl, Idaho: Beacon Books, 1999.

Arrington, Leonard J. *History of Idaho*. Vol. 1. Moscow: University of Idaho Press, 1994.

Austin, Judith. "The CCC in Idaho." *Idaho Yesteryears* 27.3 (Fall 1983): 13–18.

Bailey, Ronald. *Descriptions of the Ecoregions of the United States*. Ogden, Utah: USDA Forest Service, 1980.

Berry, Wendell. *Home Economics*. San Francisco: North Point Press, 1987.

Beston, Henry. *The Outermost House*. Garden City, New York: Doubleday, 1928.

Boime, Albert. *The Magisterial Gaze*. Washington: Smithsonian Institution Press, 1991.

Brehme, Chris. "A GIS Analysis and Model of Suitable Gray Wolf Habitat in the Northern Rockies." www.spatial.maine.edu/ucgis/testproc/brehme.html.

Brome, Harvey. *Faces of the Wilderness*. Missoula, Montana: Mountain Press, 1972.

Burke, Edmund. *A Philosophical Inquiry into the Origin of our Ideas of the Sublime and Beautiful*. Oxford: Oxford University Press, 1990.

Callicott, J. Baird, and Michael P. Nelson, eds. *The Great New Wilderness Debate*. New Haven: Yale University Press, 1998.

Caroll, Kenneth. "Prehistoric Graffiti." *Idaho Yesteryears* 37.1 (Spring 1993): 24–27.

Carrey, Johnny, and Cort Conley. *The Middle Fork & the Sheepeater War*. Rev. ed. Cambridge, Idaho: Backeddy Books, 1980.

————. *The Middle Fork: A Guide*. 3d ed. Cambridge, Idaho: Backeddy Books, 1992.

Church, Frank. Papers. Boise State University Library. Special Collections Department. Boise, Idaho.

Conley, Cort. *Idaho Loners: Hermits, Solitaires, and Individualists*. Cambridge, Idaho: Backeddy Books, 1994.

————. *Idaho: A Guide for the Curious*. Cambridge, Idaho: Backeddy Books, 1982.

Craighead, John J., Frank C. Craighead, Jr., and Ray J. Davis. *A Field Guide to Rocky Mountain Wildflowers*. Boston: Houghton Mifflin, 1963.

Cronon, William. "The Trouble with Wilderness." In *Uncommon Ground: Toward Reinventing Nature*, edited by William Cronon. New York: Norton, 1995.

D'Azevedo, Warren L., ed. *Handbook of North American Indians: Great Basin*. Vol. 11. Washington: Smithsonian, 1986.

DeVoto, Bernard, ed. *The Journals of Lewis and Clark*. Boston: Houghton Mifflin, 1953.

Dickinson, Emily. *The Complete Poems of Emily Dickinson*. New Haven: Yale University Press, 1955.

Dillard, Annie. *Pilgrim at Tinker Creek*. New York: Harper & Row, 1974.

DuBois, Eliot. *An Innocent on the Middle Fork*. Cambridge, Idaho: Backeddy Books, 1997.

Eiseley, Loren. *The Immense Journey*. New York: Random House, 1957.

————. *The Night Country*. New York: Scribner's, 1971.

Eliot, T. S. *Collected Poems, 1909–1962*. New York: Harcourt Brace, 1963.

Emerson, Ralph Waldo. *The Complete Works of Ralph Waldo Emerson*. 12 vols. Boston: Houghton Mifflin, 1903–1904.

Flores, Dan. *Caprock Canyonlands: Journeys into the Heart of the Southern Plains*. Austin: University of Texas Press, 1990.

————. *Horizontal Yellow: Nature and History in the Near Southwest*. Albuquerque: University of New Mexico Press, 1999.

Forest Fire Lookout Association (FFLA). www.firetower.org.

Fuller, Margaret. *Forest Fires*. New York: John Wiley & Sons, 1991.

Graber, Linda H. *Wilderness as Sacred Space*. Washington: Association of American Geographers, 1976.

Guth, Richard A., and Stan B. Cohen. *Red Skies of '88*. Missoula, Montana: Pictorial Histories Publishing Company, 1989.

Hampl, Patricia. *I Could Tell You Stories: Sojourns in the Land of Memory*. New York: Norton, 1999.

Hardy, Martha. *Tatoosh*. New York: Macmillan, 1946.

Harrison, Robert Pogue. *Forests: The Shadow of Civilization*. Chicago: University of Chicago Press, 1992.

Hemingway, Ernest. "The Shot." In *The Literature of Idaho: An Anthology*, edited by James H. Maguire. Boise, Idaho: Hemingway Western Studies, 1986.

————. *The Sun Also Rises*. New York: Scribner's, 1926.

Hoagland, Edward. *Notes from the Century Before: A Journal from British Columbia*. New York: Random House, 1969.

Huser, Verne, ed. *River Reflections: A Collection of River Writings*. Chester, Conn.: Globe Pequot Press, 1985.

Jeffers, Robinson. *Selected Poems*. New York: Random House, 1963.

Johnson, Alice A. *Walls of Glass on a Mountaintop*. Laramie, Wyoming: Jelm Mountain Publications, 1990.

Lane, Belden C. *Landscapes of the Sacred: Geography and Narrative in American Spirituality*. New York: Paulist Press, 1988.

Leopold, Aldo. *A Sand County Almanac*. New York: Oxford University Press, 1949.

Liljeblad, Sven. "The Indians of Idaho." *Idaho Yesteryears* 4.3 (Fall 1960): 22–28.

Lopez, Tom. *Exploring Idaho's Mountains: A Guide for Climbers, Scramblers & Hikers*. Seattle: Mountaineers, 1990.

Kerouac, Jack. *The Dharma Bums*. New York: Viking, 1958.

Knudson, Ruthann, and Darby Stapp, Steven Hackenberger, William D. Lipe, and Mary P. Rossillon. *A Cultural Reconnaissance in the Middle Fork Salmon River Basin, Idaho, 1978*. Moscow: Laboratory of Anthropology, University of Idaho, 1982.

Krakauer, Jon. *Into the Wild*. New York: Villard, 1996.

Krech, Shepard III. *The Ecological Indian: Myth and History*. New York: Norton, 1999.

Kresek, Ray. *Fire Lookouts of the Northwest*. Fairfield, Washington: Ye Galleon Press, 1984.

Lookout Network: The Newsletter of the Forest Fire Lookout Association. Priest River, Idaho. 1990–present.

Maclean, John. *Fire on the Mountain: The True Story of the South Canyon Fire*. New York: William and Morrow, 1999.

Maclean, Norman. *A River Runs Through It and Other Stories*. Chicago: University of Chicago Press, 1976.

McPhee, John. *The Control of Nature*. New York: Farrar, Straus & Giroux, 1989.

———. *Young Men and Fire*. Chicago: University of Chicago Press, 1992.

Major, Kris. "The Yankee Fork Dredge and Its Community." *Idaho Yesteryears* 32.2 (Summer 1988): 22–34.

Marx, Leo. *The Machine in the Garden: Technology and the Pastoral Ideal in America*. New York: Oxford University Press, 1964.

Maughan, Ralph. *The Frank Church Wilderness*. www.poky.srv.net/-jjmrm/wpages/frank.htm.

Maughan, Ralph, & Jackie Johnson Maughan. *Hiking Idaho*. Helena, Montana: Falcon, 1995.

Merwin, W. S. *The Rain in the Trees*. New York: Knopf, 1988.

Mitchell, Edwin Valentine, ed. *The Pleasures of Walking*. New York: Vanguard Press, 1934.

Mitchell, John Hanson. *Ceremonial Time: Fifteen Thousand Years on One Square Mile*. Garden City, New York: Anchor Press/Doubleday, 1984.

Momaday, N. Scott. "Sacred and Ancestral Ground." *New York Times Magazine* 13 March 1988: 28–30, 81.

Moore, Brian. *Black Robe*. London: Flamingo, 1994.

Moore, Bud. *The Lochsa Story: Land Ethics in the Bitterroot Mountains*. Missoula, Montana: Mountain Press, 1996.

Moye, Falma J. *Geology of the Middle Fork of the Salmon: A Wild and Scenic River*. United States Department of Agriculture, Forest Service: 1995.

Muir, John. *My First Summer in the Sierra*. Boston: Houghton Mifflin, 1911.

Nash, Roderick. *Wilderness and the American Mind*. 3d ed. New Haven: Yale University Press, 1982.

National Wilderness Preservation System. www.wilderness.net/nwps/map.cfm.

Nelson, Richard. *The Island Within*. San Francisco: North Point Press, 1989.

Nicolson, Marjorie Hope. *Mountain Gloom and Mountain Glory: The Development of the Aesthetics of the Infinite*. Ithaca: Cornell University Press, 1959.

Norris, Kathleen. *The Cloister Walk*. New York: Riverhead Books, 1996.

Oelschlaeger, Max. *The Idea of Wilderness: From Prehistory to the Age of Ecology*. New Haven: Yale University Press, 1991.

Ortega y Gasset, José. *Meditations on Hunting*. New York: Scribner's, 1985.

Palmer, Tim. *Endangered Rivers and the Conservation Movement*. Berkeley: University of California Press, 1986.

Paul, Sherman. *The Shores of America: Thoreau's Inward Exploration*. Urbana: University of Illinois Press, 1958.

Peacock, Douglas. *Grizzly Years: In Search of the American Wilderness*. New York: Henry Holt, 1990.

Peek, Pat. *One Winter in the Wilderness*. Moscow: University of Idaho Press, 1998.

Pyne, Stephen. *America's Fires: Management on Wildlands and Forests*. Durham, North Carolina: Forest History Society, 1997.

———. *Fire in America: A Cultural History of Wildland and Rural Fire*. Princeton: Princeton University Press, 1982.

———. *World Fire: The Culture of Fire on Earth*. New York: Henry Holt, 1995.

Quinn, James M., James W. Quinn, Terry L. Quinn, and James G. King. *Handbook to the Middle Fork of the Salmon River Canyon*. Medford, Oregon: Commercial Printing Company, 1981.

Ross, Alexander. *The Fur Hunters of the Far West*. Edited by Kenneth A. Spaulding. Norman: University of Oklahoma Press, 1956.

Rothman, Hal. *Devil's Bargains: Tourism in the Twentieth-Century West*. Lawrence: University of Kansas Press, 1998.

Ruess, Everett. *A Vagabond for Beauty*. Edited by W. L. Rusho. Salt Lake City: Gibbs Smith, 1983.

Sanders, Scott Russell. *Staying Put: Making Home in a Restless World*. Boston: Beacon, 1993.

Schafer, R. Murray. *The Soundscape: Our Sonic Environment & the Tuning of the World*. Rochester, NY: Inner Traditions International, 1993.

Schama, Simon. *Landscape and Memory*. New York: Knopf, 1995.

Shepard, Paul. *Coming Home to the Pleistocene*. Washington: Island Press, 1998.

———. *Man in the Landscape: A Historic View of the Esthetics of Nature*. College Station: Texas A&M University Press, 1967.

Shi, David. *The Simple Life: Plain Living and High Thinking in American Culture*. New York: Oxford University Press, 1985.

Snyder, Gary. *Axe Handles*. San Francisco: North Point Press, 1983.

———. *The Back Country*. New York: New Directions, 1968.

———. *Earth House Hold*. New York: New Directions, 1969.

———. *Left Out in the Rain: New Poems 1947–1985*. San Francisco: North Point Press, 1986.

———. *Mountains and Rivers Without End*. Washington: Counterpoint Press, 1996.

———. *A Place in Space: Ethics, Aesthetics, and Watersheds*. Washington: Counterpoint, 1995.

———. *The Practice of the Wild*. San Francisco: North Point Press, 1990.

———. *Riprap & Cold Mountain Poems*. San Francisco: Grey Fox Press, 1965.

———. *Turtle Island*. New York: New Directions, 1974.

Spring, Ira, and Byron Fish. *Lookouts: Firewatchers of the Cascades and Olympics*. Seattle: The Mountaineers, 1981.

Stegner, Wallace. *The Sound of Mountain Water*. New York: Doubleday, 1969.

Steubner, Steve. "Ruckus on a Recreation River." *High Country News* 25 May 1988.

Stevens, Wallace. *The Collected Poems of Wallace Stevens*. New York: Knopf, 1954.

Stewart, George. *Fire*. New York: Random House, 1948.

Swanson, Earl H. "Anthropological Resources of the Middle Snake." *Idaho Yesteryears* 12.4 (Winter 1968): 10–12.

———. "Folsom Man in Idaho." *Idaho Yesteryears* 5.1 (Spring 1961): 26–30.

———. "Idaho's Prehistoric Past." *Idaho Yesteryears* 9.1 (Spring 1965): 17–24.

Taylor, Murray. *Jumping Fire: A Smokejumper's Memoir of Fighting Wildfire*. New York: Harcourt, 2000.

Thoreau, Henry David. *The Correspondence of Henry David Thoreau*. Edited by Walter Harding and Carl Bode. New York: New York University Press, 1958.

———. *The Illustrated Walden*. 1854. Princeton: Princeton University Press, 1973.

———. *The Journal of Henry David Thoreau*. Edited by Bradford Torrey and Francis H. Allen. 14 vols. Salt Lake City: Gibbs M. Smith, 1984.

———. *The Maine Woods*. Princeton: Princeton University Press, 1972.

———. *The Natural History Essays*. Edited by Robert Sattelmeyer. Salt Lake City: Gibbs M. Smith, 1980.

———. *Reform Papers*. Edited by Wendell Glick. Princeton: Princeton University Press, 1973.

———. *A Week on the Concord and Merrimack Rivers*. Boston: Houghton Mifflin, 1961.

Turner, Frederick. *Beyond Geography: The Western Spirit Against the Wilderness*. New York: Viking, 1980.

Turner, Jack. *The Abstract Wild*. Tucson: University of Arizona Press, 1996.

Tydeman, William E. "No Passive Relationship: Native Americans in the Environment." *Idaho Yesteryears* 39.2 (Summer 1995): 23–28.

U.S. Department of Agriculture. Forest Service. Idaho Panhandle National Forest. *When the Mountains Roared: Stories of the 1910 Fire*. N.p., n.d.

U.S. Department of Agriculture. Forest Service. Intermountain Region. 1981. *The Middle Fork of the Salmon: A Wild and Scenic River*. Washington: Government Printing Office.

U.S. Department of Agriculture. Forest Service. Intermountain and Northern Region. *Frankly Speaking. Report of Frank Church–River of No Return Wilderness*. N.p., n.d. Washington: Government Printing Office, 1998.

U.S. Department of Agriculture. Forest Service. *Your Land: The National Forests in Idaho*. Hailey, ID: Peak Media, 1989.

U.S. Department of Interior. National Interagency Fire Center (NIFC). "Wildland Fire Statistics." 7 August 2000. www.nifc.gov/stats/wildlandfiresstats.html.

U.S. Department of Interior. National Park Service. *Wildland Fire in National Parks*. Washington: Government Printing Office, 1998.

U.S. Department of Interior. National Park Service. *Wildland Fire in the Northern Rockies*. Washington: Government Printing Office, 1989.

U.S. Fish and Wildlife Service. *Northern Rocky Mountain Wolf Recovery Plan*. Denver: U. S. Fish and Wildlife Service, 1987.

Waite, Robert G. "Zane Grey and Thunder Mountain." *Idaho Yesteryears* 39.2 (Summer 1995): 18–23.

White, Lynn, Jr. "The Historical Roots of Our Ecologic Crisis." *Science* 155 (1967): 1203–07.

White, Richard. "Native Americans and the Environment." *Scholars and the Indian Experience*. Edited by W. R. Swagerty. Bloomington: University of Indiana Press, 1984.

Whitman, Walt. *Leaves of Grass*. New York: Modern Library, 1993.

Williams, Raymond. *The Country and the City*. New York: Oxford University Press, 1973.

Williams, Ted. "Incineration of Yellowstone." *Audubon* January 1989.

Wilson, E. O. *Biophilia*. Cambridge: Harvard University Press, 1984.

Yahr, Warren. *Smokechaser*. Moscow: University of Idaho Press, 1995.

Yeckel, Carl. "The Sheepeater Campaign." *Idaho Yesteryears* 15.2 (Summer 1971): 2–9.

Zontek, Ken. "Mules Across the Mountains: Packing in Early Idaho." *Idaho Yesteryears* 39.2 (Summer 1995): 2–10.

index

AMERICAN LAND & LIFE SERIES